M000191910

BROTHER FRANCIS
OF ASSISI

Ignacio Larrañaga

MÉDIASPAUL

This book originally appeared as *El Hermano de Asis*,
Cefepal, Santiago de Chile, 1989.

English translation by Jennie M. Ibarra.

Phototypesetting : *Médiaspaul*

Cover illustration: Simone Martini, *Saint Francis*,
                    Lower Church of Assisi.

Cover : *Mike Lory*

ISBN 2-89420-246-6

Legal Deposit — 4th Quarter 1994
Bibliothèque nationale du Québec
National Library of Canada

© 1994   Médiaspaul
         250, boul. St-François Nord
         Sherbrooke, QC, J1E 2B9 (Canada)

Table of Contents

Chapter One

THE DAWN OF FREEDOM

In spite of everything, he returned free of worry. He had every reason to feel despondent. But, contrary to what was expected, a peculiar calm flooded his face, and a *certain something* was apparent in his eyes, similar to a peaceful night's sleep or a dawn that was destined to appear.

On that particular night everything was out of the ordinary, and now his dreams rested on a new center of gravity. Everything had changed as if the world had spun an unexpected 180 degrees that night. As the morning clouds stretched over the valley from Spoleto to Perugia, Peter Bernardone's son rode peacefully home. He was open to everything, and that is why he felt free and content.

It has been called the *night in Spoleto*. However, circumstances notwithstanding, the Franciscan adventure did not begin on this night. Quite the contrary occurred. It was here that a great number of obstacles reached a peak, in which persistence on the part of Grace met resistance on the part of the young dreamer. On this night our combatant was conquered.

* * *

Nothing in the life of a man is improvised. A human being is always the son of an era and an environment, as are trees and plants. A fir tree does not grow in tropical rain forests, nor does sea moss grow on snowy peaks. If in generation after generation a large human exponent were to emerge, it would not come about suddenly, like mushrooms that grow in the mountains.

Our souls are recreated from an image that reflects the ideals fostered in our surroundings. Our roots are nourished, as if by osmosis and, without our awareness, by a world of ideas that surrounds us. If we want to know a man, we must look about him, at his *immediate surroundings*.

As he looked on the world through the window of his youth, Bernardone's son found a picture full of lights and shadows. The flames of war and the colors of peace, the wish for reform, and the thirst for wealth, all were mixed in the most paradoxical fusion. If we want to decipher the mystery of Francis of Assisi, at least a few pieces—and this is the intent of this book—let us begin by observing his world.

Immediate Surroundings

The *Guelf* nationalists were, time and again, loyal to one another and allies of the pontificate for the purpose of expelling the imperialists of the Holy Roman Empire. The *Ghibellines* were then what are known as *collaborators* today, and the *Guelfs* formed what is now called the *opposition*.

It was a century ago that the *penance of Canossa* took place. For three days and three nights the emperor Henry IV of Saxony stood barefoot at the castle walls in Canossa, Tuscany, wearing the grey tunic of penitents and waiting for the excommunication imposed by Pope Gregory VII (Hildebrand) to be lifted.

This was the apex of a crisis in the long-standing struggle between the pontificate and the empire. It was also a critical moment in the *investiture controversy*. The Pope claimed the right to ecclesiastical appointments, since bishops and abbots solemnly received not only goods and property from the hands of princes, but also the crosier and ring. Naturally, things were not as simple as they initially appeared. A universe of worldly interests and ambitions lurked behind the crosier and ring.

In five expeditions of destructive force the emperor Barbarossa wreaked havoc in the Italian cities. A few years before Francis' birth, the emperor had embarked on these expeditions with particular viciousness against the city commune of Assisi, a precinct into which he entered victorious, with feudal lords swearing allegiance and the emperor inflicting his imperial hold on the restless and humiliated masses.

Upon leaving, he appointed the adventurer Conrad of Swabia deputy in order to fight resistance among the rebellious townspeople. The aristocracy of Assisi, taking advantage of the imperial protection, oppressed the *serfs* with new and severe demands, forcing them into a subjection from which they had previously been freed.

Francis was born during the time when the village was under Conrad's vigilant watch from *Rocca*, a menacing and formidable fortress erected high above the city. Francis lived his childhood in these surroundings.

It was a period full of contrast and activity. Alliances were at the mercy of words written in the sand, formed and falling apart amidst inconsistencies; small republics and large feudal estates would rise and fall. Today the emperor would ask the Pope for protection, and tomorrow he had him deposed or set another up against him or made him disappear altogether through the cracks in Rome.

The serpent of ambition reared its ugly head in battlemented castle towers, Lateran palaces, and imperial fortresses; winds always fueled the fires; the crusades resembled a storm sweeping away the violent mixture of faith and greed, sublime devotion and a thirst for riches, reverence for the Crucified One, and irreverence for the vanquished...

* * *

At the rise of Pope Innocent III to the pontificate, a man of great influence and a generous heart, the Italian cities let out a cry for independence, demanding justice and, in some cases, raising the fist of vengeance. The insurrection spread over all of central Italy like a relentless hurricane.

In the city commune of Assisi, the revolution reached uncommon prominence. It was the spring of 1198. When the townspeople got word that Conrad had surrendered in Narni at the insistence of the Pope, the Assisians went up to *Rocca* and, with their first assault, tore down the grand bastion. Not a stone was left unturned.

With great speed they erected a wall around the city with the stones taken from the dismantled *Rocca*. This is how the Republic of Assisi came into existence, independent of the emperor and the Pope. Francis was then sixteen years old.

The flames of vengeance ignited everywhere, fanned by the people's anger against their feudal oppressors. Castles were burned in the Umbrian valleys, battlemented towers were shattered, stately homes were ransacked, and the nobles took refuge in Perugia. Among the fugitives was an adolescent of about twelve years of age named Clare.

The Assisian noble refugees sought the help of an old rival, Perugia, against the wishes of the populace of Assisi, who had forced them into exile. After many years of parleys, propositions, and threats, the warlike dispute was settled in the neighborhood of Ponte San Giovanni, an area midway between Perugia and Assisi. It was the summer of 1203.

Francis was a participant and twenty years of age at that time.

Here Bernardone's son made his historical entrance, fighting in a skirmish in favor of the humble people of Assisi. The combatants of Assisi were utterly defeated and the most affluent among them were taken hostage and transported to the prisons at Perugia.

There was Francis, a prisoner of war, in the damp dungeons of Perugia.

Castles Threatened with Destruction

Francis was too young to endure this fate without pain. The soul of this twenty-year-old youth was a fragile vase. A blow from a tiny rock was enough to shatter the vase, like an interrupted dream. The winds of change and the passing of time are what shape the soul.

One has the impression that contemporary biographers mentioned the years of Francis' conversion in passing. And like the journalists, chroniclers did no better than to jot down some anecdotes. But, apparently, they did not witness, nor did they describe, the internal drama unfolding within Francis, a drama that explains those events. They mentioned nothing about his conversion until the *night in Spoleto*. Nonetheless, on this night the fruit fell because it was ripe.

For me, *Francis' transformation* began during the eleven long months of incarceration and inactivity. Before one can construct a world, another world must wear away. And there is nothing on this earth that can destroy the very core of a creation; human edifices die stone by stone. In the prison at Perugia, Bernardone's son began to die and Francis of Assisi began to live.

Zeffirelli has made a beautiful film, *Brother Sun, Sister Moon*, but this film does not come any closer to solving the

13

mystery. There is not even a hint of the profound impulses that give birth to so much beauty. The movie is like a magical world that suddenly appears out of nowhere. Imagine a plane taking off with its engines absolutely silent. No one, except perhaps the purest of masochists, can endure what Francis endured in those scenes. He led a nomadic existence, greeting embittered faces with a look of contentment, holding his head high before rain and snow, responding to asperity with kindness, to poverty with happiness... All of this presupposes an extraordinary strength of mind, which is not evident in the film. It is a journey full of pain and hope, and, in short, presupposes the transforming hand of God in the life of a man.

Grace does not conquer frontiers. The world did not appear, from one morning to the next, bathed in the beauty of spring. The passage from one world to another was a slow one for Francis, taking two to three years, and it was not a tumultuous journey. The transition was harmonious, but not without pain. Everything began in the prison at Perugia.

* * *

Before any transformation can occur there must be an *awakening*. Illusions die and disillusion remains, deceptions are dispelled and the truth prevails. Yes, all awakening is disenchantment, from the *fundamental truths* of Prince Sakyamuni (Buddha) to the illuminations in *Ecclesiastes*. Disenchantment can very well be the foundation of a new world.

If we analyze the pivotal moments in the lives of the great saints, and observe the spiritual transformations that occur all around us, we will discover that, in every case, an awakening took place at the outset. The individual is convinced that all reality is ephemeral and transitory, that nothing is lasting, except God.

In every absolute fellowship with God, there is a subconscious longing for transcendence and eternal life. In every decisive *passage* toward the Infinite there is a desire to break free from oppressive limitations. In that way, conversion becomes the ultimate deliverance from pain and suffering.

Upon awakening, the individual becomes a *savant*. He knows it is ludicrous to make the relative absolute and the absolute relative. He knows we are forever searching for limitless horizons, and that human reality is restricted to a narrow path that crushes our yearning for transcendence, hence pain and suffering. He knows that a person reaches only a certain point and no window exists from which to escape, and for this reason his most ardent desires remain frustrated. Above all he knows, when all is said and done, that *God* is what is most valuable, because only he shows the way to direct the ancient and mysterious impulses of the human heart.

* * *

Francis' *awakening* took place in the Perugian cell. There, a building was taking shape. What building? The dreamer, the one who detected, like an ultrasensitive radar, the dreams of his era, through which he projected a world full of embattled castles, of shining swords overpowering the enemy. The soldiers rode to the battlefields waving flags of allegiance, hoping to see the shadow of a most elusive *glory*. Their lances won them titles of nobility, and, like King Arthur's knights and the paladins of the great emperor Charles, such heroic deeds opened the doors to *fame* and the ballads of poets. In short, all the roads to fame were linked

15

to the battlefield. This was Francis' world, a world that *thirsted for glory*.

In pursuit of those fatuous desires, our young dreamer arrived at the outskirts of Ponte San Giovanni. The original illusion was restored to a more worthy disillusionment, one of tremendous value! To have such visions of glory and to encounter defeat is utterly humiliating. And it was here that God waited for him.

The Lord does not enter castles built on foundations made of wealth, power, and glory. In the absence of adversity, a man's only preoccupation is himself, which is regrettable because fear then takes possession of him, making him anxious and miserable at the thought of losing everything. For man, adversity is salvation.

For this reason, Lord God, if you wish to save your son who sleeps comfortably on a bed of roses, there is no better strategy than a good hard push. When worlds crumble, dust blows in all directions; this is disconcerting to a young man. But when the dust settles, the youth wakes up, opens his eyes, and sees what is true and liberating.

This is what happened to Donna Pica's son. On the plains of Ponte San Giovanni, his dreams, his castles in the air, crumbled to the ground. It is not surprising to find a bewildered youth in the midst of all the dust. But when time passed and the dust settled, Pica's son, like another Sigismund, began to see things clearly. All things are as ephemeral as dreams.

It is unbearable. A sensitive and restless youth cannot endure confinement within prison walls, chewing the bitter herbs of subjugation. In captivity there is too much time to think. There are no distractions. The one and only oppressive truth is defeat.

Nor did our young man escape the psychological perils of captivity. The captive, like a political prisoner, lives in uncertainty and fear. He has no idea how many months or years he will spend in captivity, nor the course that certain political events will take, nor what the future will bring. All that is certain is a future at the mercy of an arbitrary *paternal authority* or a hostile lobby of feudal lords.

On the other hand, our prisoner knew all too well that captivity and defeat are the bread and butter of chivalrous adventures. But it is something else entirely to have first-hand knowledge of such an experience, especially by one who has yet to suffer life's many hardships, and by so sensitive a youth.

The crisis begins. Opposite the rise and fall of buildings, opposite emperors who shine today and are gone tomorrow, opposite noblemen who are silenced forever by the blow of a lance, stands another Nobleman riding among the fallen in the fields, another Emperor who transcends glory and obscurity, another Edifice whose height is eternal. Grace keeps watch over Pica's son. His sense of security is shattered.

Biographers of long ago say that while his fellow prisoners were melancholy, Francis was not only happy, he was euphoric. How can that be? A sensitive man is easily depressed. His temperament would give us reason enough to think that he felt disheartened. However, he was not saddened.

The words of Thomas of Celano, a contemporary biographer, support what we have been saying all along: that everything began in the Perugian prison, that the Lord rushed into the wreckage of castles left in ruins, that the encounter with the Lord was gratifying, and that right there he caught a glimpse, perhaps a dazed glimpse, of a new direction for his life.

In fact, the ancient biographer wrote that his companions were amazed by his state of euphoria:

"Francis, are you crazy? How can you be happy in these rusty chains?"

His answer was this:

"Do you know why? Look, I have a premonition that there will come a day when all the world will revere me as a saint."

In the Perugian jail, fleeting glimpses of eternity pierced the darkness hovering inside Francis.

The Word Is the Life

In August of 1203, the plebs and the aristocrats of Assisi said to one another: Why waste energy fighting with each other? Let us sign a peace treaty and work to strengthen our small republic. As a result of this alliance, Francis and his fellow prisoners were released and they returned to Assisi.

Approximately two years transpired before the *night in Spoleto*. What did Bernardone's son do during this period? The biographers say very little. However, we can deduce a fair amount from what little they do say.

It is most unfortunate for us (perhaps for the Church, not to mention for all of humankind) that throughout his life, Francis, was extremely reserved about his personal life, his relationship with God. No man has guarded the secret avowal of his communications with God with as much fidelity as this man did. He was known to be communicative; that is why the movement which he began has such fraternal or familiar qualities. However, with regard to his spiritual experiences, he would wrap himself in an obstinate sphere of silence that no one could penetrate.

He never wavered, no matter what the consequences, and in his day it was called *sigillum regis*, the king's secret: "my business" with my Lord is between him and me. It is important to note that news of his death was cause for celebration. Why? Naturally, it was not because he died, rather it was the opportunity to finally discern and examine his tormenting thoughts, and touch his wounds.

For three years and with great zeal he hid those mysterious signs on his body. Everyone knew about them, but no one, while Francis lived, was fortunate enough to explore them, neither his most intimate friends, nor even Clare. Brother Leo, his secretary and nurse, was the only one who could see them.

Due to this *sigillum*, it is possible that contemporary narrators did not receive word of his *passage* or conversion. Consequently, scant information remains of this period.

* * *

So many contemporary chroniclers, as well as Francis in his own testament, readily introduce us to God's setting, as if a profound familiarity already existed between Francis and the Lord. But deep intimacy with God presupposes a long personal history, a history that has yet to be revealed.

Today, the tendency is to overlook the personal life of St. Francis. Instead we will find an ample collection of stories reflecting prevailing points of view. Frequently we will find a modern-day rebel, a *hippy* 'drop-out' from society, a sentimental nature-lover. For the most part, the books do not delve into his personal life.

In introducing Francis to a modern reader we should not be so preoccupied with scrutinizing his actions and experiences, to see which are most effective in reconciling our worries and frustrations. In so doing we would lose sight of St. Francis and betray the modern reader. Francis must be examined from within, focusing on his internal life. In that way we may uncover the *mystery* and, without a doubt, that mystery will be the answer for our generation and for generations to come.

What is the mystery of a man? What word other than mystery can we use? Secret? Enigma? Explanation? Charisma? A certain magnetic charm? I am convinced that all mysteries, one by one, are eternally buried once they are resolved. The mystery in all individuals can be found in their genetic makeup, vital impulses, ideas and ideals taking shape since infancy.

But with Francis we also find a unique personality woven with sharp contrasts which makes it more difficult to know his *secret*. However, we have a code with which to decipher the enigma of St. Francis: God, the one great word in his life.

God *passed* through Francis' realm of being. God *touched* him. God *chose* him. God *visited* him. And through this connecting theme, everything becomes clear. Now we see how contrasts can shape a coherent and harmonious personality. We can also understand how the poorest man in the world can feel like the richest man in the world, and so much more.

* * *

There exists what is known as the *pleasure principle*: according to scientific studies every human being is motivated, in a sense, by pleasure. Without the reality of God, Francis of Assisi could be categorized in any clinic as a psychopath. All of his lofty and foolish remarks, his passion for Lady Poverty, his reverence for rocks and worms, his friendship with wolves and lepers, his preaching in a scant attire, his obsessive search for the divine will...is evidence enough of any person's instability. The sublime and the ridiculous are almost always in each other's shadow. The interface that divides the two is God.

Yes, God makes the ridiculous sublime. God is that remarkable force that shatters all notions of normalcy, awakens all human potentials and directs them toward new heights that were unknown until then.

From a rock come sons of Abraham. Look any and everywhere and you will find extraordinary examples. With this word-God-the enigma of Francis of Assisi is resolved, his secret is deciphered.

Since we live in a secularized world, the temptation exists to present to the modern world a Francis without God, or a God that is present surreptitiously or almost not present at all. In this scenario, St. Francis becomes a beautiful marionette that does prodigious stunts, but it is all a fantasy. It has no substance and does not explain the mystery of Francis.

Such an interpretation of his life would perhaps move the romantics, attract a *hippy* following, describe him as the forefather of ecologists, as mentioned in historical records. But the profound mystery of Francis remains unresolved, unexplained. Just open your eyes and look without passing judgment. At first glance you will be convinced that God is the cohesive element in the backbone of the fluid personality of Francis of Assisi.

The Woman in His Life

Upon his return from Perugia, having barely set foot in the streets of Assisi, our spirited young man threw by the wayside his meditations on the transitory nature of life, forgot the demands made by the Lord, and indulged freely in youthful desires that had been stifled for a year, by losing himself in a whirlwind of festivities. The thirst for glory had died. A thirst for merriment lived.

Various cliques of fun-loving friends formed among the comrades. Those comrades imprisoned in the jails of Perugia were the rowdiest of the bunch. Bernardone's son was selected to lead the group and was given the symbolic baton because he had money in his pockets and a spirit overflowing with mirth. They stayed out until all hours of the night shouting, laughing and singing as they made their way through the narrow streets. They would stop below certain windows and sing love songs to beautiful girls while playing lutes, zithers and harps. They had an insatiable thirst for merriment and festivities.

Months passed. They were inspired and their spirits never dampened. Generally, Francis arranged the banquets. There was something mysterious in him that attracted everyone. He kept company with the richest and most extravagant of Assisi's younger generation. He participated in singing contests and equestrian tournaments, and was quite accomplished in both. He was envied by some and applauded by all. Bernardone's son was the indisputable king of Assisi's social life.

* * *

One year earlier Grace had conquered his thirst for glory, and now Grace would do the same with his thirst for merriment. The chronicler pays tribute to this moment with the words of the prophet: "...I will strip her naked and expose her as in the day she was born, and make her like a wilderness, and turn her into a parched land, and kill her with thirst." (*Hos* 2:3). The youth suffered a grave illness of strange origin, difficult to diagnose. For many months he stood on the precipice between life and death: cold sweats, high temperatures that persisted, nightmares, general fatigue, and a very long convalescence.

During the long recuperation and, in general, during this period in his life, the person who will help him to see the light appears, the woman who will imprint indelible marks of faith and hope on his soul: his mother.

Lady Pica's silhouette, made of sweetness and strength, disappears in the silence. It passes fleetingly, like a comet, within the pages of old chronicles. She makes an appearance, she shines, and she disappears. She can bear the weight of the world on her shoulders, but she does it without theatrics, simply and silently.

It is a paradox. Although sources provide only traces of information about her, we are nonetheless able to deduce and piece together a complete picture of Pica. This can be achieved indirectly. Look into Francis' soul and extract from his subconscious, piece by piece, a captivating profile of this woman, to whom the Franciscan brotherhood owes a great deal.

* * *

Traditionally, although sources are silent on this point, she is thought to be a native of Provence, the birthplace of poetry and song. Nevertheless, we have at our disposal sufficient information that allows us to conclude, by deduction, that Pica was in fact French.

At moments when a person is overcome with extreme emotion, the tendency is to express such sentiment in the mother tongue, the language on which one was "nursed." This is a *constant* in all humans. It has been said that St. Francis Xavier, in his agony, expressed himself in Basque, his maternal tongue. The Poor Man of Assisi, an intensely emotional man, expressed his feelings in Provençal

(French). Wouldn't this be his maternal tongue, the language spoken by his mother?

Let us suppose, for example, that I learned English at twenty years of age, and that I spoke it to perfection. In a moment of intense emotion I would want to express myself freely and without any mental restriction. I would naturally use my native language or the mother tongue, where word and sentiment, phonics and foreign experiences, are intrinsically woven.

If, as the majority believe, Francis had learned French in his youth while traveling on business, it would be quite bizarre and almost inexplicable to see him expressing himself in French in moments of absolute joy where words interlock with even the most primitive of feelings requiring a natural release. A person who learns a language as an adult lacks the flexibility and facility to express himself freely in that language.

We can therefore deduce, that Francis' mother tongue is French, that is to say, that his mother spoke the Provençal language (French). Hence, the words *maternal tongue*, and not paternal, since it was learned from the mother at birth.

* * *

We come to know the soul of that woman by making inferences, and, indirectly, come closer to uncovering the *mystery* of Francis. It is a game of substitution. From Francis' subconscious we extract the necessary characteristics for a composite of Pica, and in the mother's reflection we will see a portrait of the son.

According to Celano, when the father caught the squandering youth, a boy known to possess mystical powers, and threw him in the dungeon, the mother "trembled to the core with sorrow." That expression describes something funda-

24

mental and powerful: it expresses much more than the sadness the mother felt for the son. Strong currents of sympathy flow between a mother and a son. It is a harmonious mixture of consanguinity and kinship.

* * *

With regard to St. Francis' writings, the evocative images of the maternal figure, the mother in general, and subconsciously (or consciously for that matter) of his own mother, are impressive and occur frequently in his testament. The evocation is an emotional one for Francis. Whenever Francis wishes to express a human experience, an emotional relationship, an empathetic attitude, he turns to the maternal image as a basis for comparison. We need to reach the core of this man, a core that is nourished by a thousand memories—almost forgotten—of a person who gave him protection, spirit, love, faith, ideas and ideals.

In the Rule of 1221, when denoting the high standards that build and sustain the fraternal life, Francis says to his disciples "each one of you must love and care for your brother as a mother loves and cares for her son." He returns to the same verbs that connote the maternal love and care, in the second Rule, by saying "if a mother loves and cares for a son born of her flesh, all the more reason exists to love and care for those born of the Spirit."

What is surprising is not the verb *to love*, an ancient and trite word, rather the verb *to care for*, an exclusively maternal verb. *To care for* are words that are compatible with the verbs *to consecrate* or *to dedicate*, which are found in the Bible. *To care for* means to reserve a person and a time for someone else, which is what people do, especially mothers.

* * *

In or around the year 1219, Francis endeavored to establish a fundamental organization for the disciples who went up the high mountains searching in silence and in solitude for the Face of the Lord, in order to recapture inner peace.

He wrote, therefore, the norms to be followed or the brief statute called *Rules for the Eremitical Life*. Suppose a small fraternity of four brothers live up in the cabin. In order to emphasize the type of relationship each should have with the other, Francis used expressions that were shocking but that also exuded fraternal tenderness. Once again and more conspicuously than ever, the maternal figure was manifested.

Of the four brothers, "*two will be mothers* with two sons." With respect to the kind of life each should lead, "the two who are mothers will follow Martha's way of life, and the two sons will follow Mary's way of life." He later orders them, that is, he asks them, upon completing the prayers of Tierce, to break the silence "and go to your mothers." Among the many expressions there is one that is especially tender: "...and when you feel the urge, you [the sons] can beg your mothers, like poor little things, for the love of the Lord God."

Since it is a period of eremitic life, Francis advises them to guard against strangers entering the cabin, to have the mothers "protect the sons against any who may disturb the silence," and to have "the sons speak only to the mothers." Francis also instructs the brothers to take turns being mothers and sons in order to lessen the possibility of forming dependent relationships, reinforcing therefore the need for real equality, both juridical and psychological.

At the very core of a man who expresses himself in this manner there are faint echoes of a mother who was an inexhaustible source of compassion, a mother who spent many sleepless nights at the bedside of an ill child.

The Poor Man of Assisi formed a bond using two of the most dissimilar pieces of thread to be found anywhere: the eremitic life and the fraternal life, solitude and family, silence and cordiality.

* * *

For many weeks Brother Leo lived with a thorn in his side which inhibited his feelings of peace. He did not know the source of the suffering. Perhaps he had some doubts and wished to consult with Francis. Possibly he was overwhelmed with feelings of nostalgia for the father and confidante of his soul, with whom, after many years of traveling together, he had forged a deep friendship.

Francis, knowing that states of melancholy conceal voids filled with numbness, and that there is no crisis that a little affection cannot cure, took up his pen and wrote an invaluable note that began with these words: "My son, I speak to you as a mother speaks to her child." Beyond the note, "Lady" Pica was still "alive".

* * *

Surprisingly, in analyzing his writings, in particular the mystical writings, we notice that when Francis addresses God he almost never uses the word *father*, which is peculiar for a man so full of affection.

The God with whom Francis had such an intimate rapport was the Lord, the Omnipotent, the Admirable.... He used the word *father* sparingly. This word meant little to him, and subconsciously evoked the figure of an egotistical, domineering man who lingers in the darkest memories of his life. Francis could very well have addressed God using the word "Mother," but the sound of it was startling. Such a word would have been in complete harmony with every fiber of his personal history.

The woman who emerges from these pages and these memories, what was she like? Fused in this woman is the power of the oceans, the sweetness of a honeycomb, and the profound brilliance of a starry night. Long before the romantic chivalry propagated by the troubadours pervaded the Italian republics, that lovely woman had fed inspired ideas into the soul of her little boy. What words define *that certain something* in his personality that recalls an ineffable melody, that calls to mind the splendor of the dawn, or the serenity of nightfall?

Before God showed Francis his destiny and vocation, he showed them first to his mother.

The Thickness of Smoke

Tribulation knocked at the door. The heavy hand of the Lord placed Francis in the midst of affliction, resulting in sleepless nights and days of delirium.

The thirst for glory was reduced to ashes. In the prime of his youth, he no longer thirsted for pleasure. Francis was nothing and with the illness advancing steadily, he would soon fall into the abyss.

Time and again the angel of the Lord visited the sick young man at his bedside and showered him with wisdom. The angel said to him once again: Youth blows like the wind against our doors, like waves that rise as high as mountains and are suddenly foam. How thick is the smoke? The dreams of men weigh less than smoke. How much does glory tip the scales? Everything in heaven and on earth lacks weight and firmness, except the Eternal.

* * *

We are a few months shy of the *night in Spoleto* where we will find Francis in total communion with the Lord and resigned to everything. With Grace marching onward, one can presuppose that, during those months of convalescence, the angel of the Lord saw the Face of God in the sickly youth.

Young Francis, who from birth showed signs of spiritual sensitivity, began to experience a divine sweetness during these months. He began to feel a profound sense of peace, betraying traces of wisdom. In these moments the way of the Lord was the brightest.

Conversion is a race between God's sweetness and the charms of human beings, where the latter begin to lose pace with the former until the Presence is finally affirmed and declared the victor.

In the young convalescent we see signs of this interplay, where human impulses first prevailed and where spiritual desires would soon overwhelm them.

As we have previously stated, Lady Pica is without a doubt present within the framework of this crisis, collaborating with Grace to seal his destiny. During long sleepless nights with his mother at his bedside, the youth who lay at death's door pondered the many contradictions in human nature, paradoxes which he too experienced.

* * *

The chronicler goes on to say that when Francis recovered his health, although not completely, he got up with the help of a walking stick and leaning on his mother, walked about the bedroom testing his strength.

He was anxious to get outdoors and reacquaint himself with nature and with his boisterous friends. After a few days, still pale and on shaky legs, the left his father's house and headed out to the countryside. He wanted to assure himself that he was still full of vitality.

Porta Moiano is one of the few gateways in the walled city that opens to the countryside. There, Francis surrounded himself with the intoxicating beauty of nature, under a deep blue sky, just as the sun began to paint the distant hills a mysterious shade of light-blue.

Nature was just beaming with life, undulating outward through the wide expanse in harmony with the colors of insects, birds, plants and trees. The Umbrian valley stretched from Perugia to Spoleto with dazzling beauty and vitality. Francis wanted so much to surrender to that world, to be one with the throbbing pulse of life, to feel...

* * *

But the blood stopped running through his veins. Two active poles are necessary to get a spark, but Francis felt numb and it was impossible to light the flame of enthusiasm. "Neither the beauty of the terrain nor the graceful vineyards were enough to awaken his dormant enthusiasm," says the chronicler.

Celano continues, stating that Francis felt mixed emotions of surprise and disappointment at this numbness, for on previous occasions he would immediately connect with the beauty surrounding him. The narrator adds that at that precise moment our "wounded" young man began to meditate on the absurdity of losing one's heart over things that live and die in a matter of a day. He walked slowly back to his home, his soul filled with melancholy and frustration.

The explanation for this insensitivity was rather simple. He was simply suffering from a vitamin deficiency due to his illness, and all he needed was extra nourishment. Maybe it was too soon to leave his bed. He was always so impatient and so "reckless"! There was no other explanation. But beyond these biological phenomena, and even through them, God was beginning to guide the chosen one on a course that Francis had yet to understand.

Humanly speaking, Francis could not fight back. With just a few assaults, God was able to destroy his two strongest bastions: the thirst for glory and the desire for pleasure, and in this way he left the boy totally defenseless.

Upon his return home on that particular day, Francis took much more to heart the meditations on absurdity and wisdom, meditations that had been a part of him since his release from the Perugian prison. But this time those thoughts penetrated to the core, simply because he lacked the "weapons" for defense and counterattack, and so was vulnerable from all angles.

The Dreams Awaken

He was wounded but not defeated. That is the nature of conversion. No one is converted completely and forever. Wounded and all, the Old Self accompanies us to the grave as a wounded serpent will, all of a sudden, lift its menacing head.

Months passed. Francis made a complete recovery. Once again the flame of illusion lifted its blazing head, and on the wings of a rejuvenated spirit, he flew into a maelstrom of festivities and amusement. He could not be without his friends. According to the chronicles, at times he would even leave his parents sitting alone at the dinner table in order to be with his friends.

* * *

From 1198 on, all of Italy watched the course of events taking shape between the Pontificate and the emperor. This time the center of contention was in the Kingdom of Sicily.

Due to very complex reasons, the struggles took on universal proportions. Pope Innocent III appointed Captain Walter de Brienne to protect the papal policy, which was winning wide support.

The Norman commander was victorious and continued to advance the papal position with much success. The name Walter was cheered throughout Italy. From city to city, people talked of his exploits immortalized in song by the troubadours.

The war resembled a crusade. Throughout the Italian cities, knights and soldiers answered the call to arms and rode to the battlefields of Apulia, in southern Italy, to join the armies fighting under the Norman flag.

The holy flames were also ignited in Assisi. A gentleman by the name of Gentile took the initiative and prepared a small military expedition with the best of Assisi's men.

The nobleness of the cause and the possibility of wearing a suit of armor captivated Francis and, in the cold ashes of the past, chivalrous fantasies were stirring. At twenty-five years of age, Francis joined the expedition.

He prepared his equipment for battle in no time, and the day of the campaign finally arrived.

The Night of Liberty

Francis said goodbye to his parents. That morning, the small city, with all its comings and goings, resembled a busy beehive alive with activity. Hugs, kisses, tears, and goodbyes. And in the middle of all the commotion and the fluttering handkerchiefs, the small but splendid military expedition embarked on its tour of duty through the large eastern gateway toward Foligno, heading for Via Flaminia which would bring them past Rome to southern Italy.

At nightfall, the expedition reached Spoleto, the city at the foot of the Spoletan valley. But it was written that everything would begin and end at Spoleto.

* * *

Francis lay down in the midst of his gear : jacket, mesh stockings, helmet, sword and lance, emblazoned shield, and the long tunic. And all this splendor was readorned, made more brilliant in his dreams of grandeur.

It is written in chronicles from that period that on that night Francis heard a voice in his dreams :

"Francis, where are you going?"

"To Apulia, to fight for the Pope."

"Tell me, who will give you the better reward? The Master or the slave?"

"The Master, naturally."

"Then, why do you follow the slave and not the Master?"

"What should I do?"

"Go back home. There you will find the answer."

The next morning, Francis went back home.

* * *

On that night Francis experienced what the Bible refers to as a *visitation from God*. In my opinion, Francis did not hear voices that night, nor did he have visions, but for the first time and with extreme force, he felt very much *filled with the Holy Spirit*. In spiritual terms it is called an *extraordinary infused gift*, with very strange characteristics.

Yes, there is no doubt, as biographers will attest, that the dialogue between the Lord and Francis came to him in the form of a dream. It is more than likely that even Francis would later on interpret the experience as a dream or express it in allegorical terms when confiding to someone the events of that night.

This is a constant element in the history of souls: when someone has an experience that is too powerful for words, the individual instinctively turns to allegories in order to express him/herself.

What occurred that night? For reasons that are consequential, the following happened and had to happen: in a surprising, exaggerated, assaulting, and vivid manner (these are the characteristics of a *transfiguration*) the Divine Presence took possession of Francis, freely and willingly.

The man feels like a beach flooded by a relentless high tide. He is speechless, overwhelmed, absolutely enraptured, with a very clear idea of his own identity. At the same time he feels part of something immense, transcendent, embracing all of time and space; all of this *in* God's name, exploring for that infinitesimal moment what it is *to be* God, resembling somewhat to a lesser degree what can only be Eternal Life. All of this comes to fruition by way of God's infinite mercy, internally or externally no one knows how...

A mountain of words can only give an approximation of the meaning behind an extraordinary personal revelation:

security, certainty, light, warmth, happiness, clarity, intuition, jubilation, peace, strength, sweetness, liberty...

* * *

This *visitation* has tremendous meaning for the one being touched by God's presence. Francis had vivid and crystal clear evidence (that neither dreams nor locutions could ever give him) that God ("known," experienced) is All Good, Supremely Good, Entirely Good, the only One who is worthwhile, to whom titles of nobility and lords of the land do not compare.

Now, why do I say that some of what occurred that night had to transpire? Because otherwise what did occur could not be explained. And in order to understand ourselves, we must penetrate all that is personal in Francis.

He was going to Apulia as a crusader defending the Pope. Yesterday he said his goodbyes to his parents and to the town of Assisi. In this military campaign Francis was committed to the youth of Assisi, to the worthy young men who rode with him, to Count Gentile, under whose command he marched, to his parents, to whom this expedition promised a great measure of glory, to his honor, to his word as a gentleman, to his name...

A simple dream is not enough to negate the bonds of commitment. If on the following morning Francis decided to return home, completely ignoring his responsibilities as a soldier, it can only mean that something extremely significant occurred that night. Francis has demonstrated in his life that he was a man of conviction. A dream is a poor explanation for this nocturnal transformation. Only a powerful and liberating experience of God could explain this formidable retreat.

* * *

On that night all the chains were broken. Francis felt absolutely free. Nothing mattered to him except the Lord. In the immediate future he saw nothing but problems and interrogations. What explanation could he give Count Gentile? What would his comrades-in-arms say, who yesterday were his fun-loving companions, and who in just a few hours would continue on their journey southward? They would probably call it desertion or madness. They could say whatever they wished. Nothing mattered to him anymore.

Tomorrow he would return to Assisi. What would the townspeople say? the youngsters? What would the violent Bernardone say? Lady Pica? the neighbors? the prelates? What could he possibly say? No explanation was possible; no one would understand. Some, the kindest among them, would say he lost his head. Others, the malicious ones, would talk of desertion, frivolous behavior. For a soldier, the most dreaded word is *cowardice*. They would throw that word in his face, in the face of a man who was so sensitive about honor. To tolerate all that, which yesterday would have been impossible, no longer mattered. He felt absolutely free.

He was abandoning a secure and gratifying course to follow one that was uncertain, full of dilemmas and insecurity, and he was doing it alone. He would take on any challenge, if it meant following the Lord, whom he now "knew" personally.

The following morning he said his farewells—who knows what excuses he gave—to his comrades and began his journey back to Assisi. An indescribable experience such as this one, though lasting only a few minutes, stays with the person for a long time, perhaps for a lifetime.

While retracing his steps from Spoleto to Assisi, Francis, without a doubt, was bathed in the Presence. Upon entering the streets of Assisi, the incredulity of the townspeople began, then the uneasiness, later the rumors, a mixture of irony, ridicule, and sarcasm. Francis, still under the effects of the *visitation*, ignored what they said, and walked serenely through the streets.

It was the dawn of freedom.

Chapter Two

RISING SUN

It was as if young Francis had returned from a long, long journey. He saw that the world was full of compassion, mountains overflowing with mercy, and peace covering all the earth. Everything looked exquisite. The world was absolutely beautiful. To live was a privilege. He had learned that and much more on his long journey. Who can tear down the mountains or stop the movement of the stars? So be it: therein lies the source of peace. Appreciate the little things in life, just as you would the big things.

As of this moment, the physical appearance of Pica's son would change imperceptibly in three years time. The Presence was molding him in the mature hue of a golden wheat field. The transformation was as gradual as the coming of spring. One morning we notice quite unexpectedly that the almond trees are budding, waiting impatiently to burst with blossoms. Days go by and no one notices a thing. Then one day we open a window and see everything in bloom. Everything has occurred so slowly, so silently, so surprisingly...

The same thing happened to Francis. In three years time, Pica's son would unknowingly, and no one knew how, clothe himself in the vestments of peace, born, without a doubt, of a profound inner freedom. Those that looked on him would find inner peace.

He developed—I would not know how to say it—a kind of tenderness or reverence for the tiniest, most insignificant things. He would not even think of harming a fly, or stepping on a rock, or of keeping a caged bird. A flood of compassion rose in him for beggars and lepers. And a serenity, typical of mountains that are eternal, began to cover his face. This metamorphosis took place in the span of three years.

I Will Nourish You with Honey

Within a few days of his return from Spoleto, the gossip around town began to slowly dissipate, much in the same way that dust in a room collects on the furniture. Nothing made sense to Francis, but all had been decided. There was no reason to be hasty or rash. The Lord himself, all merciful and good, would open the doors and lead the way.

He resumed his normal life, occupying himself once again with his father's business. The townspeople persuaded him to reclaim his glory as the king of parties. Weeks passed. He got together with the young crowd, leading in song, cracking his share of jokes and partaking in all sorts of merrymaking. Nevertheless, unintentionally and unavoidably, he began feeling, more and more, like a stranger among them. His heart was somewhere else.

It is hard to believe. The core of his being, "visited nightly" by God, found all things to be trivial, all things to be a waste of time. He was overcome with an incredible urge to find a time and place to be alone with the Lord. This is the way the Lord teaches his prophets.

Irresistibly attracted, his prophets are first drawn to solitude. There he nourishes them with his honey, fills them with his sweetness, burns them with his fire, bruises them with his silence, and molds them like anvils made of steel. And when the prophets take on the image of God and are completely immune to any and all maladies, he delivers them once again to the multitude.

* * *

Francis was no longer enthusiastic about parties and decided he had had enough. He therefore prepared a dinner-party, making it a farewell banquet; for this reason he filled the table with all sorts of liquor and tasty dishes. Upon finishing the meal, the lads, their hearts aflame with the spirit of wine, darted down the streets of the silent city, shouting and singing, accompanied by lutes and clavi-chords. Francis, as usual, carried the ringleader's baton, but his spirit felt terribly ill.

And in this web of merrymaking and revelry, his discon-certed God waited for him with an unexpected "visit." In the narrow time frame of one month, or possibly less than one month, the Lord *visited* Francis for a second time with an *extraordinary infusion of grace*.

A heart that has been *visited* is affected by that *visit* for many days. And it is more than probable that in the midst of that Dionysian frenzy, Francis' thoughts were, to a greater or lesser degree, with the Lord.

Gradually and furtively, within his group of friends, Francis began to distance himself in order *to be* with the Lord. And in one of those idle and romantic wanderings around the city, the Presence overcame Francis, with all the massive weight of its sweetness, like a nocturnal assault. Our captain of festivities was pinned down right there in total ecstasy.

All the life forces within him, functioning on *high voltage*, in addition to his utmost abilities, efforts and labors, remained relentlessly focused on the Lord. In other words, the Presence took total and instantaneous possession of all

41

that was personal in Francis, integrating and taking hold of his whole being in a sublime fusion. There is no human experience in the world that approximates, not even vaguely, the rapture and richness of one of these "visits."

* * *

The experience lasted a few seconds, maybe one or two minutes. Suddenly, his enlightened comrades noticed that the captain of festivities was not among them. They went looking for him and found him in a daze. Naturally, they began making fun of him and shaking him to bring him out of the trance. Perhaps never in his life did Francis feel as terrible as he did at that moment. That awakening was worse than an electric shock. At that moment he would have given anything to have been on the bare summit of Mt. Subasio.

The young men teased him:

"Hey Francis! What's going on? Thinking about your girlfriend?"

He had to say something in order to conceal what had occurred. Francis answered in the same tone:

"Naturally; and I assure you that she's the richest, most noble, and most beautiful girl ever."

Some chroniclers say that he was referring to Lady Poverty. It is a gratuitous assumption. At this time in his life, Francis knew nothing about a so-called Lady Poverty. Most likely he wanted to get out of an uncomfortable situation as gracefully as possible, saying anything that came to him along the same lines and in the same tone as the questions asked.

However, another explanation is possible. During this time, Francis began expressing himself allegorically and metaphorically, usually using the image of the hidden treasure. If, in his answer, he desired to express something definitive, it was this: in the world neither wife nor any worldly possession can give greater happiness than the Lord, and I have "found" him.

His carefree companions thoroughly enjoyed that outing, and their nocturnal "street band" played on in between bouts of laughter. But something still lingered in the air, indicating that a chasm had opened between them and their noble friend, a divide that would soon separate them permanently.

Lone Dove

From this moment on, Francis was compelled to quench an insatiable thirst that would accompany him until his dying days: the thirst for solitude. It is so hard to imagine. Who would have thought that this reckless, extroverted youth who loved to wander about the streets, this lover of parties, would retire into seclusion? Among the contradictions in his personality and in his personal history, we find this: a recurring need to be a pilgrim and a hermit.

The extraordinary visitations awakened in Francis an ardent desire to be alone with the Lord. His eyes were pools of nostalgia and his soul was an insatiable chasm with the following name: *thirst for God*. A human soul that has been profoundly captivated by God and longs to be with him, suddenly has wings that reach beyond the horizon, beyond oceans and mountains, beyond cities and rivers; it does not fear the ridiculous, nor the darkest shadows, nor are there obstacles that can hinder its journey.

* * *

Biographers say that Francis began to seek solitude on a daily basis, in and around the environs of Assisi, in order to pray. Silently, he walked the short distance from his home to Porta Moiano. He walked up the slopes of Subasio amongst the ash trees, thickets, evergreen and oak trees.

When he found a location at a safe distance from prying eyes, he would sit on a rock, or at times kneel, and pour his heart out to the Presence. At times he looked toward the heavens above the Apennines where his Visitor reigned; at other times he would shut his eyes and feel his Friend fill his veins and the very core of his being.

He would go back home. He worked at the counter in his father's place of business. He went out very little. He took short cuts when he did not have the luxury of time, crossing olive groves and vineyards, quickly reaching the forest in the central valley near St. Mary of the Angels. There he remained, either leaning against an old fir tree, or sitting near some shrubs, or prostrate on the ground, depending on the circumstances.

There were days when, during those moments, he wished time would stand still, like the hands of an old clock. He wanted the heartbeat of the entire world to beat inside him, ten thousand arms with which to adore and embrace the infinite mystery of his Visiting Friend.

Since he was a novice at prayer he would easily break down and cry, according to biographers, and he would express himself in a passionate voice.

Walking up the steep streets, Francis returned to his house bathed in a mysterious peace. An astute observer would have been able to see the splendor of eternity in his eyes. However, neither his family—except perhaps Pica—nor his friends were able to decipher the secrets in his soul. The talk revolved around comments and rumors about the peculiar turn Francis' life was taking.

An Anonymous Confidante

After numerous trips to the woods and the slopes of Subasio, Francis finally came upon the ideal place for his daily retreats. The site is thought to have been a hollow, somewhat like a cavern, in the rocky terrain. It could well have been an ancient Etruscan burial ground.

During this time a curious phenomenon, one of the many contradictions in his personality, came to light. Since Francis was quite communicative by nature, he felt a terrific need to share with someone the extraordinary things his soul was experiencing. And so he chose to pour his heart out to a youth, a boy of his age, someone he liked very much, or in any case, respected a great deal.

But even with this friend he was extremely cautious. He spoke in vague terms and allegories, telling his friend that he had found a treasure that, in an instant, made the discoverer rich and happy. Despite the need he felt to communicate his experiences, Francis was reserved, as was his custom, when speaking about manifestations that were spiritual in nature.

The fortunate confidante is lost in anonymity.

He is a character who has always intrigued biographers, past and present, and despite all the research undertaken to discover his identity, nothing is known about his name or his personal history.

* * *

In any case, Francis and his confidante walked toward the grotto. Francis very kindly asked his friend to wait nearby while he prayed. His friend was obliging and polite (perhaps even curious?), and did as he was asked. Francis went deep into a cave and for hours on end he poured out his soul.

According to biographers he let out moans, sighs and tears deep within the cavern. This information could only come from the mouth of the mysterious confidante. Did he join the brotherhood later on? Was he one of the companions of St. Francis?

Be that as it may, a drama was unfolding within Francis which draws our attention. To what do we attribute his misery and tears? Did he regret the frivolity of the life he used to lead? Did thoughts that he could possibly return to that life fill him with dread? Did he feel the sting of contradictions in experiencing fervent desires for sanctity and the impossibility of achieving it?

After many long hours, Francis reappeared and his patient friend greeted him as he came out of the cavern. At times Francis looked strange and tense, and at other times he looked peaceful and full of happiness.

His confidante was anxious to hear about his revelations. But Francis did not waiver from his usual metaphors about treasures, kingdoms, emeralds... Even though they were good friends, his confidante must have grown tired of enigmas and mysteries because he soon disappeared.

After a few weeks, "he was so full of joy that everyone noticed a change," says Celano. What explanation could he possibly give his friends, who yesterday were his fun-loving companions? It was useless to say anything objective. No one would understand or they would dismiss it as nonsense.

Nevertheless, he had to say something. So with regard to his military exploits, he told them that he needed to carry them out in his native homeland and not in the region of Apulia, and for this reason he had returned. With regard to everything else, he referred to the oft-repeated images of hidden treasures or wives that are beyond compare. The chronicler makes no mention of the reaction to these explanations.

The Birth of His Compassion

In following the accounts of earlier narrators, at this stage we see a transformation occurring in which Pica's son is bathed in serenity and filled with a peculiar kind of happiness. In conjunction with this, God's sympathy awakens in him a sensitivity, very much out of the ordinary, for all things that suffer. But it was more than that: he was beginning to feel tenderness or sympathy or fascination (all together) for the poor, the insignificant or the weak.

In short, after a few months of assiduous care, the Lord took Francis out of himself and put him in the world of the forgotten where he remained until his last days. First, he had a predilection for beggars, and, without abandoning them, he went out of his way for lepers.

* * *

Francis came to God by way of man, the poor. I am very impressed by how frequently and serenely this is reaffirmed today. These affirmations are a part of today's society, but in every way they contradict the paths he took and the words he used.

If one carefully analyzes the texts of contemporary biographers, looking at all of them simultaneously, what is most prominent on those pages is Francis' extraordinary sensitivity toward the poor, a reflection of God's own benevolence toward Francis, even though in his nature a proclivity to act on behalf of noble causes was evident.

In the last days of his life, while he was happily recording in his testament the years of his conversion, he summarized them by saying: "The Lord took me among the lepers and I showed them my compassion." So we have it that first he found the Lord, and then the Lord took him by the hand and they walked among the lepers, and not the reverse. He says this from his heart.

Man is motivated by pleasure of one kind or another. People are not drawn to ideas, nor to ideals, nor do they associate with beggars or with lepers because those things are pleasing, Pica's son least of all. As we will see, he found them particularly repugnant.

In order to make the unpleasant something pleasing and commonplace, man not only needs exceptional motivation, he also needs to be in love with Someone, the one, the only one, who can change the unpleasant and make it pleasing. Due to certain inclinations and because he finds it pleasant, man loves only himself and always looks for things that give him pleasure. That is the norm.

* * *

The chronicles say the following about the Three Companions: "Although for some time he had been generous to the poor, nevertheless, since then it was his intention never to deny alms to whomever asked him in God's name, and to give it freely. So if ever he were outside his home and a beggar asked him for money, he would give it. If he did not have money to give, he would give his hat or his sash, so as not to have the beggar go off empty-handed."

Pica's son had money to spend and was very generous. His easygoing friends knew this all too well, feasting at lavish banquets paid for by the cloth merchant's son.

But now things were different. Francis displayed every measure of compassion. In giving alms, he gave of himself, of his warmth. In giving a coin, he gave quite happily his heart and a kiss.

It was Jesus. Jesus himself returned to earth and dressed like the beggars. In the portico of St. Rufinus he found Jesus under the arch extending his hand. Jesus staggered in lonely walkways. It was Jesus sleeping under the bridge by the river, shivering from the cold. Jesus emerged from the deep, mysterious chasm of every beggar, extending his hand and asking for a little kindness. Yes, the beggars had empty stomachs, but their hearts—this was vital—were cold and looked for warmth.

The alms-giver of Assisi went to each one, learned their names, greeted them by their names, asked to know something of their lives and their desires, and was concerned about their health.

These wanderers, accustomed to indifference from both great and small, shook their heads in disbelief. They could not understand why the son of a prominent merchant would be the least bit interested in their sad existence. He was very close to them. They perceived in his look and in his gestures a secret well filled with tenderness, a certain something that words could not describe, as if an angel had descended bearing the heart of God.

* * *

He walked among cypress and chestnut trees toward the forest or the cavern. Along the way he came across a beggar and gave him the money he had in his pockets. He continued walking. Around the bend he encountered a second vagabond and gave him his hat or his sash.

He spent many hours in the cavern. The fire within Francis illumined its dark recesses. He talked to God as a friend talks to another friend. He emerged from the cave like a piece of burning wood, radiant with joy, and he would walk back home.

If on the way home he were to see a third beggar, something unusual might occur. Since he promised himself that he would give to anyone who asked him in God's name, and since he had already given all the money he had in his possession, he would take the beggar by the hand and go behind a thicket. Francis would take off his shirt, and with all delicacy he would implore the beggar to accept it in God's name.

On more than one occasion Francis returned home with barely anything on. Pica would conceal her emotions, pretending not to notice. Deep inside she felt tremendous pleasure at the sight of such saintly eccentricities, because it seemed as though her intuition regarding the eminent and mysterious destiny of her son was being fulfilled.

The Mother Once Again

Fortunately, his father, the cold and arrogant merchant, was away on business in Italy and France during this period in Francis' metamorphosis. His father was busy in the buying and selling of silks imported from Persia and Damascus.

Taking advantage of his father's absence and his mother's quiet complicity, Francis said to himself:

"In the past I was very generous with my friends, even extravagant, because I wanted to be the leader of society in Assisi. Now that I have other friends, why not do as I have always done?"

So when Pica prepared the table for the two of them, Francis, without raising a fuss and without explanations, crammed the large table with all sorts of tasty morsels as if he were expecting company.

At first this strange behavior surprised Pica and she asked the lad to explain this disproportionate amount of food. Her son answered quite simply that the overabundance was reserved for his new and numerous friends, the poor.

His mother did not say a word. She neither condemned nor condoned his actions. She simply remained silent. Nevertheless, Francis knew that her silence was also her consent. This act of decency and generosity continued for weeks. Never again did his mother discuss the subject. Thoughts can be expressed without the need of words. His mother hid a secret and tacit satisfaction behind her silence.

As we have previously mentioned, the bond between mother and son manifests a profound affinity, a connection that is warm and full of sympathy and communication. There are sons who do not resemble their mothers. But there are times when the resemblance is so great that they become mirror images: reflections, impulses, reactions, ideals, in all things identical.

There is no doubt that Pica felt a certain satisfaction with the direction Francis' life was taking. Could it be possible that through her son's achievements with regard to these high ideals, she was fulfilling the dreams—impossible dreams—of her youth?

If Clare's mother entered the convent founded by her daughter, who is to say that this other mother would not have done the same and followed fervently in her son's footsteps?

At any rate, she gave to her son all that was great in her heart, not only biologically but also through her words, mood and disposition in her daily life. If she did not explicitly put her son on a path toward God, she at least gave him incentive and some encouragement. Francis' mother is also the mother of the Franciscan movement.

Into the Depths of Selfless Giving

But to give alms to the needy or to show beggars compassion was not enough. Nor was it enough to project Jesus' image onto those pitiful human beings. It has been said that to give one's life for someone else is the ultimate proof of love. Perhaps a greater expression of love exists: to live the unique experiences of a friend. The Incarnation of Jesus is a manifestation of this.

During this time, Francis, for reasons that are unknown, made a pilgrimage to Rome in order to lie prostrate at the feet of the Apostles. He entered St. Peter's Basilica and prayed for quite a long time. He gave generously. He was consumed with passionate love as he left the central nave. In the vestibule, at the foot of the mighty columns, he found swarms of beggars extending their hands as they asked for alms. And then something very unusual occurred.

Francis' compassionate gaze froze on the most disheveled among them. He took him aside. They stopped near a corner of the spacious vestibule. And in a humble tone the elegant young man asked to switch clothes with the pauper because he wanted the role of a beggar, to try out the part for a few hours. In fact—the scene is difficult to imagine— they exchanged clothing right there. And Francis, dressed in rags, went with the beggars; he sat on the steps of the portico and began to ask for alms from the passersby. When it was time for dinner, he sat at the beggars' table where he ate heartily from a bowl shared by all.

Did his passionate feelings at that moment prompt the sudden change in his behavior? Did the recent convert promise the Lord such proof of his love? Did he long to have such an experience, one that he could not have in Assisi for fear that he might upset his parents or for fear that he might not be strong enough to face ridicule?

Be that as it may, these exploits were preposterous, and if we do not find motivations of a serious nature, motivations that transform things at the root, this strange episode gives us sufficient cause to believe that the adventurer had lost his wits. The disgusting rags, the atmosphere of pestilence, the scraps of food from a shared bowl (he, who was used to exquisite meals prepared by Pica), for a person who is normally quite sensitive (and Francis was sensitive to a fault), would most likely make him nauseous and sick to his stomach.

If, instead, what occurred was cause for rejoicing, as the biographers say, if the dinner was very satisfying, then this means that in those moments a powerful driving force deep inside made what was repugnant agreeable. Francis was thinking of none other than the Lord Jesus. It was more than that. He was "imitating" and living "as" Jesus.

Pica's son mentally identified with the Son of Mary. The Poor Man of Assisi felt that he was doing as the Poor Man of Nazareth would have done, since beggars were mirror images of Jesus. Thus, we understand how Francis' burning impulses—which could not help but cause repugnance—were overpowered by Jesus' presence and transformed into sweetness.

In what way was this event significant to Francis? Was he victorious in conquering himself? Did he want to destroy the lofty towers in his dreams of grandeur? Did he wish to catch a glimpse of freedom on the horizon of the plains of poverty? At any rate, with this adventure, Francis of Assisi plunged vertically into the depths of selfless giving where he would live joyfully submerged for most of his life: everything is Grace.

Now, as a beggar, he received alms and bread, and for the rest of his life everything would come from the hands of the Great Giver.

Entering the world of evangelical poverty was also his first significant experience of self-abnegation: he renounced his clothes, his bourgeois personality, even his inheritance. In short, he was repeating a story that was thirteen centuries old, one that Jesus had experienced: although he was rich, he led a life of poverty for our sake.

An episode such as this marks a chosen person with a maturity beyond his years.

What Was Once Bitter Is Now Sweet

Upon his return home, Francis' spirit reached new heights. He felt the thirst for God with every fiber of his being, and when he had even a few minutes to himself, he would run up to the hills or down ravines, yearning for solitude.

He would climb the steep terrain of Subasio, walking on dead leaves and rocks, to a suitable height, and there he would spend the day with the Lord. His communion with God was becoming more and more serene and profound. There was no longer the flood of tears. Each time he would say less, and silence was beginning to substitute for words.

Apparently—according to biographers—Francis' spirit was branching out in two significant directions: in one, the Crucified Christ began to gradually open the deep wounds of compassion in his heart and, in the other, the Crucified Christ began to hold him in a general state of suspended intimacy and wonder with God, the Almighty. He felt freer with every passing day.

We no longer see that likeable confidante who, it seems, grew tired of this heartless dreamer's unsubstantiated fantasies. Significantly, the story of the Three Companions states that from now on Francis would confide in, consult and be consoled by "God alone." Sometimes he would seek Bishop Guido's counsel.

Francis was like a meteor that is steadily approaching and losing itself in the deep recesses of total solitude. We find him near cherry trees in bloom, keeping company with crickets and cicadas, while poppies danced in a sea of green wheat fields. Francis opened his soul to the grace of God with great affection. Little by little he began to enter a state of profound submission and docility.

* * *

The following occurred during this time. There was an old woman in the city who was hunchbacked and deformed, with a hump that was so high that it made her look monstrous. The poor old thing had a horrible figure, and it was terrifying to look at her even from a distance.

Many times the young man met her on the street during his solitary travels. Pica's son was extremely sensitive. He was immediately attracted to beautiful things, but deformed human beings made him nauseous, and this he could not deny. It is interesting to note that at this stage in his life he did not hesitate to show compassion to the poor souls in rags, but he could not bear to look at this old woman, even from a distance. The sight of her made him sick to his stomach. Lepers affected him in the same way.

* * *

Little by little, something akin to an obsessive idea was overpowering him. Francis, the elegant young man, had the notion that if he continued fasting and doing penance he would turn into a grotesque creature, like the hunchbacked woman. The obsession overpowered him completely.

Biographers call it diabolical temptation! But there is no need to exaggerate. It could very well have stemmed from a concrete idea or, perhaps, from mental fatigue resulting from his fasting. Could it be that the Lord was testing him? Be that as it may, it is not important to find the cause of the phenomenon, rather, it's important to see its effects.

One day, when Francis was in serene communion with the Lord in the cavern, he felt, unequivocally and acutely, a force within (biographers say that he heard a voice) that said:

"Dear Francis: If you want to know my will you must reject everything you have loved until now and love all that you have rejected.

"And when you begin to do so you will see that what was once bitter is now sweet like honey, and what was pleasing until now will become insipid and displeasing."

His obsession disappeared.

A Mysterious Transmutation

Within the prevalent theme, which is evident in the last few pages, these words (actually a declaration), placed between the *affaire* with the old deformed woman and the appearance of the lepers, are like a flash of lightning that brings to light many strange facts about the Poor Man of Assisi and solves the deep mystery of Jesus' exceptional witness.

We have seen, and most importantly we will see, how the Poor Man of Assisi tackles every unpleasant circumstance in his life, how he masters situations and, if you will permit the expression, "swallows them"; and afterwards, deep inside, they flow like a river of honey.

Pica's spoiled son was never interested in the destitute, because of the displeasure they aroused, nor was he motivated by any high ideals to go near lepers, nor did he deny himself any peculiar desires. The dying Francis will, in retrospect, solemnly begin his testament by remembering that in his youth lepers used to fill him with disgust, and that the Lord took him by the hand and placed him among them, and that he treated them with kindness and compassion.

And he recalled with great emotion on his deathbed how something that was so repugnant to him had become terribly sweet not only for his soul but also *for his body*.

The last expression is very peculiar. Can one explain how repulsive creatures, the sight and smell of them, can cause pleasurable sensations, both bodily and spiritually? One can presuppose from this fact that Francis, on the one hand, was endowed with a highly sensitive nervous system, and, on the other hand, possessed a very vivid and impressionable imagination.

All this is of interest with regard to understanding his personality and explaining many of his present and future experiences. But it alone does not explain why the displeasing was now pleasing.

* * *

To reiterate, Jesus' presence explains the mysterious transmutation that he felt deep inside. All of this leads one to suppose that Francis, so richly endowed, felt the divine reality in some way while vividly experiencing Jesus' personality (projecting that Person onto the leper). The power of that experience erased or eclipsed the repulsive reality in the foreground, and the divine presence remained as the only appreciable reality, superimposed on human reality.

In other words, Francis the person (mind, impulses, motives, energies) was completely preoccupied with Jesus. And this presence filled him with such an abundance of joy that his sense of well-being overflowed into the physical realm.

How can I describe this? Jesus, the catalyst influencing Francis' behavior, was of paramount importance, mentally and emotionally, and Francis' spiritual sensibility overshadowed his senses. Therefore, Francis did not smell the stench at the lepers' table, only the sweetness emanating from Jesus, for whom he went among the lepers and whom he embraced in their image.

The incident with the lepers, the absolute joy and pain of the crucifixion on Mt. Alvernia, the ashes in the food and the shuddering at the enchantment of mother earth, complete spiritual joy in abject poverty, and so many other paradoxical events that will appear in the following pages, can only be understood for this reason: the Lord God's unifying and affirming path of renewal and rebirth is vivid and true by virtue of a sensitive and gifted man who responded to the *calling* with all his being.

Trial by Fire

To reiterate, his first friends were the beggars. Before long, other poor souls would appear who would steal his heart: the lepers.

He always felt an innate aversion toward them. When he went to the fair at Foligno on business and saw the lepers as he approached, he always took another route or the long way around in order to avoid them. But even so, on more than one occasion he gave alms to a passerby who then gave it to *the sick in the care of the Good Lord*.

They were called the *damned race*. By contrast, they were also called the *sick in the care of the Good Lord* or simply *Christian brothers*, this being the most common. Those with faith saw in the lepers the vivid and anguished figure of the Crucified Christ, who, in the image of the leper, washed away the leprosy of sin.

Anecdotes full of tenderness soared on the wings of popular legend, describing how Jesus appeared to this saint or that queen in the image of a leper. For many years during the Middle Ages lepers were known to be the outcasts and the most venerated of society. They all wore grey and something by which one could distinguish them from afar. Drinking from fountains, swimming in rivers, and coming near plazas or market places was prohibited. In short, they were desolate persons.

Nevertheless, in its own way, medieval society adored them. There was not a city or town that would not build a shelter or a leper colony for these *Christian brothers*.

* * *

It is interesting to note that, at this stage in his life, in which Francis drank God's fragrance through every pore and had acquired a deep spirituality, he should still feel such an inexplicable aversion toward these *sick in the care of the Good Lord*.

Incidentally, this aversion was the yardstick which measured his sensitivity and impressionable nature. This important fact is also a way of interpreting many events in his life, giving us an idea of the intensity with which Francis experienced these events. The biographer states that, during this time, the mere mention of a leper made him react so violently that "upon seeing the leper colonies from a distance, some two miles away, he would cover his nose with his hands."

But he could not go on like this. One by one, he had conquered every obstacle and hurdle. Only the trial by fire remained. Were not those sad shadows the sorrowful silhouettes of his Beloved Jesus Christ? After all, was not the disgust he felt for those *Christian brothers* blasphemous? Could he say Jesus had not given him the most profound pleasures in his life? At best, his cowardice was ingratitude.

One day, while absorbed in consolation, Francis placed in the hands of the Lord the blazing sword of an oath: he would take in his arms, as he would a little boy, the first leper to cross his path. For him, this was equivalent to throwing his naked body on a bed of hot coals. But his word remained, like a lance thrust firmly into the earth. The rest was a matter of honor.

* * *

One morning, as he made his way along a turn in the serpentine road on the foothills of Mt. Subasio in the direction of Foligno, he suddenly came across the cursed shadow of a leper stretching out his arm full of loathsome sores.

Francis' blood boiled in an instant, like a wild beast on the attack, and the repulsion that rose in him was like a brick wall. It was too much to bear! His first impulse was to dig in his spurs and disappear. But he remembered those words: "Francis, what was once bitter will now be sweet." The quicker he accomplished his task the better.

He sprang from his horse, knowing nothing between stillness and swiftness, and for the first time in his life he was face to face with a leper. Hastily, he placed alms in his hands. He took him in his arms, not without some difficulty.

He put his lips to the *Christian brother's* decaying cheek. He kissed him forcefully time and again. Then he quickly kissed both the leper's hands and, with a "God be with you," turned and left. He mounted his horse and sped away. He had triumphed over the trial by fire. Blessed be the Lord!

He rode on for a few yards... What was this? He had never had a sensation such as this. From deep inside the earth and from the depths of the seas, from deep inside the mountains and from his own blood rose, wave after wave, an ocean of sweetness. It was (what was it?) the perfume of the most fragrant flowers, the quintessence of all the world's honeycombs. His veins and arteries were rivers of honey. His stomach and head were fountains of kindness. What do you call that? Rapture? Ecstasy? A bed of roses? A cloudless sky? Paradise? Beauty?

On his sickbed, looking back on that moment, Francis would say that he tasted "the best honey for body and soul." It was, without a doubt, one of the happiest days of his life and, at any rate, it was such an outstanding event that, in his testament, Francis considered it the milestone in the course of his conversion.

* * *

From that moment on, his *Christian brothers* would be his most beloved companions, and until his dying day he was an angel of compassion, creating an inexplicable bond of affection, not only between himself and the lepers, but also between the lepers and the brotherhood he founded.

On his return to Assisi, he went immediately to visit his new friends. He went directly to the valley by way of Porta Moiano and within half an hour he reached a famous leper colony called *San Salvatore delle Pareti*. Pica's son, his pockets bursting with coins, steered his steps in their direction in order to show his compassion. One can imagine the stupefaction on the faces of the poor sick souls when they saw the famous son of the arrogant merchant.

Nothing is as satisfying to a man as the realization that he has overcome the most difficult challenge of his life, revealing a maturity similar to that which a mother feels when she has given birth.

Francis hardly recognized himself. Only a few days before, he himself would not have believed he was capable of doing what he was doing now. His eyes were full of (words cannot describe it) kindness, intimacy, pity, and compassion all at the same time. Brother Francis looked into the eyes of his *Christian brothers*, one by one, for a long time. They felt accepted and loved.

Afterwards, he placed a coin in each of their hands, but not before pausing to kiss each hand lingeringly. They could hardly believe what they were seeing. To them, Pica's favorite son was like an angel from heaven, an agent of God's eternal mercy. It was a memorable day for the leper colony of *San Salvatore*.

After that, Brother Francis of Assisi visited them frequently. Sometimes, instead of going to the cavern, he went straight to the leper colony. He was no longer satisfied with just giving them coins. He filled a washbasin with warm water and slowly washed their feet, as though their feet were something sacred. With maternal gentleness he washed their feet and wrapped bandages around their wounds, not before cleaning them with great care.

He learned their names and addressed each of them by his proper name. He soon acquired some knowledge of nursing and brought medication from the chemist's shop in the city. In no time at all there was not a nurse in the leper colony as competent as Brother Francis.

The Restorer of Ruins

He had placed a blank cheque in the hands of the Lord on the *night in Spoleto*: what is your will? But the heavens did not open just yet. His horizons were as dark as night. No course of action came to light, so Francis simply lived his life day by day in devotion. He spent long hours with the Lord, long hours with the lepers, spreading peace wherever he went. He always remained standing, like a sentinel awaiting orders in the middle of the night, seeing what new developments may arise.

One day Brother Francis was walking down a rocky path lined with sharp-pointed cypresses and dark pines. He saw before him the plains stretching without end from Perugia to Spoleto, distant cities hidden in the morning mist.

After descending the hill, Francis suddenly came upon a small chapel lying in a hillock. For quite a while Brother Francis had been visiting all the chapels scattered along the hills and the valley. But never before had he come across this one.

The hermitage was dedicated to St. Damian. There were many cracks in the walls that threatened the stability of the old church. Ivy happily climbed the lateral walls, covering them completely. Inside, there was nothing but a simple altar made of wood, a few benches, and a Byzantine-style crucifix that served as the altarpiece. The modest chapel was attended by an old priest who relied on the charitable contributions of the townspeople.

* * *

Brother Francis entered the dusky church and once his eyes grew accustomed to the darkness he knelt reverently at the foot of the altar and stared at the Byzantine-style crucifix. He looked at it for a long time.

It was a very distinct crucifix: it did not express pain, nor did it arouse pity. The figure had wide black eyes in which one saw the glory of God and all eternity. A strange combination of sweetness and majesty sheathed the entire figure which inspired trust and devotion.

Francis remained motionless, no one knows for how long, drawn by its expression of calm and peace. According to biographers, at that moment he had a divine experience.

In my opinion, at that particular moment he had the third "visitation" or transfiguration. Brother Francis, in total submission, went with the current, downstream to the Sea, to a limitless Totality, toward the bottomless abyss of the mystery of Eternal Love, where man disappears like a pebble on a beach.

This time Love had a definite name, a definite figure and a passionate history: Jesus Christ on the Cross, giving his life for his friends. The image of the Crucified Christ penetrated Brother Francis' soul like a flash of lightning, engraved itself by fire on his raw spirit, and time never healed the wound. Presumably, here is where the pilgrimage began which would end on the rocks of Mt. Alvernia, where his consummation would be complete.

This experience served as the key to the Franciscan rule, shaping its original character and spirit. From this moment on, according to St. Bonaventure, whenever Francis thought of the crucified Christ, only with great difficulty could he manage to hold back his tears. Francis himself said this in confidence before dying.

Tradition has helped preserve Brother Francis' prayer that morning. With his eyes fixed firmly on the majesty of the Byzantine Christ, he said:

"Glory be to God, my Lord Jesus Christ! You are the light of the world. Shine your light on the dark recesses of my spirit. Give me three gifts: faith, firm as a sword; hope, as wide as the world; love, as deep as the ocean. Furthermore, my dear Lord, I ask one other favor: every morning at daybreak may your most holy will be known to me like the rising of the sun before my eyes, so that I might always walk in your light. And have pity on me, Jesus."

And suddenly, no one could say how or from where, a voice was clearly heard that seemed to come from Christ:

"Francis, go and repair my house, which, as you see, is falling down."

Never had he heard his name pronounced with such an indescribable accent, not even from the great lady, Lady Pica. The Lord had called him by his own name! This was definite proof of predilection.

In my opinion, the voice was a typical *locution* described in books on mysticism. What is it exactly? It is a voice. It could be a sound. Nevertheless, no one can say if the voice is coming from without and picked up by the eardrum, or is resonating from within. The only thing that is known is that the *locution* is entirely different from and more than just an inspiration.

* * *

Just as in Biblical times, great encounters are always followed by great *journeys*. Every intimate experience results in a mission.

"My Lord, I'll do it with great pleasure," said Francis in response to the command.

Brother Francis of Assisi reacted hastily, as he had done so many times in his life. Taking the command literally, he got on his feet, looked around and realized it was true: there were cracks in the walls. He went outside and walked around the private retreat and saw that it was true: it was in ruins. There was no time to waste. For months he had waited for a manifestation of God's will. God had spoken and had given him a command. It was time to take action.

His eyes sparkled with joy and conviction as he hurried home through wheat fields and vineyards. On the way he met an old priest. He greeted the priest reverently and kissed his hand. And, as Francis gave him all the money he had in his possession, he said:

"Father, in God's holy name, take this money. Day and night, I will be happy at the foot of the Crucified Christ. But since that is not for me to decide, at least let an oil lamp burn continually in my name. I will repay you with acts of love."

The Good Merchant

The young man continued on his way up the hill toward his house. During that brief walk his thoughts were focused on the immediate projects he would undertake. He needed money to buy construction materials. In order to get the money he needed to sell some goods. There was no better place to conduct business than the fair at Foligno, where his father took him quite frequently. He had to act quickly.

No sooner had he walked through the door when all was decided. When he entered the house, he showed no interest in food and gave no explanations of any kind. He prepared the horse and gathered much of his father's fabrics—Bernardone was probably away at the time. As he left, he made the sign of the Cross as though he were undertaking an important and sacred venture, and he went straight to Foligno, his soul bursting with joy.

It was a complete success. He sold everything in a few hours, including the horse. He retraced his steps to the church of St. Damian with a bag full of money. Poor Francis! He still believed that money was all-powerful. He would soon be deceived and would celebrate the most uncompromising divorce that ever took place between a man and his money...

* * *

He held the bag high and shook it hard so that the coins would sound like trumpets of war. Francis approached the old priest and spoke to him enthusiastically about his restoration project for the venerable hermitage. Francis begged the old clergyman to accept the money.

The good priest looked away. The whole affair gave him reason to believe that the lad was either crazy or was mocking him. He had read about earth-shattering conversions in *The Life of the Saints*. But it was another thing entirely to give credence to the transformation of this young man, who just yesterday was the sophisticated leader of the young men of Assisi.

Furthermore, he knew old Peter Bernardone's callous nature and he did not see the point of arguing with the volatile merchant. The old clergyman declined the attractive offer.

Divorce and Betrothal

In my opinion, it is was at this moment that the great divide occurred, the deep and impassable divide, that would split the history of Francis of Assisi in two. We will witness two divorces and two betrothals that will happen as unexpectedly as everything else in Brother Francis' life, and which will have profound consequences for his spirit. Here,

Bernardone's son dies and is buried, and, here, Francis of Assisi is born.

Firstly, as a result of the priest's rejection, Francis clutched the bag and threw it contemptuously, and the bag hit the window frame with a crash. At that moment, he renounced material wealth forever, and did not so much as even touch that precious metal ever again. His was among the strangest and most sacred divorces in human history. Francis of Assisi was a man who never in his life showed disdain for anything, except money.

Why was his renunciation so full of contempt? Did he suffer disillusionment when he realized that the metal was not all-powerful, that it was useless for the restoration of the hermitage? It was much more than that.

The son of the wealthy bourgeois merchant was a very perceptive young man; life had taught him many things. There is no room for God where there is money. Love cannot flourish where there is money. Money corrupts the senses, prostitutes the emotions, divides the heart, breaks up families: it is an enemy of God and an enemy of man.

Thanks to the life lessons that he learned in his youth, Francis developed a deep aversion to gold and silver. The abrupt gesture of throwing the bag, that instantaneous "liturgy," absorbed all of that contempt. And at that very moment Brother Francis began to worship our Lady Poverty. Very few romantics would have held their lady in such high esteem as Francis did his Lady Poverty.

* * *

Secondly, an unfathomable abyss had opened between Francis and his family, between Francis and society. They no longer had anything in common. No one understood him, no one could possibly understand: he lived in another world.

Family and society interrelate on the basis of a common direction within the framework of conventions and needs, at times genuine, at times superfluous: one has to marry, have children, make money, attain a respectable position in society... It is difficult, almost impossible, to be free in that kind of environment. Those who want to follow Jesus need their freedom, first and foremost, and there is no freedom without a *parting*. For Francis, the hour had arrived for his exodus: to leave his home and his family.

Brother Francis knelt reverently before the priest who had so stubbornly refused the bag full of money, and, with humility, begged to accompany him to the hermitage. The priest granted his request and, for the first time, Francis did not return to his house. He slept in the hermitage. In this very simple manner, the second divorce came to pass: the break with family and society.

Apparently, he never went home again, except for the time his father had him thrown in jail. In reference to his renunciation, Brother Francis would write the following in his testament: "I left the world." His divorce from the world meant his betrothal to Jesus and the Gospel. From that moment on, Brother Francis belonged to no one, and was free to commit himself exclusively and completely to Jesus and, in Jesus, to all the world's poor.

From that moment on, the world was his home. Lepers, beggars, and thieves were his friends. The wind, rain, snow, and spring were his brothers. The warmth of the sun and the light of the moon kept him company. He ate on the road, just like the gleaners and the larks. And he went around the world in the shadow cast by God's protective wings. He had everything. He was happy.

The Onslaught of Persecution

Old Bernardone's wounds bled for a long time, the cause being the young man's sudden and shameful retreat from Spoleto, where he was preparing for the expedition to Apulia.

An arrogant person was incapable of understanding that event and his wounds festered with bitterness and resentment. On the other hand, he did not mind seeing the lad squander his money on his wellborn companions. After all, the father took pride in such actions. But to see him squander his money on the indigents in the streets was absolutely intolerable.

Furthermore, for many months the young man was engrossed in the solitude of the woods and mountains and neglected to assist his father in his commercial endeavors. But, more than anything, the rich merchant's torment stemmed from his frustrated dreams and hopes for his son's success.

It is difficult to imagine, even theoretically, two poles so distant and so opposed to one another. And Bernardone, a merchant through and through, was absolutely incapable of comprehending the new direction in the life of the young dreamer. Day by day the situation grew more and more volatile, and there was bound to be an explosion one way or another.

* * *

Francis knew that, sooner or later, a persecution would break out. He found or prepared a hiding place near the hermitage, a shelter that served to guard against the impending onslaught. It was well concealed—so he thought—from his persecutors.

There were still sediments of fear in the spiritual rivers that flowed through him: fear of being ridiculed, fear of suffering.

The attainment of freedom creates repercussions. At that moment, Francis was overcome by fears which he had not felt on his return from Spoleto. A regression? No. Human beings are like that: when all of his energies were focused on the Presence, Francis was able to face the flames, the demons, and death steadfastly.

But the soul can be fickle at times. When a person stops looking to the Lord for help, he/she becomes instinctively self-absorbed, and, in such a case, wretched insecurities instantly begin to come out of the woodwork. Then the person seeks a hiding place to lessen the anxiety. Thousands of battles and numerous wounds must be endured before winning total confidence and complete freedom.

* * *

Bernardone returned after a long absence and heard the bad news: Francis no longer lived at home. Pica was unable to give an accurate explanation, and even if she had had one at her disposal, she would have kept it to herself, in light of her husband's explosive nature.

And so, as is always the case, the workers from his shop and his neighbors joyfully proclaimed the news: Francis has not been home for quite a while; the last time he was here he took all of your best fabrics to Foligno; they say he even sold the horse; they say he sleeps in the church of St. Damian; the other day they saw him with some beggars...

The angry merchant was profoundly disturbed by the news. He was ashamed, furious, and frustrated, all at the same time. He had to put a stop to this. That crazy lad had dragged their name through mud, had tainted a respectability that he had worked so hard to attain, and now he even threatened to destroy the business.

Bernardone was determined to end the absurdities once and for all. He had family and neighbors search for him, like dogs on the prowl, in the environs of St. Damian. The tremendous din of the hunting party prompted Francis to run to his hiding place. After long hours of searching and making inquiries, of sniffing and scraping in the most unlikely of hiding places, they failed to locate him and abandoned their search in annoyance and disgust.

Brother Francis, still an amateur competitor in the contests waged by the Lord, was momentarily paralyzed by fear, and remained in hiding for an entire month. It was, without a doubt, a moment of weakness, a moment when, so to speak, he was *not in form.*

Apparently, even the old priest did not know the exact location of his refuge. Only one person, who in all probability may have been that anonymous friend, knew the precise location. Brother Francis would leave his hiding place with extreme caution and trepidation, and for only moments at a time. He was unsure of himself and placed all of his faith in the Lord.

Shades of Kindness in the Austere

One day, according to the biographer, he was suddenly consumed by a feeling of relief, a solace he had never before experienced. Once again, God's infinite mercy snatched him from the jaws of faintheartedness. In the shining light of God's grace, Francis recalled the Knight's code of honor: never fear, never desert, confront the enemy head on....

On that day, he was ashamed of his own shame. Nevertheless, he was not self-critical. He spent hours contemplating the following:

"Man can't be trusted," he said to himself. "He's as fragile as crystal; he can give you the stars or turn his back on you like a deserter. He's made of mortal clay, but there is no need to be afraid.

"My Lord Jesus Christ! Forgive me my faintheartedness. I'm a dead leaf blowing in the wind. Protect me. Give me sandals made of steel. Keep fear from infecting my heart."

And, having said this, he emerged from the dark recesses of the cave with his head held high and bathed in peace. At that moment, he could have entered into combat with the very forces of hell. He felt strong and infinitely free.

* * *

He walked calmly up the steep path leading to the eastern gate of the walled city. He made several stops along the way. His legs could not support him. He was short of breath. His spirit was invincible, but his fasting, his internal struggle, and his worries had consumed all of his energies. He was exhausted, thin as a penitent, emaciated, and had dark circles under his eyes.

He walked through the gateway onto the narrow cobblestone streets, and, as he passed the first few houses, someone yelled from a window:

"Lunatic!"

The cry resonated like trumpets sounding in battle. In a matter of minutes, men, women and children were looking out from all the windows.

"Lunatic! Lunatic!"

The cries grew louder. Boys ran to the streets. For them, there was no better diversion than this. They snarled and whistled, some mocking him in fun, others out of curiosity, and some with malicious intent.

Apparently, nothing bothered Brother Francis of Assisi. His eyes were full of peace. Very few men have shown such courage when confronting ridicule. What was the real intention behind this piece of buffoonery? Did Francis intend to go home and give Peter Bernardone some explanation? Did he want to redeem himself in the eyes of Christ for having been such a coward? We can only speculate.

Be that as it may, Brother Francis did not lose his composure amidst the savage screams. A gentle expression covered his face. Instead of appeasing them, his gentleness was their proof that Francis was utterly insane, since a normal human being would not have reacted in that manner. His behavior only served to incite them to continue their barrage of attacks.

Brother Francis' serenity spurred them on. Pushing him, pulling his clothes, deafening him with their screams and insults was child's play. They wanted to shatter his resolve. They picked up anything that was within reach, rocks, dirt, rotten tomatoes, using such weapons to test his breaking point.

The small city resonated with the clamor in the streets and soon the echoes reached the home of old Bernardone. The merchant, as curious as the next man, looked out his window to see what all the fuss was about. Instantly, shame and rage rose like fire inside him: it was his own son. The sight paralyzed him at first. He did not know whether to curse or to cry. Both reactions were drowned by his fear of being ridiculed.

In a rage, he rushed into the middle of the sadistic mob, grabbed his son by the neck, releasing his ire in a flood of biting words as he pushed his way through the crowd. He dragged him all the way home, beat him severely, and locked him in the dark basement. Brother Francis remained unshaken amid the chaos: neither fear, nor threatening looks, nor brutality could shatter his serenity: he looked like the angel of peace.

* * *

Every day the father would go to the basement and try to dissuade the lad from pursuing the outrageous life he was bent on leading. At times he begged; at times he threatened, but almost always he reprimanded him. It was all in vain. With a calm demeanor that was admirable, and yet maddening to the merchant, Francis remained inflexible. He was unyielding. His friendship with the Lord and the humiliation he had suffered, strengthened him in such a way that he was able to resist the forces of heaven, hell and inhumane treatment.

The poor and humble Francis of Assisi was rising from the depths of these tribulations, that "little and sweet" brother whose only armor was his patience; he was the freest man in the world and the richest poor man on earth.

Peter Bernardone had to go away on business. Before leaving, he took precautions and put his obstinate son in chains, both his hands and his feet. Not only did Brother Francis not resist, he acquiesced with the gentleness of a lamb and conducted himself with the stateliness of a king.

The merchant, not yet satisfied, put a sturdy lock on the basement door. He made sure that his wife, in his absence, did all she could to convince and dissuade the stubborn youth. And he left, after giving his final instructions.

The Mother's Last Benediction

It is difficult to imagine a more uncomfortable situation for a mother and her son. Both were caught between the devil and the deep blue sea.

Pica, on the one hand, was in accord with Francis. Deep inside, her feminine intuition and her strength, as a good and honest mother, sympathized with her son, and she was happy that he was dedicating his life to God and to the poor.

However, she could not condone her son's methods with regard to his consecration: leaving home and living like a pauper. On the other hand, as a faithful wife, she agreed with her husband, pained beyond words by Peter's suffering. She desired a genuine and warm reconciliation between father and son.

She tried the most effective measures of persuasion, in an effort to make her son see that some of his methods were not right. With tears in her eyes she begged her son to come back home and to accede, at least on some issues, to the request of his father.

If the mother felt badly, the son felt worse. It must have been heartrending for Francis, a son who was so sensitive, to find himself caught between the tears of a mother who was so loving and so loved by him, and the will of God. Without a doubt, those were agonizing days for Brother Francis.

All prophets would agree: men of strong emotions, pulled this way and that by the voice of God, feel the need to break the bonds, as if the chosen one, placed at a crossing, were being pulled in two different directions. Whom does he obey?

* * *

What occurred between mother and son in the basement of the house? If we begin with the outcome, we can imagine the sudden changes unfolding in that scene. The mother begged tenderly. The son affectionately refused. The mother insisted, tears streaming down her face. The son resisted, his eyes shining brightly. The mother's words began to lose force. The son, always gentle, was ever more inspired. This was a most extraordinary battle in human history.

One by one, the great lady's arguments fell to the ground, and she soon found herself without ammunition and defenseless. She saw that it was impossible to dissuade him and she gave up the fight. Pica said no more. She was no longer a foe but rather a follower, a mother turned disciple. The noble mother began to be somewhat of a "daughter" to her son, nourished by Francis' ideals and receiving the warmth from his sun.

When Francis spoke of Jesus, his words were like time-less melodies or lullabies which lulled her to a sleepless sleep, a daydream in which her old ideals were reborn, ideals that were never elucidated nor fulfilled: to give herself completely to an immortal Love. Francis was right.

She knew very well what love and motherhood could and could not give her; she knew that spring is full of promises and that autumn is full of farewells: Francis was right. Open the doors wide, let Jesus in, lose yourself in God, fill your heart with the divine light, do not leave anything for the all-consuming death, bare your soul completely in absolute solitude and be free, have nothing in order to have everything to give, sing the last song and die in the soft breeze of twilight, a death that is not a disintegration, rather a completion: Francis was right. Take the dark road and give love to all the hungry, wear the infinite mystery where it is visible to all as you walk with Jesus across worlds and millennia with peace in your voice and in your eyes, born again with Jesus, to return: Francis was right...

* * *

The next morning, the noble mother looked all over the house for the right tools. With the proper tools in hand, she went to the basement and, without saying a word, opened the large lock to this prison cell. Then she broke the iron clasped around his feet and the manacles on his wrists.

She knew all too well that she would have to endure the merchant's wrath as a consequence of her actions. But now nothing mattered to her either. Francis' glorious freedom was contagious.

Upon seeing that he was free, the youth knelt at his mother's feet. He was profoundly moved, and without saying a word he waited to receive his mother's blessing. Pica said to him:

"Bird of God, fly all around the world and sing."

Then, as she placed her hands on his head, she added:

"My dear son, God's wings cover and protect you, just like these hands. Take my blood and my spirit to the ends of the earth. Open pathways that I can't travel. Give my lamps to the nights and my fountains to the deserts. Gather the pains of this world and spread hope. May your death be a celebration and your life a birth. May the winds rock you to sleep and may the mountains provide you with shade. Cover the earth with your compassion and transform urns into homes. I love you, blood of my blood, son of my spirit. When your naked and temporal body receives the kiss of 'Sister Death,' I'll be waiting for you under Aurora's great arch."

And, having said this, Francis' mother raised him to his feet. They embraced for a prolonged period of time and without exchanging words. They climbed the basement stairs in silence. Francis looked around at the familiar sur- roundings as one would look at something for the last time. His mother accompanied him to the door and Brother Fran- cis walked slowly down the street. Never again would he cross that threshold. Pica followed him with her gaze until he disappeared in the winding streets. Happily, she would have followed him until her death. Brother Francis arrived at his home: St. Damian.

It was an inexpressible event, and, without a doubt, one of the most moving and transcendent scenes in human history.

* * *

During the following years we lose sight of the evocative silhouette of that marvelous woman. Franciscan sources do not go beyond this point with regard to her life. Historians presuppose that she suffered a premature death. She was always in poor health. Also, there is a slight possibility that Francis inherited his poor health—Francis also died prematurely—from his mother, from whom he also inherited his exemplary soul. From now on, there is no mention of her in the Franciscan sources.

Here, we also say our grateful farewell to Lady Pica, a most admirable woman.

I Take Orders Only from God

The chronicler notes that all of these trials and tribulations gave Brother Francis a strong constitution. With the exception of one or two occasions never again did fear knock at his door.

One fine day, Bernardone returned, and, as to be expected, upon hearing that Pica had released the prisoner, he rushed upon her spewing insults, threats and tirades. He was absolutely blind with anger. Pica had prepared herself in the "Franciscan academy" and had on her spiritual armor. Her shield against the tempest was her coat of arms: patience. She did not even blink.

For Bernardone, it was hopeless. The son was lost beyond hope of ever fulfilling the father's dreams of success. He had no illusions about reclaiming that dream, and above all, about straightening his son out and making him see things sensibly. But he would not tolerate the excesses of his stubborn and crazy son who threatened to destroy his social position among the respected bourgeois, a position which he had worked so hard to acquire. There was only one solution: to have Francis banished from the country.

With neighbors and friends at his side, the merchant invaded St. Damian. This time Brother Francis did not run. On the contrary, a beautiful spectacle occurred. The humble Brother Francis, radiating peace and wearing the shield of indestructible spiritual freedom, with eyes full of tranquility and gentleness, approached his father.

And when Bernardone began with his usual threats and orders, Brother Francis remained perfectly serene and while looking into his eyes, he said:

"*Messer* Peter Bernardone: in all the world, there's no other master for me than my Lord Jesus Christ. I receive orders only from him. Neither the emperor, nor the *Supreme Magistrate*, nor Peter Bernardone, nor the forces of repression, nor the armies, nor the forces from above that give the order of death, of sickness or of hell, are capable of tearing me from the arms of my Lord Jesus Christ."

In a very humble tone and in a low voice, he added:

"Forgive me, sir. Now I belong to the ranks of Christ and the Church."

It was evident that he was losing on this battlefield as well, so the merchant confronted him on the issue of the money he made selling the fabrics and the horse. Brother Francis did not say a word. He took the merchant gently by the arm, entered the hermitage, and, with his index finger, pointed to the recess in the window. After two months, the bag that the priest had refused still lay there intact. The old man grabbed the bag and left in silence.

Since he saw that it was impossible to win his son back, it occurred to Bernardone that he could at least recover monies that the squanderer had perhaps divided among the many hermitages or charities. He went directly to the municipality of Assisi and brought formal charges against his son.

The consuls sent constables to Francis' retreat. He was issued a summons to appear before the tribunal. Brother Francis, with humility and courtesy, said to the constables:

"Gentlemen, you and the consuls should know that, by God's infinite mercy, I am free. The consuls no longer have jurisdiction over me; I am a vassal of the Almighty Lord Jesus Christ and of holy Mother Church."

* * *

Upon receiving word of the juridical situation, and knowing that only one ecclesiastical authority could judge Francis, the merchant went directly to the bishopric and took the case against his son to Bishop Guido.

The bishop agreed to arbitrate the matter under debate and sent an emissary to notify Francis that he was to appear before the bishop. Brother Francis was overjoyed. I will go with pleasure, he said, because the bishop is my master and father of souls.

Francis' imagination was burning with delight. To him, the upcoming scene was like a chivalric ceremony in which gentlemen swear loyalty and obedience to their lord, in the eyes of the public. An eternal alliance with the Lord Jesus Christ called for a celebration before the bishop and the entire township of Assisi. It was a wedding day.

What was Peter Bernardone trying to achieve with this summons? If he failed to have Francis banished from the municipality, he intended, first and foremost, to disinherit his son under a judicial decree, unless his son had intentions of voluntarily disinheriting himself. Second, he wanted to recover the property he still had a right to claim.

Nevertheless, in his heart of hearts, Bernardone's intention was to disown his son, to no longer acknowledge the perverted youth as his offspring. By doing so, he would cleanse himself of his humiliation.

Like the Trees in Winter

It was a beautiful and transcendent moment. Very few spiritual events have had the impact and atmosphere, the uniqueness and significance of the scene that took place on that winter morning.

All of Assisi flocked to the plaza of Saint Mary Major, some out of curiosity, and others in anticipation of seeing the irksome merchant suffer humiliation. The small city trembled to the core. Those who used to laugh at Francis would now break down and cry. Somehow, on that day, the holy city of Assisi was born.

* * *

At the appointed hour, the plaza was packed with people. A throne adorned with the episcopal coat of arms was placed in the center of the plaza. Bishop Guido, Peter Bernardone, and Francis made their appearance almost simultaneously. A murmur of emotion rose and fell in an instant. Bishop Guido was smiling; Peter was tense; Francis was calm. The chroniclers say that Francis was greeted warmly by the bishop.

It is interesting to note that the bishop was a privileged witness to the Franciscan epic, and also witnessed Francis' death and canonization.

The bishop, as acting judge, directed his statements first to the accused, saying:

"My son, your father is very upset and his heart is filled with bitterness. You have squandered a great deal of his property and this lack of consideration has annoyed your father. Since it is your desire to serve God, it is advisable that, prior to taking this step, you return to your father what is rightfully his."

Bernardone looked at the ground. Francis' clear eyes were fixed on the bishop's face. Not for a moment did the spectators divert their attention from the protagonists.

The bishop continued, directing his statements once again to Francis:

"You do not know whether the monies were obtained by fair means or, if on the contrary, collected at the expense of the weak, in which case it would not be just to erect hermitages with the blood of the meek. My son, return to your father what belongs to him. This restitution will quiet his anger and peace will flourish in his eyes. Also, place your worries in the hands of the Lord. Fix your eyes on the eyes of God. Fill your pitcher with everlasting waters. Anoint your heart with the oil of fortitude. Ward off fear. Do not be afraid, and each morning, next to every hermitage in ruins, you will find ample bricks and rocks. It will be the work of the Lord."

Francis took a few steps forward and said:

"Your Excellency, I'll do as you have asked, and more than you have asked."

An expectant silence fell among the spectators. All were avidly experiencing these moments and no one wanted to miss even the most insignificant detail.

* * *

Francis made a small reverential gesture asking permission to withdraw, and in an instant his small frame disappeared within the episcopal house, which was just a few meters away. Apprehension seized the crowd that had gathered, including the bishop. They all looked at one another inquisitively.

In less than a minute Francis returned completely naked, except for the hair shirt that he was wearing. To everyone's surprise, he walked calmly through the multitude toward the tribunal, delicately carrying a bundle of clothes in his hands. The crowd was seized with a tense and anguished silence.

Francis approached Bernardone. Without a word, he placed the bundle very carefully at the merchant's feet, and placed the little bag of money on top of the clothes.

In his nakedness, he turned to the crowd and began to speak very slowly, while his gaze was lost in the infinite. His words were from another world.

"Citizens of Assisi and young friends," said Francis, "I hope that my words will be engraved in fire on your memory. There's no word in this world that carries a melody like the word *father*. Since I was first able to speak and walk I attached that blessed word to Peter Bernardone, who is present. I called him father and gave him kisses. He looked at me and I looked at him. He loved me and I loved him. He made sacrifices so that I might become a successful merchant, as great as he. But God chose me and loved me for all eternity, putting a wall between me and my career as a merchant. Blocking my path, he said: Come with me. I have decided to go with him. Now I have another Father. So then, the possessions I have received from Peter Bernardone are now at his feet: the clothes, the business, the inheritance, and even the family name. From now on, the Lord, who is in the heavens, is the only one in this world whom I will call *my Father*. I came into this world naked and naked will I return to the arms of my Father."

Those who just a moment before had been mocking him were now crying. The bishop was crying. Bernardone did not know where to look as he fought the infectious rush of emotions coming from the assembly. There was such simplicity and sincerity, such integrity and conviction in this scene, a scene that is unique in the history of souls. The magnitude of this impression took possession of the crowd's spirit.

The abrupt changes in the collective spirit accounted for the city's fascination with Francis, surpassing what they felt when he was the leader of the young men in society or when they considered him mad. He was achieving in his own city the heroic deeds he longed to accomplish in the region of Apulia. The fame that was formerly his most ardent desire came at a moment when fame was of little interest to him. The entire city was at his feet. He could recite the words with Brother John of the Cross: "I had it all when I wanted it the least."

* * *

Bernardone bent down, picked up the clothes and the bag, and disappeared without saying a word. A murmur of disapproval rose from those who had gathered and the noise lingered for quite a while.

Bernardone arrived at his home. A sword, forged by contradictions, had wedged itself deep inside the merchant: ire, shame, and remorse. Although he was as tough as nails, it was impossible to remain unaffected. What we would give to know Pica's reaction upon hearing about Francis' prophetic gesture! Without a doubt, she, as well as all the world, could not fight back the tears.

The last days of winter were upon them. Francis was totally disrobed and trembling from the cold. With warmth and affection, Bishop Guido wrapped him in the abundant folds of his cape.

Bishop Guido, to whom the Franciscan movement is greatly indebted, did not lead Francis away, nor did he direct his steps toward the priesthood or the monastery, which was usually the case in those days. That holy man, through sagacity or shrewdness, had a feeling that a different future was in store for that unique young man. Instead of offering advice or showing him a path, he left the decision in the hands of God, so that the Lord could direct Francis personally on a new path.

When the crowd began to disperse, they all headed to their homes amidst a flood of remarks. The bishop asked one of his servants to bring something for Francis to wear. The servant soon returned with a tabard, a type of one-piece sleeveless cloak.

Francis asked for some chalk which he used to draw a cross on the garment. He put the cloak on joyfully. Afterwards, he knelt at the bishop's feet and received his benediction. Francis got up and the two of them embraced each other warmly. Brother Francis left the city by the nearest gate and soon disappeared behind the first foothills of Mount Subasio.

Naked, Free and Full of Joy

He was the freest man in the world. Ties could not bind him. He had nothing so he had nothing to lose. What was there to fear? Why worry? Is not an army in defence of material wealth that is at risk a source of worry? What can perturb the person who has nothing and wants nothing? Brother Francis did not have clothes, food, or a roof over his head. He had no father, no mother, no brothers or sisters. He did not have prestige, friends, neighbors, nor was he part of high society. And there, in the barren and denuded earth a tall tree of liberty was born and grew.

The Poor Man of Assisi had nothing, no projects or clear ideas about his future, not even ideals. And here lay the grandeur and drama of the prophet. Here was a poor man launched on a path—by a superior force—that no one had yet traveled, with no guarantees of a final success, and no inkling as to the dangers that lurked at the next crossroads.

And since he did not have a clue, he had no idea how to show his loyalty to God from one day to the next. He was content to show his faith a minute at a time, to follow a path, step by step, obstacle after obstacle, without knowing the next step he would take. He slept under the stars caressing poppies in his hand, not knowing which poppies he would come across tomorrow; he would open his eyes each morning and begin his solitary walk on unknown paths....

When all means of security are lost, when all human support systems collapse, when finery and clothing are no longer within reach, man, naked and free, having barely made an attempt, finds himself in God's hands.

A naked man is a man who has surrendered himself, like the flightless birds that are joyously perched in the warm hands of the Lord. When one has nothing, God becomes everything.

God is always at the core. When vestments fall, God appears. When friends vanish, when confidantes become traitors, when social prestige crumbles to the ground, when good health is jeopardized, God appears. When all hope is lost, God raises the arm of hope. When scaffolds fall, God transforms himself into support and security. Only the poor possess God.

* * *

When his mother was no longer there, the Lord took Brother Francis and pressed his head against his chest, showing him more warmth and tenderness than Lady Pica herself.

At daybreak, still in the lap of "Mother" God, Brother Francis heard the world's palpitations. He opened his eyes and looked into the eyes of all of God's creatures, and, as though it were the beginning of creation, he immersed himself in the virgin world. Although he did not have blood brothers or sisters, all of God's creatures *were given* to him as his sisters. There was not a man on earth with more "relatives," in more fraternal company with God's creatures than himself, so warm and friendly and so welcomed. No one enjoyed as he did the warmth of the sun or of fire, the fresh breezes in the shade and near the fountains, the splendor of the stars and the joy of spring... In the absence of his family, creation became his family, the blue sky and celestial vault were the roof over his head.

In having God, he had everything. But to have God he had to dispossess himself of everything.

Having nothing, Brother Francis entered the immeasurable current of God's gift: he received everything. He deserved nothing. All was Grace: his clothes, his food, a look, affection, sympathy.

He who receives everything feels unworthy. He does not protest. He does not make demands. On the contrary, he is grateful for everything. Gratitude is the first fruit of poverty.

Brother Francis was like an almond tree extending its branches to the sun, from which he joyfully and gratefully received life and warmth. But if the sun hid behind the clouds, he did not complain. There were no violent reactions. This is the second fruit of poverty: peace, a sweet-tasting fruit.

Feeling unworthy, Brother Francis threw himself at the feet of the masses, as though he were the most insignificant among them. For Brother Francis, humility was not a lack of consideration for himself, it meant being considerate to others, treating them like "gentlemen," so as to *serve* them, throwing himself at their feet in order to wash them, waiting on them at table...

In the Beginning

Instead of heading for Foligno, Brother Francis took the path toward Gubbio and began to climb the first spurs of Subasio. It was still winter, but the first signs of spring were in the air. The world was like Francis: naked, pure, clean, virgin. A harsh winter had blown like a relentless gust of wind over the rostrum of Creation, unsettling the forests and razing the hillocks, transforming gardens into cemeteries.

The high crests of the Central Apennines were still covered with snow. There was also snow in some of the rural gorges.

"Winter is good for one's health," Brother Francis said to himself. "It fortifies and purifies. Winter is the cradle of spring. These are strong fir trees. They dare to grow so tall and without fear because when they were small they were severely punished by the north wind and so they gripped the earth with all their strength to keep from falling. Blessed be poverty, nakedness, and the misunderstanding that makes us hold onto God."

Brother Francis was absolutely overjoyed. Spring was running through his veins. It was as if his soul were staring out at the universe for the very first time. Everything looked brand new. Never had he relished—and been so grateful for—the warmth of the sun; it tasted like God's caress.

He was waging a decisive battle. The Lord, in all his mercy, helped him and made him the victor. It was the work of the Lord. As for man, he was the embodiment of fear and incoherence. Francis had the impression of being submerged and tucked in the bosom of universal harmony; his soul was one with the soul of the world. A joy totally unknown to him had consumed his entire being, he had this incredible urge to sing, and, above all, to give thanks. He was simply enraptured.

* * *

He continued on his way. All at once, he spied a centipede slowly making its way across the road. In an instant, he felt an indescribable feeling of tenderness. He bent down and put his finger gently in the creature's path. The little centipede began to crawl slowly up his finger. Francis looked at it admiringly, and he observed its undulating movement for a long time. He saw a bush, and with extreme delicacy and patience, placed the centipede on a leaf, recalling that in the Scriptures the Crucified Christ is likened to a worm.

Small yellow flowers, whose name Francis could not recall, were blooming everywhere. Throughout the day he took care not to step on any of them on his excursions to and from the mountains.

It is interesting to note that on that day, he felt an extreme affection toward God, but he also felt the need to channel those emotions, and express that warmth to all of God's creatures and, above all, to the most insignificant among them.

"One sees God," Brother Francis said to himself, "in the eyes of these creatures, especially in the eyes of those that are most vulnerable. But, without a doubt, the Lord is most visible and most at home in beggars and lepers. These are his favorites."

Ambassador to the King

The happiness he felt was so overwhelming, that he just could not help himself and he burst into song. He sang in French. They were Provençal songs about the chivalric life that he had learned a long time ago. Later on he learned to improvise and he dedicated songs to the Lord. At first it all sounded quite peculiar because the echoes reverberating from the hillocks took a while to reach his ears.

When he grew accustomed to the acoustics, he interjected glorious cries of gratitude to the Lord God in total exaltation, as though he were in a trance. He was the happiest man on earth.

* * *

By mid-afternoon he reached the deep, rough gorge that leads to the small town of Caprignone, midway between Assisi and Gubbio. Without warning, out of nowhere a band of robbers jumped him, shouting:

"Halt! This is a holdup! Identify yourself!"

Brother Francis responded joyfully:

"Men, I'm the herald of the great emperor."

When the thieves, always on the look out for loot, saw that he was outlandishly dressed, half naked, wearing that ridiculous tabard, but at the same time fearless and taking a bold stance, they said:

"This one's out of his mind!"

So they decided to vent their frustrations by shoving and pushing him around. They took his tabard. A few meters away they saw a deep ditch covered with snow, and they threw him into it, saying:

"Stay there, you croaking imperial herald."

During this tragicomical episode, Brother Francis remained at peace. He did not resist, he did not lose his smile; this only served to convince the bandits that he was in fact out of his mind.

When he saw that he was buried in the snow, Brother Francis said to himself:

"The ancient knights who fought for King Arthur suffered the same misadventures. It's to my advantage that I have chosen to suffer these small exploits for the Glory of the Great Emperor."

He got up. He saw that the ditch was deep and that climbing out was going to be difficult. He would start to climb and then he would fall. He tried many times. He dug his nails into the rocks. He fell again. After several attempts, he finally made his way out. He wiped off the snow and dirt and looked in all directions to ascertain the bandits' whereabouts. There was no one in sight.

"These men," Brother Francis said to himself, "assault and rob because they lack food and affection. They, too, should be among the favored. First the lepers, then the beggars, then the bandits; in short, the outcasts of society."

Among the Pots and Pans

As he continued on his way, he thought about these things, and felt happy to be worthy of suffering in the name of Jesus. He soon forgot about his adventure and continued to sing the praises of the Lord, in French. By the grace of

God, at this moment not even the forces of Mt. Alvernia were capable of frightening him.

"God is merciful," he said in a loud voice.

It was getting dark. He was hungry and had not eaten all day. He was cold since the bandits had taken his cloak, leaving him half naked.

There was a Benedictine monastery further down the road. It was called *St. Verecondo* and belonged to the district of Vallingegno. Brother Francis headed in that direction. He was not sure whether he would spend a few days there or just stay overnight. He knocked and a monk came to the door.

"I'm one of God's poor and I wish to serve the Lord," said Francis in all humility. "I have no home and no clothes. It would please me to work for my daily bread, and if it's possible, I'd like something to wear."

* * *

He spent several days there. The monks put him to work in the kitchen. Since Brother Francis declined to give any explanations concerning his identity, the monks concluded that he was a peculiar sort but not dangerous. They gave him a room to himself and one or two blankets. He spent practically the entire night with the Lord, as though he were on a honeymoon. He barely slept and was extremely happy.

During the day he did chores in the kitchen and shared in their meals; but they did not give him anything to wear. Obviously, they treated him at all times like one of the poor, as he appeared to be.

Therefore, he decided to find another way of getting the clothes he needed. One day Brother Francis met up with the prior in the cloister. He knelt reverently before him and said:

"My father, I give you my humble thanks for allowing me to work and for giving me nourishment during my stay. I ask God to send the angel of peace and spread his wings over this house every morning. I ask for your blessing before I take my leave."

And Brother Francis left, wearing no more than when he arrived. The narrators say that this same prior, a few years later when Francis was well known, went to Brother Francis to ask forgiveness for having been so inconsiderate to him on that occasion. And it surprised him to hear Francis say that very few times in his life was he as happy as in the days he spent at St. Verecondo.

The Garments of a Pilgrim

As he left the monastery, Brother Francis remembered the name of his good friend Federico Spadalunga who resided in Gubbio and who would gladly give him something to wear. He walked in that direction.

On the way, he reflected on his days in the monastery.

"Yes," he thought, "it's good to be poor and to have no identity. Those that are well-bred, titled, and have a prosperous business are the only ones that are respected in this world. The poor are scorned and, at best, ignored.

"But the Lord made himself one of the poor," he said out loud.

While he walked he was tempted now and then to speak out, under his breath, against the monks of St. Verecondo. But he resisted by saying:

"The poor have no rights, they're only thankful, and don't complain. Will the day ever come when I'll feel perfectly content in suffering tribulations?" he continued pensively.

* * *

He arrived in Gubbio, a noble city with an aristocratic look. People laughed at him as he walked through the streets. But he did not let that bother him.

"It's only natural that they laugh at me," he thought.

He walked toward the home of the noble family, the Spadalungas. They welcomed him with open arms. He told them about a gold coffer that contained emeralds of enormous value; about God's affection, that no woman on this earth, be that woman a wife or mother, could possibly give; the freedom of birds in flight; peace in the late afternoon; in all, the riches of poverty.

Messer Federico was extremely moved. Brother Francis allowed the Spadalungas to dress him in a garment worn by pilgrims and hermits long ago: a tunic with a leather belt, shoes and a pilgrim's staff. Brother Francis was touched, and with very simple words he expressed his gratitude. They said their farewells and Brother Francis began his journey back to Assisi.

"It's very difficult to have money and to be free," he said to himself as he walked. "However, there are those who are rich and whose hearts are filled with tenderness and compassion, like my friends, the Spadalungas. Most importantly, it's a gift to be able to converse with them because they express themselves with the utmost courtesy, and courtesy is the language of the angels. Nevertheless, to my Lord Jesus Christ, paradise is at the other end of the spectrum. Wealth is an irremediable whirlpool where the rich drown before reaching the shore. That's the truth. But God's compassion is much more powerful than the force of irremediable whirlpools. For God, nothing's impossible. The wealthy will also be saved."

And he added in a loud voice:

"The Lord's compassion is invincible."

With a Mother's Affection

Upon arriving in Assisi, he did not go directly to St. Damian. Instead, he went to San Salvatore delle Pareti to see his friends, the lepers. So much of God's tenderness welled up inside him that he wanted to give it all to those who suffered. Indeed, he needed to do so.

When his *Christian brothers* saw him enter, they jumped for joy and began teasing him about the pilgrim outfit he had on. They congratulated him, since they too had been informed about what had taken place in the plaza.

He began by saying, "You, the favored of my Lord Jesus Christ. Many months ago when I first came here, I came with pockets full of money because I was still the son of the successful merchant Bernardone. But now that I'm the son of my celestial Father, I bring a mother's love. And now I want to tell you a story: 'Once upon a time, up in the skies, the Lord called his wisest archangel and asked the following:

'Guess who are my most favorite creatures in all the world.'

'The children!' replied the archangel.

'No. But I do love them very much,' said the Lord.

'The poor!' exclaimed the archangel.

'I love the poor, but there are others I love more.'

'Your *Christian brothers*!' said the archangel.

'That is right!' exclaimed the Lord as he rose. 'They are the ones who remind me most of my Son when he gave himself in total submission to death.'"

The lepers were overcome with emotion. Some even cried.

He spent several days with them. No mother on earth could have shown them more tenderness. His affection poured from his hands, his eyes, his mouth, like an infinite number of dew drops. He washed their feet. He bandaged their wounds. He removed the scales from their skin. He touched their wounds when he washed them, but he took great care not to cause them any pain.

He knew what each one liked for his meal. When it came time to wash their feet, he knew who liked warm water, and who liked the water a bit warmer. He knew the personal history of each of the sick. Francis had the distinct impression that he was touching Jesus himself, that he was easing his sorrows or healing his wounds. He would stay up until all hours of the night washing their clothes. He would get up early and clean house and prepare their meals. He wanted those days at the infirmary to be festive occasions.

Reminiscing

The Lord himself had ordered him to repair the hermitages. First, he concerned himself with restoring the existing hermitages that were in ruins. One morning, after saying his farewells and a *so long* to the lepers, he took the path leading to St. Damian.

"Seven or eight weeks have passed since the time I received the order to construct hermitages," he said to himself as he walked slowly along the path. "My God, so many wonderful experiences in so little time! It looks like rubble-work erected under the arch of eternity. It's the ever present and undeniable compassion of the Lord, more constant than the mountains, which are eternal," he said in a loud voice.

One by one, Brother Francis recalled the many adventures that had occurred since that time, and he wanted to cry out in pure gratitude. As he walked along the path that led outside the city walls, he looked up, he looked down, he looked all around, seeing everything so clearly as bestowed by Grace. The Lord had so willingly conferred on him amazing gifts in such a brief period of time.

He had no intention of entering the monastery, nor of entering the priesthood. The Lord had molded him into an explorer of solitary and unknown paths. His future looked like a day covered in a blanket of fog.

"But the One who has put me on this path," he thought to himself, "will know how to direct me, taking me by the hand through this fog and solitude."

He felt free, confident, and happy.

* * *

Francis arrived at St. Damian in that same frame of mind. He went immediately in search of the priest. He knelt reverently at his feet and asked for his blessing. He explained how the Lord had sent him to repair hermitages, beginning with St. Damian, and how the bishop, in the tribunal, had encouraged him, giving him his benediction in order that he might carry out these divine orders with the utmost success. The priest did not find these explanations convincing.

Francis then entered the hermitage, and at the foot of the Byzantine-style cross he relived that moment of divine grace that he had experienced weeks before.

While inside the hermitage he began to formulate the ways and means of reconstructing the damaged walls.

"I must have been dreaming. To think that just a few weeks ago I used to trust that money was the answer. Without a doubt, I must have been blind to think that I could shore up the walls of the hermitage with the lustrous and noisy coins I held in my hand. What vanity! Hands, toil, sweat, love, the tools of Lady Poverty, are what build the works of the Lord."

Oil for the Lamp

Dressed in the vestments of a hermit and with a joyous heart, Brother Francis climbed the rocky path, and within a short while he found himself walking along familiar city streets.

He had a look of peace and serenity as he walked through the plazas and cloisters. For many, he was undeniably God's new prophet. Others were a bit suspicious as to his intentions and his mental stability. To a few, he was still the crazed lunatic and they laughed in his face. With regard to those who mocked him, Brother Francis thought:

"It's only natural that they doubt me."

* * *

Another time, the money in his pockets had illuminated the lamps that burned before the crucifix. Now that he had no money, he went from door to door asking for oil.

He knew of a proprietor of large olive groves who made oil in his basement. So he went to the man's house. As he approached, he noticed that the vestibule was full of people engaged in animated discussions: they were his old friends.

What remained of his vanity rose from the ashes in an instant, stopping him dead in his tracks. He immediately turned and walked down another street.

"Think, Bernardone's son," he said to himself. "What do you call a knight who denies his lord?"

And, while saying this, he turned right around with the intention of burying once and for all what remained of his worldly vanities.

Francis walked back to the house. He greeted his former companions very naturally. Everyone delighted in their reunion. Francis said to them:

"Friends, almost everyone thinks that I'm a saint. I'm going to tell you what occurred just now. A few minutes ago, I was walking directly towards this house to ask for oil. When I saw all of you, I was too ashamed to approach, and like a coward who deserts, I slipped away down a back street. And if it weren't for God's infinite mercy, I would have probably done considerably worse."

His friends remained silent.

For the love of his Lord, he asked the owner of the house for a little bit of oil. The gentleman gave him several liters, and, with this precious load, Francis went back to the hermitage. He was happy not about the oil, but rather about his triumph over self.

"What would become of me if I didn't have God's compassion?" he asked himself. "The beast, pain and suffering, and all, lurk behind the door, ready to make an assault at any given moment. But the Lord is stronger than the beast," he added out loud.

A Rock and a Reward

Everyday he went up to the city, walked through the streets and gathered the townspeople around him. He told them about the inexplicable joy God gives those who go to him. He sang old songs of chivalry, changing the lyrics to reflect his new situation. And he invented a chorus and melody, and sang it as follows:

"Give me a rock and I'll give you a reward.

Give me two rocks and I'll give you two rewards.

Three rewards to the one who gives me three rocks."

He formed a circle and had everyone sing this refrain in chorus.

The townspeople were joyful as they carried rocks and other construction materials on their shoulders as they made their way down to the hermitage. He needed wood to construct a scaffold, and within a few days he had what he needed. He climbed the scaffold and began laying bricks. The peasants who worked in the neighboring vineyards offered to help him for a few hours, without any reward. Francis' happiness was contagious and the restoration progressed at a quick pace.

Some of the inhabitants of Assisi, impressed by the transformation of the well-known merchant's heir, went all the way to the hermitage to see how things were going and lingered out of curiosity. And in good humor Brother Francis invited them to join him, saying:

"Friends, what are you doing just staring? The kingdom of heaven isn't for the curious, rather for those who get down and work. Get up here. I'm unable to give you a single coin as recompense, but your hearts will be filled with solace."

The priest, by nature, was very skeptical. It was difficult for him to trust and he was reticent when it came to circumstances and people. He felt that in order to trust, things needed to be not only tried but also proven. He was also very reserved with Brother Francis and observed him scrupulously for many weeks.

"It's not right," he said to himself one day. "At birth he was placed in a luxurious crib, raised with all the advantages of a privileged upbringing, and he renounces everything, all the comforts of the bourgeoisie in order to live naked and poor in the Lord's name. It's not right that I be so reserved with him."

One day he called him over and said to him:

"My son, you've lived a very privileged life. Your hands weren't made to mix mortar and carry boulders. Masonry, as a trade, is very difficult work. You're happy but you look exhausted. You don't have the strength of a giant oak tree. I fear that you'll get very weak. Don't worry about it, my son, and allow me to take care of you."

Ever since that day, the old priest took great care to prepare the best dishes with his limited knowledge of the culinary arts. He loved Francis more than he would his own son. They forged a very deep and warm friendship.

* * *

At nightfall, Brother Francis would return to the hermitage. He spent long hours in heartfelt communion with the crucifix, illuminated by the pale splendor of the oil lamp.

For now, Brother Francis expressed no other sentiments but gratitude. He was like a boy, guided by the firm loving hand of his Father. He would have gladly spent the night repeating the following words:

"Thank you, my Lord!"

He was not afraid of anything. His future was uncertain, but he had no worries.

Everyday he found time to visit San Salvatore. He needed to be among the lepers and show them the same affection he had for the Lord. The beggars who walked along the roads in the valley were his equal. Their friendship grew stronger and stronger. He visited them frequently. He and the beggars would sit on the rocks along the road and talk amicably. The exterior walls of the hermitage were soon restored.

Cup in Hand

One night, as he looked intensely at the large black eyes of the Crucified Christ, Brother Francis said to himself:

"Look at him lying on a cross instead of a bed. He's naked instead of dressed. He nourishes himself like a mendicant and sleeps under the stars. He was born in a cave and buried in someone else's tomb... And you? The venerable priest has you living like a prince. This can't be!" he then said in a loud voice. "Bourgeois' son," he said to himself, "remember: a beggar is one who gratefully receives all the leftovers, like a little dog, and eats all of it without complaining and without making faces. If the Lord made himself a beggar for your love, it is proper that you make yourself a beggar for his love. Starting tomorrow we'll go from door to door in all humility and gratitude."

* * *

After working all morning, at midday he walked up to the city and with a cup in hand, went from door to door saying:

"For the love of Love, give me something to eat."

Within a few minutes his cup was overflowing with food.

The people said:

"And to think that only yesterday he was that magnificent gentleman who prepared banquets for his friends!"

With his cup filled to the brim, he walked along the walls of the city and sat on a rock in the shade. He began to stir the mixture and was about to eat it when, all of a sudden, his stomach began to turn and he felt like vomiting.

"There is no escaping the bourgeois, is there!" he exclaimed in a loud voice.

And, having said this, he got up, left the food on the rock, and tried to regain his composure and overcome this crisis.

"The same thing always happens," he said in reflection. "When my thoughts are not focused on Jesus and my mind is elsewhere, the former self appears unexpectedly, with its instincts and impulses. I'm liable to commit a felony, even spit at the poor. Man is made of mortal clay, but this should not be cause for alarm."

He started to calm down little by little and think about Jesus. With extreme sensitivity he imagined Jesus walking, begging, hungry, thirsty, eating quite happily all that was offered in alms. While in the middle of these thoughts, the Presence, with all its strength, took hold of him, body and soul, thought and sentiment.

"Just like you, my Lord!" he said in a loud voice, and he went back to the rock.

He took the cup, and without letting his thoughts stray from Jesus he quickly devoured the strange mixture, finally wiping the vessel with his tongue.

* * *

He stood up and walked slowly down the path leading to St. Damian.

"The Lord works wonders! The Lord works wonders!" he said over and over in a loud voice. "The heart of man should be an ocean of surprises. The human mind will never fully appreciate the powerful and loving arm of the Lord God."

Suddenly, Brother Francis felt extremely happy, as never before, and he had a tremendous urge to sing.

An intoxicating spring covered everything with a glorious canopy. Brother Francis took a few steps and then stopped, absolutely engrossed by the pulse of life around him. The cherry trees were in bloom and the flowers looked like oriental queens. Soft breezes stroked Brother Francis' face, and he responded by saying:

"Caresses from my Lord!"

Little green lizards sunbathed on blistering rocks. In an instant they would disappear when they heard Brother Francis' footsteps. The wheat fields were turning a golden color. Suddenly, the air was filled with the scents of rosemary and thyme. Brother Francis inhaled deeply, taking in those fragrances, saying:

"Gifts from my Lord!"

And in this frame of mind, he returned to the hermitage.

"It's been four hours since I was here last. So much Grace, my God, in so little time, so many *happenings*, so many wonders! Poor is the one who spends the day saying, 'Thank you!'"

Bless me, my Father

Day after day, Brother Francis faced new challenges. The Lord set him on an unknown path and it was normal that at every turn he would come face to face with the unexpected, with unforeseen crises. Every battle front called for a fight, and every fight inured him with a very slow flame.

On that day in the late afternoon, Brother Francis entered the semi-darkness of the hermitage. A feeling of gratitude filled his heart like a majestic cascade. He opened the floodgates and reeled off monotonous words, overloaded with gratitude. The hours passed.

Little by little he was becoming conscious of an intense disquietude.

"What road do I take? It would be discourteous," he said to himself, "to refuse the meals that the good priest prepared

105

with so much love. I'd be denying my Lady Poverty if I have my meals served to me everyday. What should I do? Only those who have nothing can experience the gift of freedom from that Being who nourishes birds and flowers. Birds are free because they don't have granaries. Only those that receive know how to give. One must be poor in order to love. It's poverty that transforms this world of ambition and influence into a grand home where some give and others receive, while those that give are the ones that receive the most." And he concluded by proclaiming out loud, "And the most important reason of all is that my Lord Jesus Christ was poor."

Immediately the next morning, he went in search of the old priest and after kissing him reverently on the hand, he said:

"My father, I ask you to forgive me for the decision I've made tonight. I want to experience, vividly and directly, my Father's affection. He'll personally nourish me everyday. I'll beg from door to door, like a son of God, without ever straying from the joyful hands that give so freely. My father, please forgive me. From now on, I can no longer dine at your gracious table."

* * *

Brother Francis was seen daily, at about midday, walking through the streets knocking on doors, his eyes filled with a profound serenity, gratefully eating anything that was given to him by the Great Giver. Months passed. The moons waxed and waned. There were still many painful thorns down the road.

One winter morning, Brother Francis went up to the city with the intention of attending mass. He entered St.

George's Church where he had learned to read and write; it was a short distance from his paternal home.

A frost had lingered during those days, and Francis, in the garments of a pilgrim, trembled from the cold. Suddenly, someone tapped him on the shoulder, and said:

"Brother Angel sent me to ask if you might sell him some sweat."

Following the speaker's lead, Francis used the same tone, smiled, and said:

"Tell him I'm sorry but I simply can't, because I sold it at a very high price to the Lord."

A few minutes passed, and the irony began to hurt him deeply. Brother Francis was very sensitive about family issues. But soon he reacted, and thought:

"Is it his fault that the Lord hasn't visited him? Without a doubt, I'd have done much worse in the same situation."

And these thoughts consoled him.

* * *

What bothered Francis much more than the course joke was Peter's hostility. His father was anchored to the proud class of the Bernardones. He could not tolerate seeing Francis begging from door to door. It was more than he could bear.

Perhaps Peter was not as callous as he was made out to be. Perhaps, too, he was an honorable citizen. But he was a member of the bourgeoisie and full of the prejudices associated with that class, paid for by his name and his status as a rich merchant. All in all, he was a slave to the *vanities of life*, which consist of linking the individual with money and with social position, taking all of these elements and erecting a statue, to kneel in its presence and to bow in submission. He was a slave just like the majority of the rich.

Whenever father and son met in the city streets, whether the encounter was up close or from a distance, Peter would chide Francis, spewing all sorts of profane remarks. Despite all the progress he made in conquering self, despite having grown in the "knowledge" of his friend Jesus, Brother Francis could not withstand his father's criticism. He felt it deeply. Nothing could console him in those moments, not even the memory of the Crucified Christ. Therefore, he devised a stratagem that was both surprising and original, and full of tenderness.

From among his friends, the beggars, he chose the oldest and most congenial one, whose name was Albert, and told him:

"Listen, my friend, from now on I'm going to love you like a father and I'm going to nourish you daily with alms that are given to me. In exchange, you're going to always accompany me when I walk through the streets. And when Peter Bernardone curses me, you'll be my beloved father. I'll kneel before you. You'll put your hands on my head, make the sign of the Cross on my forehead, and bless me."

The scene was dramatic, amusing, and profoundly moving. At about midday, Brother Francis would go from door to door accompanied by his *adoptive father*, who was like a faithful dog at his side. The old beggar kept a watchful eye out for the arrogant merchant. When Bernardone appeared and began to curse his son, Brother Francis would immediately drop at the old beggar's feet. He would put his hands together on his chest, bow his head slightly, and say:

"Bless me, my father."

The scene was full of tenderness and goodness.

The Hermitage in the Woods

Francis finished restoring St. Damian. He then began and completed the restoration of another hermitage dedicated to St. Peter. Meanwhile, he also began restoring, that is, revitalizing, the image of Jesus Christ within himself. The voice he had heard in Spoleto was very far away, some three years in the past. The successive battles that had since transpired had given Brother Francis an unalterable maturity and peace.

It had been a while since he toyed with the idea of commencing the restoration of the little chapel lost in the woods in the middle of the valley, about two miles from the city. The little chapel was practically overrun by clinging plants and there were cracks everywhere.

It belonged to the Benedictines of Mt. Subasio, but they too did very little to maintain it. No wonder Brother Francis asked himself now and then if the restoration was worth the effort. But the chapel was dedicated to the Mother of God, to whom he professed a special devotion, and for this reason he happily started the restoration.

* * *

The hermitage was (and is) seven meters long and four meters wide. Since it was very, very old, and a solitary structure in the middle of the woods, it stirred people's imagination and became an object of popular myth. Legend has it that in Assisi, on the eve of certain solemn celebrations, an innumerable chorus of angels descended singing hallelujahs and held magnificent feasts. This version is unanimously accepted.

For this reason, since time immemorial, it has been known as the chapel of St. Mary of the Angels. It was also known as the *Porziuncola*, because, according to tradition, the Benedictines resided there, provisionally, before settling in Mt. Subasio. As a way of fulfilling monastic obligations, they were assigned a *little portion* of land.

Francis, then, began the reconstruction of the hermitage following the same methods used in previous hermitages. First, he gathered the necessary materials, mainly brick, lime, sand, gesso, and mortar. Then he looked for volunteers. He built the scaffolds, consolidated damaged walls, and knocked down those that had suffered severe deterioration and replaced them with new walls. He restored the exterior walls first, and then the interior ones.

Exodus and Wonder

The work was progressing at a good pace. Early in the restoration he would spend the night at St. Damian. However, he was soon possessed by the seductive magic of that wooded environment, and decided to remain in solitude in the hermitage, day and night.

To make the picture complete, his most favored people, the lepers, were just a half-hour's walk from the chapel, and he had the city nearby where he would go, from door to door, begging for bread. And every now and then, in his comings and goings, he would meet up with his beloved old friends, the beggars. All in all, he had everything at Porziuncola: God, the poor, the woods.

* * *

It was a solitude lived in God and governed by peace.

"It doesn't surprise me," Brother Francis said to himself, "that the angels celebrate their holidays in this paradise."

The weeks passed. The restoration was progressing slowly, because there were fewer volunteers this time since the hermitage was far from the city.

But Brother Francis was in no hurry to complete the restoration. On the contrary, he was so happy in that chapel that in the meantime, he resolved to stay there and adopt the solitary life of a hermit. As we well know, Brother Francis made no plans for the future. He did not know the direction his life would take. He simply made the effort to be faithful and wait for the manifestation of the divine will.

Taking mortar, lime and sand, Brother Francis devoted several hours to the restoration, several hours to the poor and many hours to the Lord. The moons waxed and waned. Francis was full of joy.

During these months, his soul was undergoing profound changes. God had chosen Francis. He was predestined to be the teacher of spirituality and the leader of the people. Although his destiny was many years in the making, God gave him an intense preparation a short time before he took on these duties.

* * *

It was an exodus. How can this be explained? How can this phenomenon be described? Can it be classified? The Poor Man of Assisi made himself smaller than ever, more submissive and more docile than a child. He let himself be seized. He did not resist his rise from the abyss. He was a little leaf being dragged by a river that had overflowed its banks.

His hinges and pivots were coming undone. His support systems and center of gravity erupted. And Brother Francis *emerged*, better yet, surrendered. To whom? Does it have a name? To something that was more than admiration, something other than vertigo. It can be called amazement. He measured the height of the Almighty. In contrast, and inadvertently, he measured himself. And then, the *Poverello* was born at the feet of the Almighty. And also in this way, the *Wise Man of Assisi* was born as he acquired a harmonious vision of reality (God, world, I).

Emergence, wonder, fascination, annihilation, fear. This is a statement full of contradictions. Who are you and who am I? It is a question, an answer, it is admiration, affirmation; to adore, to accept, and with humility and in all seriousness, that the Lord is the Almighty and that Brother Francis is the most insignificant; to adore, to accept and not resist all wonders with immense gratitude, beginning with one's own insignificance; to adore, to kneel at the feet of creation in order to wash its feet, bandage its wounds, put little caterpillars in a safe place, serve at table, revere the insignificant, appreciate everything, be the smallest brother among the small brothers of creation; to adore, to accept that the Presence is the Distant One, and that the Being who is the essence of my existence is also the Other Reality; to be still, mute, ecstatic, to love.

It is the revolution of adoration in which all labels are removed and all human boundaries disappear.

* * *

After the working day, Brother Francis rested as dusk approached. As the first stars appeared, he prepared himself for his communion with the Lord. To Brother Francis, the divine presence was most intense and refreshing in the mystery of the night.

Generally, he sat at the foot of a larch and he would curl himself into a ball, with his forehead touching his knees. Concentrating was not a difficult task. He allowed himself to be impregnated (it is difficult to describe) with the throbbing life and energies of the world. He would plunge happily into the chasm of the Almighty, and he spent many hours, sometimes the entire night in this position, saying slowly in a soft and awed voice, and with silent pauses:

"Lord, my God! Lord, my God!"

That was all he said, ever more slowly with each utterance.

Afterwards, he would lie prostrate face down, with his arms extended, immersed in the essence of the world, and Brother Francis would fall silent. Never was his adoration so profound as in those moments when he said absolutely nothing.

* * *

Many times Brother Francis would lift himself from the ground, and acquire an astral height. A clear sky, thought the Poor Man of Assisi, in a nocturnal forest, is something else entirely.

To contemplate the stars under fir trees, oak, chestnut, beneath their tangled boughs, put him under a spell that is difficult to explain. It left him very emotional and very grateful. It is useless, he would say. One has to be poor.

"For those who live in comfortable homes," he would say to himself, "and sleep on soft, luxurious beds, it is difficult, almost impossible, to understand the language of the stars, and the ecstasy of wonder. Only the poor are capable of discovering, in wonderment, the unfathomable riches of creation. Praise to you Lord for the liberating and holy Lady Poverty!"

The Woods and Its Inhabitants

Brother Francis wanted to give in return for all that he received. And he gave of himself, first and foremost, to creation itself. And herein lies the second dynamic surprise: his sensitivity toward all living things.

While there was something innate to his being that predisposed him to vibrate with the beauty of the world, at that time Brother Francis experienced a current of tenderness and sympathy with all creatures. God, the creatures, and Francis, were enveloped by the same reverberations in the most pleasurable and profound fusion.

During this time he acquired a special receptive capacity, a hypersensitivity (it is hard to describe), as though he had grown ten thousand reception antennae, as though he were equipped with a magic radar equivalent to the power of a thousand ears and a thousand eyes. He was capable of distinguishing, perfectly and simultaneously, the movement of every insect, the temperature of the air, the forms and colors of ferns, nettles, mosses, lichens, mushrooms, and castor-oil plants. He felt everything and it filled him with a rapture and a feeling of plenitude that was overwhelming.

As I have said before, it was in his nature to feel so intensely, but during that time it reached a magnitude beyond all measure. And, above all, there a rose from him a sense of compassion and tenderness for all the little creatures, especially the most vulnerable among them.

* * *

One day he went walking in the woods and he suddenly came across a beautiful spider web in some thick shrubs. He stopped to look at it, studiously and admiringly. All of a sudden, an unwary fly flew into the web and began to shake violently in order to free itself. A spider quickly appeared, with eyes arranged in the shape of an arc, four pairs of legs, and a large abdomen. It rushed at the fly with extreme speed, and it disappeared dragging its prey. Brother Francis was truly amazed at the spider's dexterity.

A few seconds later he felt profound sadness, and he could not place his finger on the cause. At that moment he felt a deep aversion toward the spider, and he lifted his hand with the intention of destroying the work of symmetry and beauty, but he stopped himself, and said in a loud voice:

"Everything is all right!"

Generally, seeing creatures devour other creatures affected him very deeply. For example, he did not like birds of prey, and when he spied one, instead of admiring it in flight, he would look the other way.

Nevertheless, he thought perhaps that the pity he felt was a criticism of God's wisdom, of his way of organizing life. For this reason he tried his best not to dwell on this issue of biology. He simply did not think about it. However, he always felt sadness when observing the capture of one creature by another that was larger or more aggressive.

In this case, he would suppress the sadness by repeating the following phrase several times out loud:

"We don't know anything! Everything is just fine!"

* * *

There were times during the year when there was no need to go begging in the city streets. The Lord himself prepared Francis' meals in the woods. Depending on the season, he would nourish himself with wild strawberries, blackberries, buds from trees blooming in the spring, the roots of certain plants....

With every strawberry he ate, especially the large ones, he would say in a loud voice:

"Thank you, my Lord."

Once satiated, he would return to the hermitage thinking how man complicated his life when the children of man could easily live off the bounty of the earth.

However, when he thought about these things, he would stop himself immediately since he felt that the first rule of creation was the appreciation of all things. And when he thought about himself, he had the distinct impression that he knew less than everyone else.

Every outing to the woods, especially on sunny days, was an extraordinary adventure. He discovered thousands of worlds. Every square meter held a chasm of mystery and surprise. The most insignificant things that others overlooked, amazed Brother Francis and he would look on them gratefully.

He felt that man was not the king of creation, rather the smallest brother among all things, because he was the only one capable of admiration, and in admiring, man becomes—unintentionally—smaller, more brotherly, more human.

"That's also adoration," he thought.

It is not known exactly why the chirping of crickets made him feel an unusual sensation, as though his entire being were experiencing almost cosmic vibrations, sounding something like the strumming of a harp.

He would make his way through the woods very slowly, barely touching the ground, taking the utmost care not to frighten the insects. Suddenly, he would step on a little twig and break it. The cracking sound silenced the cricket. Francis would remain absolutely still. Soon after that, however, the cricket began to rub its front wings together and once again it burst into song. Brother Francis would come very close and remain a long while, his lips parted, listening attentively.

"What marvels of the Lord!" he would say in a soft voice and continue on his way to the hermitage.

* * *

One day he came upon a strange phenomenon. He saw a long opening in the green grass. It was as thin as the blade of a sword. Brother Francis bent down to get a closer look. It was a pathway for ants on excursions to and from their laborious activities.

Brother Francis got on his knees to get an even better look at this new marvel. He was amazed at all the activity: the ants carried strands of herbs on their backs, a load that was five or six times their own body weight; they worked incessantly and were extremely organized, a perfect society. They emerged from subterranean colonies, and to those same colonies they would return with their load. Brother Francis was full of admiration and he exclaimed in a soft voice:

"Lord, Lord!"

Afterwards, without even realizing it, he began to reflect on the ants' marvelous organization and execution just to make provisions for the future. He thought that such zeal hid traces of cupidity and a lack of faith. Above all, he thought that this conduct was contrary to Jesus' belief that what every day brings is sufficient.

His admiration for the ants froze right there. When he started to think adverse thoughts in relation to them, he got up quickly so as not to fall into temptation. As he walked directly toward the hermitage, he said in a loud voice:

"Everything is just fine!"

On his way there he thought:

"No, no, I can't allow myself to behave so rudely (with hostile thoughts and feelings) in such universal harmony." And he said in a loud voice, "Reconciliation, yes; conflict, no! Love unites, aversion separates; and admiration is the gateway of love."

* * *

One day, while walking on a narrow path he came upon a frog that was jumping awkwardly. He felt instant repugnance and looked away. Then, in order to redeem himself and satisfy the frog, he looked at it admiringly, for a long time and with great affection. In general, he professed a special tenderness for the most repulsive and fragile creatures.

He was able to recognize and distinguish by name, scent, specific coloring, and special characteristics, all the plants and shrubs of the forest: rock rose, myrtle, juniper, hawthorn, willow, creeper, box. He would stand and look at any of them admiringly, bending down to smell their fragrance. On behalf of each one he would give thanks to the Lord because they could not speak, he thought.

He would get very emotional when he saw glowworms, watching them appear and disappear like aimless stars.

"How does that little light come on?" he would ask himself. "Do they light up during the day as well? No, they most likely sleep during the day."

He also felt great admiration for grasshoppers. He would study them for a long time. He would quiver at the sight of their formidable jumps.

"They're so small, yet so strong!" he thought. "If I were to jump that high, proportionally speaking, I'd reach the height of Mt. Subasio, or the height of *Rocca*, at the very least."

There were times, especially at night, when he remained absolutely still, as though he were part of a static implosion in the ocean of life. In that complex symphony he was able to perceive not only the distinct voices, the frog's pain and suffering, as well as that of other insects and all of God's

118

creatures, but also the sap running through trees and plants. He felt deeply fulfilled.

The Favored

On that day, after leaving town and spending four hours with his beloved lepers of San Salvatore, Brother Francis returned to St. Mary of the Angels.

The usual look of serenity disappeared from his face and a vague melancholy veiled his eyes. His walk resembled that of a person who was carrying the weight of the world on his shoulders. Albert—the beggar who responded with a blessing to every curse uttered by Bernardone—and three other beggars were looking for Brother Francis in order to tell him their troubles and to be consoled.

"When I used to walk with you," said Albert, "everyone looked at me affectionately. Now they look away. The *Supreme Magistrate* has given us an order: we can beg only in specified locations and at specified hours."

"There are times," they continued, "when, to our surprise, we would receive a bountiful sip of water and four olives. But it gets worse, Brother Francis. I prefer a smile instead of food, and affection instead of alms. When people give, the majority do it with repugnance, with disdain, reluctantly, extending the arm and looking away..."

* * *

These troubles had robbed Brother Francis of his happiness. He was always careful not to fall into the hands of contempt, not even in his thoughts. But this time he was somber and gave free rein to dark thoughts.

"It's always the same thing!" he said threateningly and in a loud voice. "People shrink in front of those superior to them and act superior to those who are smaller than they are. I used to do that too," he added, lowering his voice. "There's a knock on the door, and they come to see who it is, and the lineage of the visitor, shown in the manner of dress, fame or beauty, would determine in like proportion the smile, the ceremony, and the courtesy that was extended by the hosts. The lower the visitor's class, the more the attention he receives goes downhill, from courtesy to coldness, from coldness to neglect, from neglect to disdain. The Lord brought us into this world naked! There are no categories. The rest is nothing but convention and superficiality. Will there ever come a day when men will value the naked substance of the children of God?"

He raised his voice and declared:

"What's the point of loving the lovable, venerating the venerable, liking the beauty of a handsome person or kneeling at the feet of a champion? Money classifies. It erects walls of steel between brothers."

He was about to say: damned money! but he stopped himself. In spite of everything, he felt greater horror for contempt than for money.

"Clothing classifies," continued Francis, "fame classifies, so does beauty. To hell with classifications! What awaits those of God's children who have no money, beauty, titles, health or fame? Neglect and scorn."

Never had he been so angry. His breathing was agitated and ire was glistening in the depths of his eyes. He knew that these thoughts were destructive. These reflections did not sit well with him, but there was nothing he could do; they were a strange force outside his control.

* * *

He arrived at the chapel of St. Mary. Something told him that peace had darted like a frightened dove.

"The heart," he thought, "should never give free rein to fury, not even in the name of a sacred cause."

He felt the need to kneel. But for whom? He did not know. After meditating for a moment, he said:

"I will seek reconciliation with mother earth who nourishes and strengthens all children equally."

And, having said this, he knelt slowly. Afterwards, he put his lips to the ground and kissed the earth. Then, as he continued to kneel, he put his forehead to the ground and stayed in this position for several hours. Moreover, this was his prayer position.

"My God, first of all, place your hand over your servant's heart so that he can reclaim the peace. Remove the sword of fury and heal the wound. Calm my heart and my insides before your servant has a chance to utter grievous words. On this golden afternoon, I place in your compassionate hands these red roses of love:

I will not scorn those who scorn.
I will not curse those who curse.
I will not judge those who condemn.
I will not hate those who exploit.
I will love those who do not love.
I will exclude no one from my heart.

But now, allow me to say a new word and accept it plainly and appreciatively:

My favorites will be those that are overlooked.
The more of an outcast of society they are,

the deeper they will be within my heart.
When reasons to appreciate them start to lessen,
the more they will be loved by me.
I will love exceedingly those that are not loved.

And allow me to reserve the warmest recesses of my heart for the lepers, the beggars, the street thieves, and the sinners. And in this way, I will have the privilege of following in Jesus' footsteps."

Humanism

In fact, these were his favorites throughout his life: the outcasts of medieval society, those who, according to the laws of the world, were not "attractive" or pleasing. In the years of his youth, Brother Francis had observed the world and life from within and came to the conclusion that attraction plays a key role in human relationships.

"A person," thought Brother Francis, "may not have beauty, money or goodness, but that person might have fame. In this case, fame is the source of attraction and those who find this person attractive will come in droves. Another person may not have fame, beauty, a pleasant disposition or gentleness, but that person may have money. In this case, money is the source of attraction. In other cases, it may be beauty or disposition. Another person may be lacking everything, but the person's gentleness is the basis for attraction."

* * *

Brother Francis realized that people never love an unblemished man or a naked being.

"They love the qualifications superimposed on a person. But when the sources of attraction begin to fail, one by one, and all that is left is the naked and pure being, who will love him? Who will look at him? Who will come near him? Only a pure and impartial heart. A pure heart is one that has been visited by God."

Brother Francis realized that, normally, if the heart has not been purified, man goes looking for himself in other people. He is served by others instead of serving others. There is always a secret and an unconscious game of interests.

One of the more obvious examples is the case of politicians who are always proclaiming an interest in the poor. But, in fact, generally speaking, the poor are there to serve the politicians (like a trampoline) in promoting themselves, in creating a social figure, and, therefore, in enabling them to prosper economically and politically. And if they no longer suit that purpose, the politicians abandon them with splendid explanations. And the poor remain at the mercy of the elements as they wait for the pure of heart.

Humanism? Humanism is a tribute or dedication to what is *purely human*, to the naked being that is free of finery and sources of attraction. True humanism cannot exist where the process of the purification of the heart has not occurred.

It would require a long explanation, but pure humanism cannot exist without God, save on a very small scale. As things stand, only God can make a revolution in the heart, turning value judgments upside down, cancelling installments and appropriations, and designing new interest scales.

For this reason, there are very few true humanists, and for this reason the hopes of the poor remain frustrated as they hold a pile of pointless words in their hands.

In the history of mankind very few men have practiced humanism as Brother Francis of Assisi did. He venerated where there was no reason to venerate. He appreciated where there was no reason to show appreciation. He showed more than his share of love to the unlovable. The less attractive the person was the more affectionate he was, increasing his affection by inverse proportions. In this, as in everything, he did nothing more than follow Jesus' example.

Throughout this book, we will come across many emotional episodes in which we will see the resplendent humanism of the Poor Man of Assisi.

Chapter Three

THE LORD GAVE ME BROTHERS

One Surprise after Another

Brother Francis thought about adopting the lifestyle of a hermit and entering the restored hermitage of St. Mary. These thoughts or intentions were provisional. At that time, his life consisted of the following components: a contemplative life around the hermitage in the woods; devotion to the lepers and beggars; and, once the restoration of the hermitages was completed, also farming of the land with the peasants in exchange for bread, not only for himself but also for the poor.

Looking from our vantage point in time, in all that has taken place up until this moment in his life, there are many things in the singular life of Brother Francis of Assisi that are absolutely impressive.

He lived totally immersed in all that was provisional. His only preoccupation was to be faithful in the present moment. His mind was not focused on tomorrow, not even in terms of devotion. He threw himself into God's ocean and let the divine currents navigate the waters. He was always thinking: the Lord will manifest himself.

He never—not now, nor later in his life—organized his thoughts in order to analyze or synthesize the signs of the times, associating them with theological reflections and sociological statistics, and designing a plan of action within the framework of probability. He was the antithesis of a theoretical or an intellectual man.

He was—as a basis for comparison—like an explorer. Upon climbing the first mountain, the explorer discovers at that height a prominent elevation in the distance. Upon tackling that climb, towering peaks, that went unnoticed before, now make their appearance. Or, like an explorer of subterranean passageways, he bores through rock, advancing five meters, and he suddenly comes across stripes of unknown value and color. He continues to pierce a few meters of rock and, to the right, he comes across a new vein; and a few meters more, to the left, he hits a bed of a new and pure metal. He lives the unforeseeable.

This is how the Poor Man of Assisi lived, especially during these years, always on the brink of discovery, expecting the unexpected, ready and waiting, without presuppositions or conditions. Today he would receive a divine inspiration and immediately put it into practice. After a few hours, a new challenge would greet him around the corner and Brother Francis would take action, without complicating the issue.

He did not like to theorize, and he liked to rationalize even less. He liked things to be concrete and to the letter. We have seen that his life, in the lapse of time that we have analyzed, unfolded at a rapid pace, jumping from one surprise to another, from one novelty to another, without looking back and analyzing, without looking forward and projecting, always lying in wait. As soon as he received a divine order, he immediately put it into practice and waited for another. It was extreme simplicity made of concreteness and faith. A theorist can become a rationalist quite easily. History has shown us that many of these theories simply do not hold water.

He was a man made for improvisation, in the best sense of the word. How can I say it? The improvident man? Let us say he was the man who loved surprises since, initially, he was the man of wonder. His dramatic gestures were effected in perfectly ordinary ways, that is to say, in an unaffected manner. The grandest things were done with simplicity, and the most insignificant things were done with a certain solemnity.

Total Solitude

What is most surprising to the writer who delves into the sources is that Brother Francis embarked on this journey in total solitude. This is most unusual given that the man was so communicative. The writer has the impression that the Lord treated the Poor Man of Assisi with extreme prodigality, an approach that was very special and almost exceptional. Perhaps for this reason, Brother Francis never felt the inclination to stray from his solitary pilgrimage. The Lord himself was his personal guide and companion.

He consulted with no one. He did not look for spiritual guidance. He did not walk down the beaten path. He did not follow a particular plan. Neither monk, nor priest, nor cenobite. God launched him into total darkness, uncertainty, and solitude, to roam where no man had roamed before. He had no objective and did not suspect that there might be a trap waiting for him at the crossroads. How did Francis know that he was on the right track? He ran the risk of losing it all. Everything was at stake. I do not recall another prophet, no matter the times, who embarked on a journey fueled by so much uncertainty.

Was he reckless? Every adventure is branded by some recklessness. Most certainly Brother Francis behaved recklessly a number of times later in his life. But I am not sure that this is the appropriate word. What preceded seems now and then to resemble self-sufficiency. Intuition? Inspiration? There may have been some of that. But it was something else entirely.

From the abyss God cried out to him:

"Jump!"

And Brother Francis did not think twice about it and jumped.

From the darkness, God called to him, saying:

"Come, my son."

And Brother Francis entered the darkness without hesitation. His faith was exceptional and his trust was exceptional. It was the type of faith that moves mountains: the faith of a child in an adult.

The Lord said to him:

"Brother Francis, go into the jungle and lead the way; do not fear, I will be with you."

And he entered the depths of darkness.

It was an adventure in faith.

The Revelation

Autumn arrived with its golden fruits, and then it was gone. Winter came with its frost and freezing temperatures. The Poor Man of Assisi stayed in the hermitage in the woods during the cold months. He felt free and happy.

The beautiful and liberating journey lasted three years. It was also extremely painful, much more than was readily apparent. The Lord was guiding him, step by step, and preparing him with the utmost care for that to which he was predestined, his sublime providence. At this stage in his life Brother Francis was the broken sod, oxygenated and purified. Everything was ready.

He lived day by day. In the outer reaches of his conscience not one worry clouded his clear skies. Nevertheless, a human being is composed of many planes that are juxtaposed to one another. And there, in those very deep layers beyond the light of consciousness, Brother Francis waited for something. But he did not know what it was. He had premonitions of something unexpected. He was calm but he was lying in wait.

Although it was very much expected, the revelation appeared unexpectedly.

* * *

One day Brother Francis arrived at the Benedictine monastery on Mt. Subasio. He told the monks that the hermitage had been restored, and that it would be fitting to have a celebration of the Eucharist in order to restore divine service. They agreed that a priest would go on the following day.

It was the 24th of February, the feast of St. Matthias. The previous night had been very cold. Brother Francis spent many hours with the Lord to dispel the cold. He got up at the break of dawn on what would probably be the most significant day of his life. He made all the necessary preparations for Mass with extreme devotion. He summoned the peasants in the neighboring fields, and they all waited together for the priest.

The service began and Brother Francis assisted at the Mass with great devotion. Every prayer, every reading he tucked very carefully in his heart. Then everyone rose for the reading of the Gospel. It said:

"Go and preach throughout the world. Do not carry any money in your pockets. Do not carry any provisions. The shirt on your back is sufficient. You do not need shoes, nor a walking stick. Live by the labor of your hands. Upon arriving in a town, ask an honorable family to give you lodging. When you enter a home, always say: Peace in this house. Be as ingenuous as doves and as shrewd as serpents. If you are rejected, go somewhere else without protesting. There are many wolves out there; you are young lambs among them. They might force you to appear before civil tribunals; the Father will put precise words of defense in your mouths. Do not be afraid. I will be with you until the end of time."

A bolt of lightning before their eyes would not have caused nearly the same effect that these words produced. Brother Francis was operating on high voltage. He was fascinated beyond description. He felt as though his blood had solidified in his arteries. It was as though dead words so often said could suddenly come alive and raise the dead.

For three years a dark curtain seems to have covered his eyes. Suddenly, the Gospel drew back the curtain and a clear, limitless horizon appeared before his eyes. It was as if the Benedictine priest had melted away and Jesus himself was pronouncing the words.

* * *

The Mass continued. Brother Francis was profoundly moved. At the end of the Mass, the villagers went back to their homes. Brother Francis approached the priest with his usual extreme delicacy, and said:

"Minister of the Lord, the words of the Gospel have reached the depths of my soul. I'd like to hear them again, and, if possible, have a pertinent explanation according to your interpretation."

They took the missal and walked out of the hermitage. They sat in the sun along a rocky path. The priest read the

Gospel once again. He commented on every verse. Then a general commentary was made on the context. Brother Francis asked some questions and the priest answered them. They both remained silent for a while.

Suddenly, Francis got on his feet. He looked inebriated. His eyes were shining and he looked much taller than his actual height. He lifted his arms, which resembled two very taut flames, and he exclaimed in an emotional voice:

"For a very long time I felt my way through the shadows, looking, looking feverishly for the will of God, and I have finally found it. Glory be to you Lord! I see the horizon, the road traced before me. It is the work of my Lord Jesus Christ. I will walk this evangelical road even though there might be thorns in the flowers that stretch from here to the end of the world. And on this road my candle will flicker and die."

They returned to the hermitage. He took the walking stick and threw it away.

"What else does the Lord Jesus Christ command?" he asked himself.

And, without answering, he removed his shoes and threw them as far as he could into some thickets. He loosened the buckle on his belt and threw it with all his might, making it look like a flying serpent. He took off the hermit's cloak and put it under a bush.

"What else does the Lord Jesus Christ command?" he asked himself joyfully once again.

He took an ordinary sack and cut it in the shape of a cross and added a hood. It was similar to the vestments worn by the shepherds of Mt. Subasio. He tied a piece of rope around his waist, and he went out into the world as he made the sign of the Cross.

The First Outing

As he walked toward the city, the Poor Man of Assisi had the distinct impression that he was Christ's knight in armor. He exulted in this thought.

"There is no nobler order of knighthood in the world," thought Francis as he walked, "than to roam the world at the command of the Great Emperor Jesus Christ, to carry Lady Poverty on a sea of dreams, to help all those wounded by sorrow, to undo the injustices of selfishness, to look for the truth in fallacy, to attack dejection in the pessimist, to rush at the fortresses of sin, to carry the banner of peace on the point of a lance, to reach for the stars..."

These thoughts made him drunk with happiness as he set out on his first evangelical outing.

As he approached the city, he did not even stop at San Salvatore to visit his *Christian brothers*. He kept on going, and he said to the first peasant he bumped into:

"May the Peace of the Lord be with you."

And from then on, instead of saying a "good morning", he would give the same evangelical greeting to everybody he met on the road or in the street.

He went straight to the plaza. Two or three people walked up to him, drawn by his peculiar garment. Instead of explaining the change in attire, he began to extemporize on the motives of Love. Soon after that, two or three curious passersby gathered around him upon hearing his raised voice. He then stood on a large rock in the plaza, and his words intensified in tone and in inspiration.

Brother Francis knew his listeners' weak spots very well, and he directed his words to those areas with great spiritual freedom. It was not the first time the inhabitants of Assisi heard a layman improvise in the plaza. They were accustomed to listening to Valdo's followers.

* * *

They were simple words that penetrated like the edge of a sword. He never got carried away by oratorical flights of fancy. That did not suit his personality. On the contrary, his words were brief, preferably the textual words of Jesus, with an additional commentary here and there. His exhortations were reiterative and practical. He never lost himself in flowery speech, nor theological discourses. Concise, brief, practical.

His person and his life were made for preaching. There was warmth and conviction in his words because he spoke from experience. When he finished speaking, his listeners would go to their homes in silence. There were still a few who did not take him seriously, and their mocking smiles were never far from their lips. But when they saw his sincerity, their smiles froze and they were defenseless. It was difficult to resist his serenity. It was so captivating and contagious.

He whet the appetite for eternity that sleeps in the deepest recesses of the soul. He answered fundamental questions about life with brevity and simplicity. It is not known exactly why, but under the magic effect of his voice, souls would regain the shadows of peace that cooled their interior flames. They all felt happy.

Brother Francis went to the city everyday. Wherever a group of townspeople were gathered, out of idleness or other reasons, he would present himself as the ambassador of peace, and he took the liberty of telling them the demands of evangelical life. He did it with such humility and simplicity that no one took offense at having their get-togethers interrupted.

One of his favorite places for proclaiming the Word was the portico of the Temple of Minerva, next to the Corinthian columns.

Eventually, the entire city was eager for the evangelist's visit since the townspeople felt that those words were what they needed to hear, and they would go back to their homes with calm and peaceful souls. Furthermore, this messenger did not criticize anyone, not even the *Supreme Magistrate*, nor the clergy, nor the civil authorities. He did not look like one pushing for reform, but rather like one who had discovered a treasure and wanted to share it with the masses.

The First Companion

It is a constant in the history of religion that the prophet renounce family and country once he has taken on his mission. He rarely went back, and never as a prophet. Normally the word and spiritual work of the prophet shine on distant shores, far from his native land.

In this, as in so many other things, Brother Francis was an exception. Apparently, he never felt the need to leave his people. The words of the Gospel transformed him into an inexhaustible itinerant, sowing words of eternal life in faithful and faithless lands. But he never pulled up stakes from the valley of his birth. The Franciscan epic always had its epicenter in Assisi.

* * *

With regard to social standing, Bernard was a few notches above Francis. He was a gentleman, and a chronicle tells us that "it was recommended that he take charge of the city of Assisi." A merchant like Francis, but of greater wealth, Bernard's nature was prudent and reflective. He was not very excitable and he kept most of his impulses in check. He was reflective, cautious and a bit reserved.

He had that particular quality that enabled him to distinguish the essential from the unessential. He reflected many times on the contingency and the transient nature of all that is created, and, mysteriously enough, this thought filled him with peace.

Convinced that nothing mattered in the ebb and flow of life and that everything lacked permanency, his heart began to detach itself from worldly values and adhere to eternal roots, and to cultivate that thirst for God which, in addition to Grace, was an innate disposition in his personality.

This was the beginning of Francis' first mystical relationship. Bernard was a calm man, so he watched and waited. Months and years passed, and Bernard began to think:

"Francis has hit the nail on the head. He had everything and he let it all go. He looks happier than the rest of us. He has nothing yet he has everything. And his conversion was not a passing fever. All of this would not be possible if Francis did not have a loving friendship with God. I'm going to observe him closely in order to verify the depth of his transformation."

One day, Bernard invited him to dinner. When the meal was over he said:

"Francis, it's very late and the Porziuncola is quite a distance from here. I'm going to have them prepare a bed in my quarters so that you can rest."

Above the headboard, Bernard had placed a picture of the Lord, illuminated by the faint light of a lamp.

Francis went to bed and pretended to be asleep. Bernard also pretended to be asleep while faking a convincing snore. Then Francis got up very quietly, knelt before the image, extended his arms out in the shape of a cross, and slowly and softly began to say:

"Lord, Lord!"

It was as if those words resounded from the very depths of the earth, carrying the world's adoration. He did not say anything else.

Never was there such an absolute fusion of person, word, and content within the word. Bernard was profoundly moved and even altered by this scene. He looked at Francis furtively: in the pale light of the lamp he saw Francis' silhouette, which was like adoration carved in marble.

Francis repeated the phrase over and over again. But there was such a variation in tone in his pronunciation, that it always sounded different as if each utterance was the very first time he pronounced the words. Sometimes his voice was powerful, but the sound had nothing to do with guttural inflections, rather it resounded from his soul. Other times he would stop and remain silent. Many times the tone was so forceful that it resembled a deep sigh or sob, and upon hearing it Bernard would get such a lump in his throat that it was almost impossible to hold back the tears. Francis sustained this posture until the light of dawn. It was a memorable night.

* * *

The next morning, Bernard said to Francis:

"Brother Francis, the Lord has made me wealthy. It's apparent that wealth has separated me from my Lord. And I want the Lord to be my treasure. How do I do this?"

"It's true, Bernard," Francis replied. "It's difficult for the Lord to be the soul's treasure if the soul is preoccupied with treasures. It's all about choices, Bernard: God or money."

"Then, what must I do?" Bernard insisted.

"Tomorrow morning we'll go to church and the Lord himself will manifest His will," Brother Francis replied.

The next day, they set out first thing in the morning. They passed by the episcopal residence of Peter Cataneo, canon of St. Rufinus, who had also expressed the desire to follow in Francis' footsteps. They walked through the city's main plaza to the church of St. Nicholas. All three attended early Mass and prayed until nine, realizing the significance of that moment.

Then Francis got up in a manner which signaled that his next gesture would have tremendous impact. He approached the main altar with reverence and took the missal in his hands. With the mere motion of opening the book, Francis put the delicate question before God with amazing candor and with the kind of faith that moves mountains, fervently asking the Lord to manifest his will.

Then, he opened the missal for the first time and his eyes fell on these words: "If you want to be perfect, sell all you have and give it to the poor; then come and follow me." He opened the missal for the second time and read: "Do not take anything with you, be it a bag, money, walking stick, or clothes." He opened the book for the third time and found these words: "If you want to follow me, deny yourself, take up your cross and follow me." The words had the force, brevity and clarity of a lightning bolt.

Francis calmly placed the missal back on the altar. He then joined the two neophytes, sensing the transcendental nature of the moment. His eyes shone with the brilliance of the dawn.

He stood on the highest step of the altar and said to them:

"Friends, the Lord has spoken. Comments are superfluous. Even more, a remark at this time would seem rather audacious, even profane. The Lord himself has made the decision. The Gospel will be our only inspiration and rule, not only for us but for all those who wish to follow us. Let's go brothers! May the Gospel retain all its freshness and newness as we proclaim the Word. Glory be to God the Almighty and to you Lord Jesus Christ, whose mercy is ever present, for showing us the way and opening the doors to the world."

* * *

Brother Francis was filled with emotion.

"Bernard," said Francis, "there's the answer to your question."

The three left the church and, having crossed the plaza, went directly to Bernard's mansion. There they devised a kind of lottery: these things and that amount of money for the leper colony at San Salvatore. Those linens and this amount of money for other needy infirmaries. The rest would be divided this very day among the poor in St. George's plaza.

It was a spectacle capable of moving a rock to tears. In the name of the Gospel, the city's most affluent gentleman renounced all of his material wealth in order to follow Christ, in the footsteps of the Poor Man of Assisi. It was the 16th of April. Widows, the elderly, beggars, in short, all the poor, gathered in the little plaza to receive their portion.

Shock waves ran through the city. Nevertheless, not everyone was in favor of that prodigality.

"If all the merchants of Assisi were to follow suit, the city would be in ruins in no time," said one individual.

"Bernardone's crazy kid is spreading a deadly virus," said another.

"Maybe this extravagance is the solution to the problem of the city's poor," another thought to himself.

With no roof over their heads, not a coin in their pockets, with nothing that they could call their own, no family, no country, the three pilgrims left the city through the gates of the western wall, and walked toward St. Mary of the Angels, full of joy and with a feeling of freedom. They were literally foreigners on this earth.

Brother Francis was very happy. He never analyzed events nor did he think about the future. The possibility that this little group would be, should be or might be the beginning of a great movement did not even cross his mind. He was a man who lived for the present. He was happy to think that great gentlemen were entering a new order of chivalry under the command of the Great Emperor, Jesus Christ. These thoughts filled him with joy.

The next day they built three small huts with trunks, dry branches, weeds and some clay. Each hut was the height of an average man; the length was that of a reclining body, and its width measured a meter and a half. Afterwards, they dug a furrow, shaping it into a large square, in which they planted a clump of trees. They built a large hut in the center of the square, similar to the huts used by the shepherds who live in the Apennines.

In short, a few months later we find ourselves in the woods with a hermitage restored by Francis, a large hut within a clump of trees, and a variety of little huts, growing in number, scattered within the grove.

Bernard and Peter made long robes similar to Francis', in "a color that blends with the animals of the region," somewhere between steel and dark grey, following a very simple design: one piece with a hood, and a rope fastened round the waist. The vestments resembled those worn by the shepherds of the high Apennines.

139

The New Member

Assisi was buzzing with gossip concerning the events that were unfolding. The send-off of the most learned priest and the most influential gentleman vividly impressed a country lad named Giles, a soul as transparent as water and with a gaze as candid as that of a child. It was the 23rd of April, the feast of Christ's knight, St. George. Giles attended Mass and was an enthusiastic participant. Afterwards, he directed his steps toward the plains.

When he got to the Porziuncola in the woods, there was not a soul around. As he was about to leave he saw Brother Francis emerge from the woods. Giles rose to his feet and said to him:

"Brother Francis, great friend of God, I also want to be a friend of the Lord. Take my hand and lead me to his heart."

The lad's purity and simplicity moved Brother Francis very much. His eyes were moist with tears. With tremendous warmth, he put his hands on the young man's shoulders, and said:

"My dear, dear brother, do you know what went on in the city this morning? The Emperor has arrived in Assisi and from among its citizens he has chosen a knight to be his personal steward in his imperial castle, and you are that knight. May the hand of the Lord protect you and may he send the angel of peace to you every morning. What's your name?"

"Giles," said the other.

"How would you like to have a forest full of Giles!" added Brother Francis.

"Wait here a moment, Brother Giles," Francis said.

And as he said this he went into the woods to summon Peter and Bernard, who were at prayer.

"Come brothers; come quickly to see the gift that the Almighty has sent to us."

Francis' happiness was as abundant as cascading waters. He took Giles by the hand and introduced him to his two friends. Francis said to them:

"Let's have a celebration greater than the one for the birth of a new baby into a happy family."

Francis, Peter and Bernard smiled and kept their smiles during the entire love feast.

From the very first moment, the new candidate felt as though he had fallen into the lap of a warm and loving family. They ate what they had: some olives and slices of bread left from the previous day. Bernard got up to fetch water in an earthenware pot. As Brother Francis looked at Giles with affection in his eyes, he said to him:

"From this day on you no longer have parents nor brothers or sisters. We will be your mother, father and brother."

* * *

After the love feast, Francis and Giles went to the city to get some material with which to make a robe for the new member. Brother Francis radiated so much sincerity and natural charm that Giles took great pleasure in his company, as though they were old friends.

As they headed toward the city, a little old lady came up to them begging for alms. Brother Francis had nothing to give her and he went on his way. The old woman was insistent. Francis and Giles continued in silence. Finally, moved by the woman's persistence, Brother Francis turned to the newcomer, looked at him affectionately, and said:

"Brother Giles, would it be possible, in the name of God, to give this little old lady some article of clothing?"

Instantly, Giles took off his cloak and gave it to Francis, and he in turn gave it to the old lady. Later on, Giles mentioned that he felt a strange happiness, as if an intoxicating perfume had permeated his entire being.

Alive and Active

The four brothers began their new lives. They did not concern themselves with making a schedule nor writing a set of rules that all should follow. Despite Peter's intellectual abilities and Bernard's organizational skills, it was Brother Francis' personal touch that was the distinguishing characteristic of that group. Their lives evolved spontaneously with the passing days and weeks.

They devoted long hours to the Lord, each in his own hut. At times they would go deep into their wooded retreat. Frequently, Brother Francis spent entire nights in prayer, like his Master. During the day, one or two of them helped the peasants with their work. As a reward, they accepted food but never money. One of the disciples always returned to the hermitage with little bags of nuts, olives, apples or grapes, depending on the time of year.

Another brother went to the leper colony to attend to the sick. Another went up to the city to preach peace and love. Before returning, he would go from door to door asking for something to eat. The disciples would alternate these activities.

Every morning, Brother Francis decided the day's activities for each brother. This delegation of chores was inexpressible: it was not a command, not even a request. Brother Francis spoke to each one about Jesus' attitudes, which motivated them to do their assigned chores. He did so with so much love, giving each a warm farewell embrace and a heartfelt blessing, that the brothers felt as if they could walk to the ends of the earth. To be given a command was equivalent to being loved.

* * *

The disciples were anxious to return to the hermitage. There, Brother Francis waited for them with open arms and a smile on his lips. They returned, one by one. Brother Francis took each one by the hand and led him to the feet of Our Lady. They greeted the Mother of Christ ardently and asked for her blessing.

Afterwards, they gathered in the main hut. Francis asked each one about his day and the disciples narrated the adventures they had braved on their journey. Brother Francis applauded their efforts and praised the Lord. He constantly reminded them of Jesus' behavior. Everyday he mirrored Jesus before their eyes, and they encountered his presence daily.

Those family reunions lasted for hours. They were like open doors, each welcoming the other. It was Brother Francis himself who ignited this feeling of mutual trust. Brother Francis loved them so much and with such sensitivity, that he was absolutely transparent. Inevitably and moved by his pure example, they responded in the same way, with the same feelings of warmth and acceptance. They spoke about the Lord among themselves as though he were a mutual friend who was ever in their thoughts: they could not help but speak of him.

Thus, Francis infused a special kind of spirit into the little group.

The First Great Adventure

One night, after their family reunion, Brother Francis took his three friends before the altar of the hermitage. They prayed together for several hours. Francis got up and stood under the Byzantine-style picture of the Virgin, and said to them:

"With loving scissors we have cut the most beautiful ties that link us to this world: the family. We have buried and given unto death the fiercest beast in the human jungle: money. We are forever betrothed to Lady Poverty. Our shoes are rotting under shrubs and our tunics are decomposing on thickets. We have left the doors wide open for Love. We have freed the heart. In so doing, we have followed the mandate of the Almighty Son of God. But we have yet to write the last verse: Go into the four winds and sow the seeds of the Gospel in the mountains and in the valleys. Sons of my soul and knights of my Lord Jesus Christ: we are now a golden wheat field. We will follow the mandate of the Lord and go two by two wherever the Spirit takes us. We will give to everyone those four golden coins: love, peace, happiness, and freedom, all in the name of the Gospel.

"Bernard and Peter," he said in conclusion, "will go where the compass points North. They're strong. The Lord will walk by their side. I will be accompanied by the sweetest flower, Giles. Tomorrow, at daybreak, when the blackbirds sing their first tunes, we'll be on our way. Our mutual affection for one another will grow in each other's absence."

Afterwards, he knelt down before the Virgin, looked at her face, and entrusted them to her care with such moving words, that tears appeared in their eyes.

That night Brother Francis did not sleep. It was a night for prayer. The knights of Christ were about to embark on their first journey, and it seemed normal to him to spend the night in vigilance on their behalf. At the first light of dawn, Brother Francis waited for his friends, and the final embrace, at the door of the hermitage. Afterwards, Bernard and Peter headed for Perugia; Giles and Francis toward Spoleto.

It was inevitable: Brother Francis' eyes filled with tears, and he began to sing old songs of chivalry in order to compose himself. He feared that Giles would get too emotional. He never thought that their farewell would be so painful. He was not aware that he loved them as much as he did.

* * *

After passing Foligno, they went deep into the valleys between the wide gorge of the Eastern Apennines, which centuries ago was named the Marches of Ancona. On the first night, they slept in the portico of a church, under the Roman arches.

At nightfall, two beggars also arrived at the church, with the intention of spending the night. Francis was glad to share their company and began to converse with them.

"Giles," Brother Francis whispered in his ear, "it's important that you know that every beggar carries Jesus under his rags."

Brother Giles fell into a deep sleep. Francis slept very little. He spent many hours looking at the stars, while he repeated with admiration and gratitude:

"Lord, my God!"

At daybreak, Brother Francis woke Giles up, touching him gently on the shoulder, and he said in good humor:

"Valiant knight of Christ, on your feet! To arms!"

They walked together. It was a crystal clear morning. The sky was full of playful swallows and black swifts doing amazing pirouettes in the air.

"Brother Giles," said Francis, "let's walk separately until we reach the next hamlet; I'll walk in front, and you'll walk about fifteen paces behind me. We need to fill our souls with the Lord's spirit and his divine strength."

For every swallow he saw, he repeated:

"Praise be to God. They have enviable wings," he thought to himself, "but they don't have a soul. I'll be their soul."

Every time they met along the road, Brother Giles smiled enthusiastically, raising his voice and saying:

"May the peace of the Lord be with you."

Whenever he saw villagers cutting the grass or weeding corn, he would yell jubilantly from the corner or as he approached them:

"May the peace of the Lord be with you all."

The villagers did not know what to say. It was the first time they were ever greeted in that manner. Giles repeated the scene many times.

"This one's nuts!" a few reapers finally retorted, and, feeling as though they were being mocked, they replied with harsh language.

Giles was frightened at first. Then he felt humiliated. Later on he felt momentarily disheartened about his chosen vocation in life.

He approached Brother Francis somewhat fearfully and said to him:

"Brother Francis, they don't understand this greeting. They think I'm mocking them. Why can't I greet them as anyone else would?"

In the time it takes to blink an eye, or for a bolt of lightning to split the night sky in two, thousands of thoughts rushed through Brother Francis' mind.

"It's easy," thought Francis, "to throw a bag of gold out the window. It's very easy to withstand thirty-nine lashings without blinking an eye. It's relatively easy to walk to the ends of the earth barefoot and in the snow while being beaten by harsh winds. And, with the help of the Lord, it's possible to throw oneself into the flames or onto the sword, to offer one's neck to the scimitar, to suffer torture on the rack or to be dragged by horses or to be devoured by wild beasts, even to kiss a leper on the mouth.... But to remain calm when the grotesque figure of ridicule appears, not to get upset when they drag ones precious tunic through the streets, not to blush in the face of humiliation, not to shudder when one is disrobed of name and social stature...all of that is humanly impossible, or a miracle of God's mercy."

* * *

Brother Francis was growing very fond of the young and transparent novice. But he was afraid for him. He feared that, in the long run, he might be incapable of confronting the great test of dishonor: mockery and ridicule.

"Man," thought Brother Francis, "identifies with his image as though it were his shadow. Almost inevitably the person and his or her image are confused in an indissoluble symbiosis. Man is wounded in his image, and he is also wounded by his social environment. If we get more newcomers, this will be the most difficult foundation stone to preserve: humility."

Giles asked permission to greet people in another manner. Brother Francis did not know how to respond at first, and fell silent.

"It's the fear of ridicule," he thought, "the eternal problem of a social image."

Suddenly he thought of telling him about Jesus' serenity when he was slandered and mocked.

"He's not ready to understand," he said to himself, "and even less prepared to put it into practice."

So he decided to respond using the same line of reasoning as the one, who is controlled by superficiality, uses:

"Don't be afraid, my young lamb," said Brother Francis. "That greeting will be forever famous throughout the world. Don't worry, my son! The day will come when even the most exalted princes will kneel before you at the sound of this greeting."

It was not an evangelical response, rather a somewhat "worldly" one. Giles was not mature enough to shoulder a valiant evangelical attitude. He was still a beginner in the things of the spirit, and Brother Francis, understandingly, treated each one in accordance with his level of spiritual growth.

They continued on their way. Brother Francis noticed that the novice was not as sure of himself as before, since his greeting lacked the usual radiance. But he pretended not to notice and dropped the subject. For miles and miles, he spoke about Jesus.

That same day they ate only plums and bread made of barley, and they drank water from the numerous springs found in that mountainous region. They slept near the entrance to a public kiln used daily by the villagers to bake bread.

Before going to sleep, they spent time in deep adoration. Brother Francis noticed that the novice was much calmer, but that some tension lingered, like one who has fought his first battle. With deep affection and devotion Brother Francis placed his hands on the newcomer and imparted a long blessing. Giles immediately fell asleep. Brother Francis remained deep in thought, reflecting on many things.... Before falling asleep, he vehemently begged the Lord to grant them, him and his followers, the supreme gift of humility.

* * *

The days that followed were full of adventure. They entered villages, walked up slopes crowned by crenellated castles, penetrated the very heart of these cities. They stopped where a group of people had gathered. Brother Francis spoke to them about love, peace, and freedom. Above all, he talked about Jesus himself, and on occasion his words overflowed with emotion. His words penetrated the taverns with evangelical force, and he spoke imaginatively about love and peace.

His favorite places were the plazas. The same thing happened every time: Brother Francis would begin a very warm conversation with one or two people. More people would gather. And as the crowd grew, so did his tone and inspiration.

As Francis spoke, Giles would circle the plaza and the streets repeatedly, inviting people to come and listen:

"Go and listen to Francis of Assisi. He's God's servant."

When Brother Francis concluded his words, Giles would step forward and address the crowd:

"My brothers, what you have heard is the truth in all its purity, and there is no better expression of it than this. Believe him. I assure you he is a saint."

"They've lost their minds," some said.

"It's the spirit in wine that has overpowered them," said others. "They must be heretics," said some.

"It's neither this nor that; they're poor simple souls, little boys almost, who do not know what they are saying," a few replied.

Barefooted, wearing vestments that were neither clerical nor monastic, resembling the style of the followers of Valdo, with fearlessness of spirit, with the freedom of the children of God, and with the happiness of one who has everything, the two brothers walked through the villages and valleys of the Marches, raising a dust cloud of polemics.

The most sensible said:

"Calm down; don't judge so hastily. These aren't words of an idiot, nor words of a heretic. These men do not speak against the clergy or nobility or anything. They only speak about God and peace. Furthermore, any observer can perceive a radiant joy in their souls and an unusual sense of freedom. Our mockery doesn't upset them. Without a doubt, all of this is from God."

Some venerated them. Most stayed away, suspecting that the brothers could be just about anything. The women, above all, thought they were sorcerers. When they saw the brothers from afar, they would give high-pitched screams and hide in their homes.

On their return to Spoleto they were not permitted to enter certain valleys that they had so often frequented. Villagers chased them away with rocks and wild dogs. They were hungry by day and shivering by night. They slept in stables on haystacks. But at times they were not even afforded that luxury. When that was the case, the brothers would go out into the fields, gather armfuls of dry grass and sleep next to trees under the stars.

Delight, Precaution, Productivity

During all this time, Brother Francis was caught between two powerful and opposing forces: on the one hand, he was immensely happy in striving to imitate the life of the persecuted and slandered Jesus; on the other hand, he was very preoccupied with his beloved newcomer. Apparently, Francis was little bothered by people's reactions. Instead, he was constantly attentive to Giles' state of mind.

He feared that the young man might be incapable of absorbing such powerful "nourishment," that he might become discouraged, and suffer an incurable wound. It was the concern of a mother for her child who was in harm's way. For him, a brother was as important as a whole town or troop. Giles, for example, was just as important as the county of Camerino or Ancona.

At night, once the lights of the world and human voices had faded out, Brother Francis took advantage of their intimacy, under the stars, in order to inject enthusiasm into the beginner.

"Son of my soul," he said, "happy are the knights of Christ who are covered with red wounds and blue scars. They will shine like emeralds for all eternity. Happy are we who are considered worthy of walking the same path as our blessed captain, Christ. What would you say, my son, if the emperor were to walk into the large plaza and, pointing to you, say: 'I invite you to walk beside me, but note: we are going to run the same risks, be at the front lines in combat, but I will go first: are you ready?'

"Giles, my son," he continued, "I'm going to open my heart to you, and share some intimate things with you. When I think about my Redeemer's humility when he was slandered and remained silent, when he was beaten and did not retaliate, when he was insulted and did not protest...when I think of my Lord Jesus Christ's infinite patience, I feel like crying and I go crazy with the desire that they throw mud, dirt, rocks, dogs, and profanity at me. I'd be the happiest man on earth. And when I think that he suffered all of that for our love, oh! I go nuts and feel as though I've grown wings and can fly all around the world yelling: Love is not loved, Love is not loved."

Under a moonlit night, Giles was able to observe Francis' eyes and they were full of tears. Sharing such confidences was profoundly moving for the novice. He slept happily and woke up feeling energized. Francis was like an eagle holding the eaglet by the throat and dropping him into the abyss, saying: Fly! Giles matured considerably in just two weeks.

* * *

In terms of productivity, that first apostolic outing was a complete disaster. No conversion, no proselyte and, apparently, no popular commotion. Francis spent so much time in deep meditation with the poor and Crucified Christ that he had no time to worry about wonderful and tangible results. He never thought—not then nor at anytime—in terms of effectiveness. But Giles, in addition to being a beginner, was a peasant, accustomed to analyzing things from the perspective of tangible results. He was visibly depressed by the apparently fruitless results.

One day, when Brother Francis' words were the subject of mockery and laughter, Giles began to give explanations to the townspeople and historical facts about Francis' identity, in order that his words produce the greatest impact. Brother Francis did not like his methods, but he did not say a word.

That night they slept within the ruins of an old castle. It was a beautiful and brilliant night. They did not feel like sleeping. Brother Francis was happy and his soul was filled with inspiration. That night he wanted to say the most profound things to the novice, but he did not know how to say them. He approached him and, with great affection and expressions full of emotion, he said:

"How can I say it, my son, how can I say it? He was a tree burnt and split in two by a bolt of lightning, its wood serving no purpose, neither for lumber nor for fire. That was my Lord. He was a garland made of carnations that was dumped in the garbage and covered with flies. That was my Lord. He was a burning forest and dormant forever in sand and ashes. That was my Lord. No voice, no splendor, nailed and helpless, defeated and motionless, extinguished lamps and hushed harps, while all of humanity, like an endless procession, passed before his lifeless shadow repeating in chorus: 'it's hopeless, it's useless, it's the end of our dreams'..."

At that moment, Francis stood up in the darkness of the night, acquiring a celestial height and, raising his voice, he continued:

"From that garbage dump, from that silent helplessness, from the Son's useless submission, the Lord God won Victory, Usefulness, and Redemption, forever; in short, all the energies that will transform the world until the end of time. Giles, my son, pride's old banners are waving in our underground passageways. We will raise on high the flag symbolizing the Glory of God and, in the most humble symbiosis, we will identify our glory with the Glory of God, our interests with the interests of God. Let's say the county of Fabriano has converted, and we're immensely happy. Are we happy about the triumph of Grace or our own success? Let's say this village has rejected Grace, and we're saddened; but why? Is it because they have rejected God or because they have rejected us?"

Brother Francis was impulsive. While reflecting on the destitution and humility of the Crucified Christ, he had discovered, by way of contrast, the motivation behind human behavior. But he never shared his conclusions with anyone, and, in doing so now, he felt relieved, as though a tremendous weight had been lifted from his shoulders.

"Let's elaborate," he continued, "on a theological treatise in order to lay the foundations of the *Christian Republic*, and to say in the end: It deals with exceptional and divine interests. When the papal forces triumph, we say right away: God is victorious. Our mouths fill with resounding words: effectiveness, productivity, organization, interests of the Church, results. These are our value judgements and criteria for action. And to the degree to which these values change, so does our degree of satisfaction. It's a horrendous and strange type of mixture," said Brother Francis in a very low voice, so that Giles could not overhear. "We all want to triumph, and shine, and we do it in a consecrated but profane manner, mixing personal desires with the interests of God. When I think of this, I just want to cry.

"My son, we forgot about the Cross. It's difficult to free oneself of something. To make oneself poor is no easy task. No one wants to be little. We think we can and we think we should *do* something: redeem, organize, transform, save. Only God saves, my beloved Giles. At the hour of truth, our plans for salvation, our apostolic strategies tumble down the slopes of frustration. There are many recent examples of this but we never learn from them. Believe me, my son, it's infinitely easier to mount a successful apostolic campaign than to make oneself little and humble. We're like the apostles when, on their journey to Jerusalem, the Lord spoke to them about Calvary and the Cross. 'They didn't understand a thing,' they didn't want to know, and they looked the other way. My son, in our initial emotional reactions, we feel intense repugnance toward the Cross.

"That is why," Brother Francis said in conclusion, "at the sight of the Cross we instinctively close our eyes, justifying our anxiety about conquest and victory with rationalizations. To make oneself little: therein lies salvation. Let's begin by acknowledging that only God saves souls, only he is omnipotent and needs nothing from no one. If he were to need, it would be from insignificant slaves, poor and humble, who imitate his Son in submission and obedience, capable of loving and forgiving. This is all we need to do. The rest is God's doing."

Little by little Brother Francis, approached the conclusion of his colloquy. They were both profoundly moved and were silent for a long time. Giles did not feel the need to ask for clarification. Everything was clear.

They spent most of the night looking silently at the stars, and thinking about the poor and Crucified Christ. They were extremely happy.

Reunion and Festivities

Francis and Giles returned to the Porziuncola. Bernard and Peter were awaiting their return. It was their first reunion. It is difficult to describe the scene: eyes moist with tears, long embraces, not a word was uttered...

After the initial emotional moments had passed, they went to the hermitage. They knelt before the picture of St. Mary. They prayed in silence. Afterwards, Brother Francis raised his voice and expressed ardent words of gratitude to the Mother of Christ. Then they went to the main cabin.

It was a family reunion full of freshness and spontaneity. Each one recounted his exploits during the apostolic excursions. The four were radiant. They celebrated their adventures. They glorified the Lord. Now and then Brother Francis interjected words of encouragement. It was a family celebration, and it would not be a celebration without a banquet. Peter and Bernard had a few days set aside to prepare the feast for this momentous occasion: an abundance of olives, some nuts, bread made of barley and fresh water. They were overjoyed.

* * *

Within a few days, three more citizens of Assisi came to join them. As the first order of the day, Brother Francis set forth the evangelical words of total renunciation and, with Bernard as an example, they renounced their worldly possessions and joined the brotherhood of the Porziuncola.

The family grew. For Brother Francis, this was not a cause for concern. On the contrary, each citizen who knocked on their door was a gift from God. Brother Francis neither called nor chose them. He simply received his disciples from the hands of the Lord.

He never worried about the future of that incipient movement which was growing at an accelerated pace. Moment by moment, he concentrated only on encouraging, restraining or molding each brother, one by one, according to his needs, moods and personality. Tomorrow he left in the hands of God.

* * *

If Brother Francis did not worry about the future of that little group, for sure the inhabitants of Assisi surely did. The fact that prominent citizens were renouncing all the comforts of the bourgeoisie sparked public opinion from the very beginning. But as is always the case, with the passing of time, all those heated emotions ended up covered in dust, and the fickle opinions of the public underwent a complete change.

They were under the opinion that it was an epidemic of lunacy, provoked by one lunatic who was a complete failure. At this pace the economy would dry up and the city would suffer financial ruin, resulting in a catastrophe much worse than the plague. One can tolerate the renunciation of goods to the poor only to a certain point, but that the city should have to feed these new beggars was absolutely intolerable. There were just too many. In short, this *new craze* went against the established order and common sense. It had to be stopped.

One day, Francis went up to the city and, instead of giving bread, people threw rocks. Anyone else would have been totally dismayed. What was worse, the inhabitants had every right to be irritated. On the surface, it appeared as though Francis was snatching family members and, after demanding that they squander all their belongings, was casting them into the world with nothing to call their own.

Common sense tells us that this idealism was not only folly, but also a dangerous conspiracy. Even his most ardent supporters were less than enthusiastic and felt that something had to be done in order to contain the epidemic.

Caught between Submission and Resistance

The citizens of Assisi took their complaints to Bishop Guido. In the final analysis, he was responsible for the recent developments, and he held in his hand the sword with which to cut the chain, if he so desired. One day, he summoned Francis to discuss a change in strategy.

"My son," he said, "I don't have to say anything. Go and speak with the first person you meet in the street, and you will notice immediately that a discontented deaf person has gained influence over the citizenry. This disgruntled person is against you. In some eyes you will also perceive the flaming coals of anger. What is so serious about this unrest is that they are holding me responsible. But this is not what is hurting me; in the final analysis, I am but a poor mortal. What I want to say is that this serious indignation is dividing the people from the Church and from God himself.

157

"I do not agree," he continued, "with some of the complaints. For example, they have no right to complain about all the gentlemen who are following you. They are not following you; they are following Christ. The people also have no right to say that these men are squandering their riches, because in reality, they are renouncing their goods in order to follow the dictates of evangelical poverty. However, I do find that some complaints are justified. They complain that your begging is becoming a tremendous burden. Many of them are poor; they have very little to live on. My son, permit me then to offer you some advice. You need to reassess your group's way of life. I consider it of fundamental importance to provide means of sustenance. Your life is hard, very hard. Francis, my son, an individual like yourself and a few others are capable of sustaining your way of life without heroics. But most people stand far below that summit. Groups of people move to rhythms that are similar to their own. Above all, be sensible, my son; keep your feet on the ground.

"I can help you," the bishop said in conclusion, "get some land, an olive grove, a vineyard, an orchard. Work that land as God would have it and live honestly and poorly by the sweat of your brow. To live everyday by one's labors is the principle behind a Christian and also a monastic life."

* * *

The bishop said no more. Brother Francis remained silent. Once again he found himself in the middle of a drama, the drama of all prophets. He was not born for conflicts nor for battle. He was a man of peace, by nature and by grace. He would have been happy living forever as an anchorite in the rough gorges of Mt. Subasio. Nevertheless, the hand of the Lord, placing him in battle after battle, had just put him in the middle of two conflicting currents: submission and resistance.

Whom do I obey? Did not the Lord himself reveal this way of life through the evangelical word? But, is not the Church the agent through which God's will is revealed? Whom do I obey? Could the evangelical word and the voice of the Church contradict one another? Herein lies the temptation: the Gospel opposite (against) the Church. An intellectual would have been lost, trapped between a thousand questions and irrelevancies. A bishop *is* the Church? The Pope or council *is* the Church?

Brother Francis did not get tangled in subtle reasoning nor was he tempted to compare the Gospel to the Church. While looking at Bishop Guido, he spoke in a low voice, confidently and naturally with humility and reverence:

"My lord and father. When we get the olive grove, we'll have to construct an oil press. Once we have the oil press, we'll need oxcarts to carry the oil and sell it. When we sell the oil, we'll have some money. We'll buy a few new acres of land with the money. More acres means more laborers to work the developing property. With time, the expanding property will need walls to defend it. Later on, the walls will require soldiers to watch and protect them. The soldiers will need arms. And one day the arms will march us inevitably into conflicts and battles. From property to wars is a synopsis to this story," concluded Francis.

It was that infernal chain of events. Bishop Guido listened enthusiastically, and while he listened his arguments and words of defense fell from his hands. It was an unanswerable response. Francis, the man of peace, touched the raw and bloody wound of human society: all property is potentially violence.

* * *

Brother Francis was never a typical thinker, much less an intellectual. But the wisdom of the Gospel, together with his natural intuition, held the key to the solutions of life's fundamental problems. To have possessions establishes a correlation between property and proprietor, that is, an appropriation. When the property is threatened, it calls on the proprietor. The proprietor becomes alarmed and arms himself in order to protect the threatened property.

From defense we jump easily into offense. There are ambitions, which are dreams of major conquests that require the use of more effective weapons. Only with arms (be they emotional, verbal, legal, or made of steel) can property be defended and conquered and, in that way, *property* and *war* become one and the same thing.

However, since all of this is covered by a grotesque visage, it becomes necessary to rationalize, to cover a rotting interior with attractive gowns. And so, sacred banners of combat are woven, such as mother country, ideologies, vain interests, and the so-called interests of the Church. The words lose their original significance; polychromed words are used to distort and deceive until society (from the smallest to the greatest) is no more than a monstrous ensemble of disguised interests, ulterior motives, ambiguous words, unscrupulous diplomacy. A tremendous adulteration.

Only in total and abject poverty is there peace, honesty and brotherhood.

Hirelings and Witnesses

Bishop Guido pressed the issue no further. His silence was a tacit authorization to continue on the path of abject poverty. At the very least, the evangelical spirit of this prelate must be recognized and admired. There is no doubt that he was a man of faith and intuition. Once again, under the present circumstances, he did not wish to go against divine plans and, stepping aside, he let God guide this strange prophet along unknown paths.

Brother Francis returned to his family at the Porziuncola. Once he appeared, the general mood, one of discontent, soon vanished. In all likelihood, in light of what had occurred, the disciples took precautions so as not to aggravate the townspeople, readjusting their way of thinking during their reunions and devising ways to interweave evangelical poverty with daily sustenance.

The months that followed were a period abounding with inventiveness; and the Franciscan way of life incorporated fruitful experiences and new routines. These next two years were probably the golden age in Franciscan history, and on his deathbed Brother Francis would evoke those times with nostalgia. There were no paths. The paths opened as one walked.

"The bishop is right," Francis said to himself. "One's labors must be the means of sustenance."

But Bishop Guido was thinking about the work that monks do on their large farms.

"Not that!" Francis said to himself. "No possessions."

And so? The answer presented itself quite readily: work for wages on someone else's farmland. This was a brand new concept, an almost revolutionary idea, proposed by Francis as part of the routine of religious life, in the name of evangelical poverty. He achieved two significant results, almost without intent: daily sustenance and the brothers' prophetic presence in the midst of God's village, particularly among the workers.

* * *

The life of Brother Giles, as one of the first Franciscans, was exemplary, typifying their manner of working. A few years later, we find Giles in Fabriano making furniture and weaving baskets and other wickerworks. He would then take his wares to the city and sell them, receiving in return for the sale food and clothing for himself and his companion, instead of money. With these labors he managed to clothe many disciples.

When he lived in Rome, he would go to the woods every morning after Mass and return with lumber stacked on his shoulders and sell it in the market. During the grape harvest, he would gather grapes, take them to the grape press and press them with his own feet. Every morning he would go to the plazas where they hired laborers.

A landowner wanted to hire workers to gather nuts. But no one wanted to go because the walnut trees were too high and the plantation was too far from the city.

"I'll help you," said Giles, "if you give me nuts as wages for my work."

Giles arrived at the plantation, made the sign of the Cross, and climbed the robust walnut trees. He labored all day long. He received so many nuts as a reward that he found it impossible to carry them in his bag. So he removed his robe, tied the sleeves and the hood together and made a large sack. He threw the nuts into the sack and took it home, distributing some among the poor as well.

He would go to the country during the grain harvest and gather ears that had been left behind. If a farmer wished to give him a sheaf, he would decline the offer, saying:

"I don't have a granary for the wheat."

When he would arrive at a hamlet or city, he first preoccupied himself with finding work as a laborer. He always reserved his most productive hours for prayer. He was happy and efficient during the hours that he labored.

* * *

The other disciples emulated the same or a similar way of life in those first years. We find them dedicating themselves to the care of lepers. This was one of the most popular occupations, if not *the* most popular. Brother Francis allowed them to have the proper tools for each vocation.

In the first years we find the disciples employed in the most diverse array of activities, depending on the locale and time of year: they carried drinking water from the springs to the villages; they cut trees in the forest for wood or lumber; they buried the dead, especially during the outbreak of epidemics; they repaired shoes, wove baskets, polished furniture; they helped the peasants gather grain, fruit, olives, nuts, grapes, depending on the time of year, and receiving whatever item they gathered as their wages. Later on, and in other regions, we find them scattered among the fishermen and mariners, maneuvering heavy oars or fish nets; we even find them in the kitchens of the feudal lords.

Brother Francis had deep respect for individual temperament and capability. He gave them complete freedom with respect to hours and manner of working, but he always stipulated one condition: "Make sure that your work does not extinguish your spirit of prayer and devotion."

As we have said, they never received money, save medicine for the sick. In addition to helping the lepers, they asked for alms on their behalf, and in this way the labors of the disciples provided the leper colonies with economic assistance.

Upon entering the Brotherhood, they did not deviate from their original context; on the contrary, they considered their original profession as the normal area where they ought to exercise their apostolate. According to Francis, the first ideal of the young brother who had been *called* was to return to his place of origin as God's witness, once he was transformed by prayer and the brotherhood. However, Brother Francis did not demand that everyone pass this test. On the contrary, he studied the potential of each individual, weighing his strengths and had the individual take risks according to his own capabilities.

* * *

As they went out into the world to preach the Gospel, they took care to do manual labor to provide sustenance and also as an apostolate. It was natural that the disciples help the peasants during the day, and at sundown preach the Word to those they labored with or to others in the small square in the village. They went in pairs through the villages and cities, barefooted, with no horse, no money, no provisions, no protection, no fixed abode.

At nightfall, they would retire to a hermitage, a leper colony or other provisional refuge in order to rest and devote long hours to the Lord. On other occasions they would go to the monasteries and ask for lodging. However, they normally sought shelter in the porticos of churches or of houses, in abandoned huts, in caverns, in public kilns... There they would sleep on some hay on the floor. Very early the next morning, they would go to a parish church or to the nearest chapel, and then begin the day's labors and apostolate.

In these first years all the disciples emerged from Francis' personal kiln. He was each brother's teacher, father and brother. So long as Brother Francis remained the primary influence over each brother, the brotherhood was a sight to behold, especially when they went out into the world. Almost all were young, poor and happy, strong and patient, austere and amiable.

They were courteous and affectionate with each other. They did not speak out against nobility, nor clergy, nor anyone. Only words of peace, poverty and love flowed from their lips. They enjoyed being among the sick, poor, and outcasts of society. Their words had moral authority because their example had preceded over the word.

Master of Spirits

However, all of this did not come about with the wave of a wand, nor was it always golden. Let us go now to the seven disciples at the Porziuncola.

Francis was well versed in human nature. Familiar surroundings and his own experience taught him about human frailty. He remembered his fluctuations and his ups and downs during his first years in the sphere of Grace, despite the powerful "visitations" of the Lord. If God demonstrated this much compassion despite his own resistance during the years of his conversion, should he expect the others to act differently?

"In the molding of a brother, one has to show respect, a lot of patience and, above all, invincible hope," Brother Francis thought to himself. "As long as man can breathe," he would say, "there can be wonders."

He also knew that catastrophes can occur, but he preferred not to think about that.

He treated each one as Lady Pica had treated him: with unlimited patience and affection. He was never hurt by her rebukes. They were more of a directive than a reprimand.

"Love!" he thought to himself many times. "Therein lies the key, love! To mold is to love. Love makes the impossible possible."

Brother Francis was born with the sensitivity to love. He received endless affection from his mother and exceptional emotional strength from the Lord God. All this made him happy and free. Life taught him that the only invincible weapons on earth are those made of love. In his last years he always gave this advice for those impossible situations: "Love him as he is."

"What merit is there in loving a captivating person?" he would ask himself.

Very soon rough "stones" began arriving at the Porziuncola, men who had tremendous desires to be consecrated by God and be polished by Francis' maternal hand.

As in every group of human beings, among the transparent young men who arrived at the Porziuncola's *Mother House*, other young men also came who locked themselves within their walls, who left doors ajar to observe rather than to be observed, who stored explosives in their vestibules, and those who, without realizing it, hid serpents on their verandas.

Brother Francis studied each case individually. He did not synthesize nor generalize, nor did he like to deduce. He dealt with each brother in the here and now. Yesterday he was happy, now depressed. The day before yesterday he was tempted, now liberated. The man does not exist, thought Francis, nor the person. This brother woke up radiant this morning; now, at nightfall, he appeared somber. He was a different person altogether.

* * *

And so began his labors, polishing each with the delicate and patient hands of a mother.

"Delicately, that's the word," he thought many times.

It was essential to bump and bruise the rough stones, but he suffered more than the wounded stones.

He had the rare gift of being able to invert roles and distances. He managed to make the disciple feel like the "master." At the end of his days, he used to say that the minister should treat the disciples in that way, especially when they are admonished, so that they feel like "gentlemen." This would be the chief characteristic of a teacher or coordinator. Brother Francis most certainly got those results.

"There is no reason to fear anything," he thought to himself.

He had the wisdom to know not to accelerate the process of development, not to progress too rapidly:

"Patience and wisdom are one and the same thing," he said to himself.

The problems with the brotherhood that he was unable to remedy he left in God's hands.

"For him, all is possible," he thought.

He polished Bernard's "wariness," Peter's doubts, Giles' insecurities, John Capella's peculiarities.

He tested the brothers' strengths by sending them to preach or to work. He spoke with them upon their return, asking about the decisions they had made and the difficulties they had encountered on their excursions. He stimulated them by using examples from the Gospels. He excited them by speaking about the Lord. He knew that special comparisons impressed them. He gained their trust with extreme ease. He dramatized quite often and was practiced in that most difficult art of being able to open doors by simply opening his own.

Why Do You Cry?

Months passed. Autumn and winter were but a memory. There was a new member among them and his name was Philip Lungo. Legend has it that the angel of the Lord had purified Brother Philip's lips with a smoldering brand. For this reason, whenever Brother Philip spoke of God, he used superlatives and inspiring words.

Frequently Brother Francis spent entire nights in prayer. The memory of the Crucified Christ burned in his heart, causing mixed emotions of joy and pain, sadness and happiness. Deep within his soul he felt the flourishing of a scarlet wound. Whenever he thought about the Crucified Christ, the wound reappeared and bled, and he would break down and cry, giving no thought to being seen.

On a Friday, he said to the disciples:

"My children, see to your activities. I will stay here."

On that day, he did not eat or drink, nor even take a sip of water. He curled up on the ground next to a fir tree. He spent the entire morning thinking and feeling the Passion of the Lord. At around three o'clock in the afternoon, he could not contain himself any longer and he broke down and cried. He cried his eyes out, sobbing and wailing uncontrollably. He got up and went into the forest wailing and crying. All of a sudden, he bumped into a peasant and, instead of composing himself, he went on crying. He was not the least bit ashamed.

The peasant asked him:

"What's wrong, brother. Why do you cry?"

Brother Francis responded:

"My brother, my Lord is on the cross and you ask me why I'm crying? At this very moment, I'd give anything to be the biggest ocean in the world, and to have as many tears as drops of water. At this very moment, I'd like the world's floodgates to open, cascades and torrential rains to come crashing down so that I could borrow some tears. But even if we were to gather all the rivers and oceans, there wouldn't be sufficient tears to cry for the pain and love of my Crucified Christ. I'd like to have the powerful wings of an eagle and cross the mountain ranges, screaming over the cities: Love is not loved! Love is not loved! How can men love one another if they don't love Love?"

The peasant could not control himself. He also broke down and cried. And the chronicle concludes with these words: "We knew that man. And he shared his experiences with us, friends of the blessed Francis, to console our hearts."

Intense Preparation

There were eight disciples all together. Spring arrived. The winter months were spent exclusively in the retreat, caring for the lepers and helping the peasants. They were now sufficiently mature in their faith. In order to comply with the mandate of Christ, they had to go out once again and announce to the world the reasons for their happiness and the paths to freedom. The swallows arrived with spring in their wake. They, the swallows of the Lord, had to go out carrying spring in their souls.

But Brother Francis was worried. He had not forgotten the hostilities he endured in his first outing to Ancona and, above all, the scare that Giles had given him. These memories filled his heart with dread. He began to remember those old thoughts.

"At this stage, I'm sure that the brothers are capable of suffering from hunger and cold," Brother Francis said to himself. "But disdain? absurdity? Uselessness? Like the clothes on our backs, man clings to his image. The hero fears humiliation. Once again before the mystery of the Cross!"

What is to be done? The Lord had placed these little ones in his hands and in his care, to help them grow into robust trees, the same as the Lord had done with him. But he was scared. He was the eagle who takes his eaglets and releases them over the abyss, saying: Fly! And if they failed to fly? What if their wings were not strong enough? And what if the winds carried them, hurling them against rocks? He was afraid, afraid of going ahead in leaps and bounds, afraid that they would succumb to the weight of the cross, afraid that they would fall into the arms of discouragement.

He decided to have them undergo intense preparation before sending them to the world. The chroniclers give us ample sketches of Brother Francis' teachings. The melody that carried and sustained his words was humility in persecutions.

* * *

One day, the disciples returned at dusk. Some had returned from weeding out vineyards, others from the leper colonies, and others from begging, with their sacks over their shoulders. They looked somewhat fatigued but were very happy. They ate dinner. There was a feeling of trust and warmth during the fraternal meal. Afterwards, Brother Francis summoned them to the hermitage. They knelt down and prayed for hours. Then, Brother Francis asked Mary of the Angels for permission to speak. The disciples sat on the floor. Brother Francis, as always, stood below the Byzantine-style picture and began to speak to them:

"My sons, have you ever seen the wind trapped in a ravine or in a cavern? If there aren't wide open spaces, the wind stops being wind. In the same way, God's spirit stops being strength and life if it doesn't radiate outward. We have tasted the bread of peace and the wine of happiness. It would be selfish of us to take a nap now, wallowing in satisfaction. The hungry and the thirsty are waiting for us."

It was a lackluster introduction that was also a bit artificial. Their eyes were wide with incomprehension; they were not sure of the meaning behind his words. The Poor Man of Assisi did not feel inspired. That is, his inspiration was blocked. All of them had suffered so much in their first outing. He was afraid to speak to them openly about the second outing. He was like a mother who suffers knowing the suffering that her children will have to endure.

He made every effort to inject warmth into his voice, and continued:

"Brothers, the Gospel is our Rule and our commander is the blessed Lord Jesus Christ. Praised be your Name forever! In the Gospel, the Lord commands us to go out into the world and proclaim the words of life. We haven't been called only to save ourselves. People are hungry and cold. Let's take bread and warmth to them. This afternoon I have spoken intimately with the Lord, and we have arranged a second outing for our family, going two by two in the four principal directions. Next week we will embark on our journey. In the meantime, it's necessary to strengthen ourselves spiritually, face to face with the Image of our blessed Lord. You can interrupt your activities if you wish, and go up the cliffs of Mt. Subasio to the *cells*, and remain there several days in profound familiarity with the Lord."

Brother Francis said no more. He had more important— and more frightful—things to tell them, but he could not bring himself to say them. As an appetizer, this was sufficient. Some disciples were a bit restless, but the majority were calm. He blessed them and took his leave to go and rest. Brother Francis kept watch all night, asking for the oil of fortitude for his disciples.

* * *

On a daily basis he would speak to them at night about Jesus' *disposition*:

"Christ never boasted about his divine nature. Being Omnipotent, he didn't dream of omnipotence. He stripped himself of his rank and put on the vestments of a slave. He renounced the advantages of being God and plunged himself into the disadvantages of being man. He bowed his head humbly before death and lifted himself silently onto the cross. He didn't open his mouth when he was slandered. He didn't threaten when he was beaten. He was like a defenseless and inoffensive little lamb. He didn't express any bitterness, any fury, any harsh remarks, any hostility whatsoever when caught in the middle of insults, lashings and injustices. He came to the Passion dressed in silence, dignity, and peace."

The disciples were profoundly moved, and Brother Francis much more so. At times, his voice broke. After speaking to them about Jesus' humility, he would leave them in silence for a long time to allow Jesus' great and humble image to permeate their souls. After this period of silence, and before retiring to rest, he would say in conclusion:

"Don't forget, our blessed Lord will walk barefooted ahead of us and we will follow."

* * *

Intuitive and clairvoyant, Brother Francis knew what awaited these little orphans out in the world. In tattered clothing which was neither a clerical nor a monastic habit, they looked like rustic mountaineers descending the high Apennines. They did not belong to any religious institution, nor did they wear any seal of the Holy See or of any bishop which would at least identify them as Catholics. Their clothing and their way of life conjured up images of Valdo's followers and other heretics.

It was the eve of their outing. They all knew it. Their faces were full of emotion, a mixture of fear and happiness. Francis looked spirited. He took care to hide his fears. They gathered in the hermitage. It was the *send-off*. Brother Francis enjoyed making this ceremony a solemn occasion. It evoked memories of chivalric ceremonies, when knight-errants celebrated the adventures to come.

It was time to drop them into the waters and drown their fears by frightening them. He said to them:

"My sons, tomorrow we go out into the world behind our captain, Christ, who is also barefoot. They won't be waiting with roses nor applause. We are ignorant and insignificant. Our sword of combat is neither science nor intellectual pursuits, rather humility, sound examples, and the strength of faith. Don't be afraid. The Lord himself will arm you with the right words for every circumstance. And because you are little, your names will be inscribed in the Book of Life in letters of gold. Be happy."

* * *

Brother Francis observed their reactions by studying their eyes and, so far, everything was fine. And so, he penetrated to the core:

"You will find good decent men who will accept your words with admiration and gratitude. But they will be part of a minority. The majority of them will dismiss your words

173

as ridiculous, and will think you ignorant and empty-headed, imbeciles and busybodies. Even some of the clergy might look at you askance. But worse things are to come. There are those who will resist you and respond sarcastically, not to mention those who will chase you away with dogs and rocks, or by throwing cold water. Some will gather and circle you as if you had lost your head."

He sprung it on them outright, barely making eye contact. When he finished his last sentence, he looked up and saw the look of alarm reflected in their eyes. It was too much. They were unable to absorb the blow. They were not ready. In a state of fright, some began to ask questions, others trembled, and panic took hold of the group. Once again the world and the cross clashed within man!

Brother Francis stepped back. He took down the cross and let *the world*, which lived inside them, have its way for now. He said to them:

"I see that you're afraid. You're almost ashamed to belong to our ranks. It's true that we're few in number and insignificant. But you ought to know that very soon we will be many, and that numerous nobles and scholars will join our ranks, preaching to princes, kings, and emperors, and many will follow the Lord because of our word."

It was a long-winded "worldly" speech, a true compromise on the mystery of the cross. But this is precisely the way Brother Francis should proceed—given human frailty—carefully measuring the thickness of each brother's evangelical fortress.

Brother Francis could not help feeling some frustration, but he reacted instantly and suppressed it. If he were to become discouraged, where would he find encouragement? He continued, saying to them:

"If they ask to know who we are, simply respond by saying that we are 'penitents of the city of Assisi.'"

* * *

Brother Francis did not sleep that night. Kneeling and with his arms crossed he ardently asked the Crucified Christ for humility and strength on behalf of his disciples, so that none should fail the test.

The next morning, the Poor Man of Assisi was smiling as he awaited the evangelical travelers at the door of the hermitage. All appeared to be spirited and happy. Praised be the Lord!

He gave them his final instructions. Then he cut a branch from a bush, held it in his hand and stood in front of the hermitage, and said:

"In the name of the Lord!"

And as he said this, he drew a large cross on the ground, making the four principal points. And in each direction he placed two disciples, sending all eight of them in different horizons.

One after another, they knelt at Brother Francis' feet. He gave each a moving blessing. Then he helped them to their feet and, as he embraced each of them, he said:

"Give all your worries to the Lord. He will be your fortress."

Deeds and Adventures

Francis and another brother, whose name we ignore, went toward the Rieti Valley. If we adhere to the descriptions given by the *Three Companions*, there were fewer fears and many more ill-fated adventures than Francis had imagined.

Wherever they went, be it city or castle, hamlet, town or a group of dwellings, the disciples always greeted people with "May the peace of the Lord be with you." And, without asking permission, they unfurled a flag of peace conferred by the Lord on those who followed him. All were taken aback by their unusual clothing, asking one another about this strange race of men who appeared out of nowhere.

Some were glad to listen. Others used obscene expressions and comical remarks. The majority harassed them with questions:

"Who are you? Where are you from? What do you do?"

As Francis had instructed, they humbly responded: "We are the penitents of the city of Assisi."

All kinds of opinions were expressed:

"You're imposters and full of deceit," some said.

"You poor idiots," said others.

The majority considered them dangerous and no one accepted them into their homes fearing they might be thieves. Many places even denied them hay on which to sleep and they had to take shelter in church vestibules, in abandoned castles and in public kilns.

* * *

Brothers Bernard and Giles went in the direction of St. James of Compostela. They had amazing adventures as they passed through Florence. They did not concern themselves with the others. According to Francis' teachings, when they spied a dome or a church tower in the distance that indicated the eucharistic presence, they would kneel on that very spot and, with their hands pressed together and eyes focused on that church, they would say:

"We adore You, Blessed Lord Jesus Christ, here and in all the churches of the world, and we praise You because Your Holy Cross has redeemed the world."

The chronicles mention that many people, great and small alike, either threw insults or rocks. Once, some people who were extremely disrespectful pushed them around and tore off their clothing. In accord with evangelical demands, the disciples only carried one tunic. When this one was pilfered, they were left half-naked. Even so, the disciples did not protest this despoilment. If the rags were returned, they expressed their gratitude as if returning their clothes had been a favor.

Some threw mud at them, others put dice in their hands and invited them to play games of chance. The lads would grab onto their hoods and drag themselves behind their backs. The disciples got used to it and, in the end, carried on unperturbed, exercising great self-control. They experienced hunger, cold, nakedness, all kinds of abuses and taunts.

Such vicissitudes prompted the disciples to recall Francis' examples and words, and these recollections encouraged them to suffer in peace. They were educated in Francis' evangelical academy. These episodes occurred repeatedly in the first ten years on successive missionary expeditions to Christian lands and later on to lands of the unbelievers.

Usefulness and Uselessness

We repeat that in terms of apostolic efficacy, that is, with respect to statistical results, the first apostolic expeditions resulted in nothing; moreover, they were a complete disaster. But the Poor Man of Assisi always put himself above statistics and the concepts of utility and efficacy, in the name of the Gospel. For him, the great apostolic mission was to live the Gospel, simply and completely. To live the Gospel meant to comply with the words of the Master and imitate his life.

* * *

"The Kingdom of God," thought the Poor Man of Assisi, "*is* Jesus himself. And the Kingdom grows in relation to the degree to which we imitate Jesus' impulses and reactions, reflections and attitudes, the life style and the general behavior of Christ Jesus. The Kingdom grows to the degree to which the disciples imitate and reflect the profound impulses, the preferences and viewpoints, and the general objective of the life of the Lord Jesus Christ."

Brother Francis imitated and taught them to imitate, almost miming, all that the Lord did and commanded, with the simplicity of a child and with the loyalty of a knight-errant.

Naturally, Jesus did and commanded many things. But there were many mysterious facets concerning Jesus that vividly impressed the sensitive soul of Brother Francis of Assisi, dimensions which can be summed up in these combined words: *poverty-humility*; a view which, in turn, encompasses the whole reality of Bethlehem, Calvary, and the Sermon on the Mount.

For example, for Brother Francis, martyrdom was the supreme apostolate. Exalted apostolates, in his estimation, included forgiving offenses, experiencing joy in hardships, praying for persecutors, having patience when taunted, doing good in return for bad, not to suffer distress in the face of slander, not to defame those who defame; in short, to live what the Lord had lived in the Passion and had taught on the Mount.

The omnipotent savior of the world is God himself. He does not need anyone (in order to save), except servants, like Jesus, who give themselves to the executioners in faith, a faith that is pure and invincible; servants obedient to the point of death and death on the cross, in total abandonment and submission to the Father in the midst of painful crises beyond our control; servants who are happy to suffer in the name of Jesus.

In fact, Brother Francis and the first disciples followed essentially this apostolate: the evangelical life. They also preached, but this was secondary: they did so with brevity and simplicity, always subordinating preaching to example.

This kind of apostolate is much more difficult than the organized and ministerial one, because here we do not see tangible results and one has to proceed in pure faith. It has much more to do with an apostolic life than apostolic activities. What is necessary is not intellectual preparation, rather a profound and lasting conversion of the heart. Neither is it necessary to be a priest. For this reason, in the brotherhood's early years we find very few priests and, in any case, for this *plan* or *form* of life, the priesthood is an accessory. What is essential is to be a *little brother*.

* * *

Returning now to the missionaries who were travelling around the world, the narrators continue to tell us that they took joy in their tribulations, that they were assiduously dedicated to prayer and to manual labor, never receiving money in recompense, and that they were extremely cordial to one another at all times. When people took notice of this, they were convinced that those *penitents of Assisi* were neither heretics nor rascals and, repentant, they approached them asking forgiveness. The disciples said to them:

"All is forgiven."

And they offered advice.

What served to convince these people that these were truly evangelical men was their mutual affection for one another, attending to each other's needs "like a mother who lovingly attends her one and only beloved child." This was probably the most original aspect of the Franciscan revolution, and here was the genius of that simple and wise man: taking the disciples from abject poverty into the arms of brotherhood. This will be discussed at length later on.

The chroniclers of this expedition offer fascinating accounts that illustrate this point. One day, two disciples were walking along and saw a mad person approaching who began to throw cobblestones at them. One of the disciples, the one standing on the other side, ran to the aid of his brother who was being attacked, and intervened, allowing the rocks to hit him and not his companion. "They were ready to give their life for their brother."

Onward to Rieti

As previously mentioned, Brother Francis and his companion headed toward the Rieti Valley. They passed Spoleto but did not enter the city. They slowly penetrated the rough gorges of the Sabine Hills.

Francis sang and spoke about God during the whole trip.

"Brother," he frequently reminded his companion, "our blessed companion Christ walks barefooted ahead of us, and if we had a little bit more faith, we'd see that every now and then he turns around and smiles at us. What would our lives be like without him? With him, we're the freest, happiest, most fulfilled men in the world; without him, we'd be the most wretched orphans on the earth. Praised be Jesus forever!"

Whenever they saw a church tower in the distance, up in the hills, he would stop and take his companion by the arm. Usually his eyes would fill with tears when he thought about Christ in the Blessed Sacrament. They would kneel and pray "We Adore You" slowly, several times. And on rising he always had vivid thoughts to share as they resumed their journey.

"Can you believe it, brother?" he said once. "I lose my appetite when I think of the blessed Christ. I could be shaking from the cold, like the other night; I think of my Lord Jesus Christ and a warm sun enters my veins."

* * *

One day, as a small valley opened before them, they saw Terni in the distance, and a monastery up in the hills. As usual, Brother Francis knelt and prayed "We Adore You." He maintained that position for quite a while. Then, he took his companion by the hand, kept his eyes focused on the monastery, lowered his voice, as if he were about to say something terrible and mysterious, and said:

"And to think that in the Blessed Sacrament Christ has given everything to us, everything! The least that we can do is to give ourselves entirely to him. Forgive me, my companion. Allow me to walk alone."

He walked ahead about twenty paces, and walked alone for many hours, totally absorbed in God. At about midday, he went to a house and asked for something to eat. They gave him alms. In turn, he gave it to his companion. Francis did not eat a thing that day. It seemed as if his soul had reached the ends of the earth.

Days passed. Their path alternated between valleys and mountains. Spring was everywhere, alive with splendor. They passed Stroncone, Le Marmore, and Piediluco. Brother Francis spoke of Love wherever he went. They had experiences and escapades typical of chivalric adventures. One day, he walked up to a house to ask for something to eat, and they gave him a dead rat. He took it in good humor.

They slept wherever the night happened to greet them. At times they shivered from the cold. Some nights, Brother Francis would remove his tunic and pass it to his companion, then he would go and pray. Praying filled him with warmth.

Constantly, especially before going to sleep, Brother Francis spoke to his companion about the other six disciples. He would remember them in his prayers.

"I wonder how Giles is doing?"

And in this way he recalled each one of them. At times, his eyes would fill with tears as he thought of the abuses that each would suffer.

He treated his companion with motherly affection and love. Before going to sleep, he would give him a blessing that was full of warmth. There was no better preparatory school than to spend a few days with Brother Francis.

* * *

As they emerged from among the hellish gorges, they saw before their eyes, as if it were a dreamlike vault, the Rieti Valley. It was a high plateau, made of splendor and serenity, flanked on all sides, by the Sabine Hills, like invincible sentinels. This plateau would come to be known as the *sacred valley* of San Francisco, flanked by four hermitages that would stand like spiritual fortresses. This site should give rise to great events in Franciscan history.

"Brother," said Francis to his companion, "what peace, what silence! This isn't a valley. It's paradise. For surely angels live here."

The verdant valley contrasted beautifully with the snowcapped peaks of the Sabine Hills. Fresh, clean water flowed in the rivers and streams, releasing a quiet murmur through the valley and giving life to the countryside. Brother Francis was completely intoxicated.

He saw the highland hamlet of Greccio appear before his eyes, resting on the side of a mountain. Brother Francis knelt and prayed "We Adore You." As he got up, he said to his companion:

"Brother, if the Almighty were to permit it, how I would love to transform this valley into a temple of adoration!"

He looked to the other side and, suddenly, his eyes fixed themselves on something. What did he see? On a bare, rocky mountain he saw a tiny village. He asked some peasants the name of that hamlet, and they responded:

"Poggio Bustone."

"Let's go there, brother," he said.

And they headed in that direction.

It took them several hours to scale the mountain. After every one hundred paces or so, Brother Francis would stop and look back. The valley began to acquire an enchanting appearance. On the right, a ravine ran down the mountain like a deep fissure. It was emotionally moving and frightening. The bare and snowcapped mountains could be seen in the distance.

They finally reached the hamlet. Francis was not in the proper frame of mind to impart peace to the townspeople. Evidently, he did not find himself at peace. For days he felt depressed, as though dark clouds hovered above.

"No one can pronounce the word peace if it is missing from one's soul," he said to himself.

They passed the hamlet without stopping and continued to climb.

Within the last peaks, at a height and distance past Poggio Bustone, more than one thousand meters above sea level, and almost inaccessible, they found a *speco*, that is, an overhang or a grotto. Implacable desolation and extremely rough terrain surrounded them: an ideal place for a battle, thought Brother Francis. Just by looking out and upward, his eyes beheld an indescribable horizon. His soul was overwhelmed with the grandeur before him.

"Brother," Francis said to his companion, "anxiety has pressed itself against my soul like a wet garment. How can I be the light of the world if I'm in the dark? How can I help peace to flourish if I'm suffocated by anguish? What solace can I give the brothers if there is no solace in my soul? I need to have it out with God. Brother, I need to be alone. Don't concern yourself with me for a few days. Go to the hamlet. Ask for bread and impart peace. When peace has returned to my soul, I'll go looking for you in Poggio Bustone."

Desolation and Consolation

Without a doubt, we have here a spiritual crisis in the life of Brother Francis. In my estimation, the present crisis was a taste of that great crisis which he was going to suffer in the last years of his life. In both cases, with respect to his resilience, the crisis and its aftermath shared the same characteristics. For the purpose of revealing even some fragments of the mystery behind Brother Francis of Assisi, investigating and discovering the nature of that crisis is of paramount importance.

In order to accomplish this, we need the context of his life and, above all, to study carefully Chapter XI of Celano's first biography. His personal motives and those having to do with the brotherhood are indistinct and recur in this chapter.

It is significant that Francis felt such pressure to return to the Porziuncola once he overcame the crisis. The content of his discourse, just simply to return, was without a doubt the motivating factor behind his doubts, insecurities, and lack of trust.

Moreover, by looking at the ample context of his life and this chapter, it is clear to me that in the *speco* of Poggio Bustone Francis of Assisi made a resolution to found an Order. Moreover, it is necessary to underscore the fact that Brother Francis' moments of crisis—as with the great prophets—are clarified, now and always, in complete solitude with God.

* * *

In the present crisis, his personal insecurity and his inability to influence a town come together. Let us look at them separately.

It is a terrible mystery of man: "this unknown." A human being has thousands of layers, the majority of which remain buried in dark passageways, and never come to light. How can I say it? There is no comparison to the layers of the earth, nor to the depths of the oceans, nor to the vastness of space. It is much more complicated than that. All human beings harbor unexplored regions that are almost impregnable. Antagonistic elements, in the most contradictory of unions, engage in mutual warfare within the person.

Brother Francis knew the mystery of God's eternal compassion. Solace and divine gifts fell like torrential rains on his soul. He knew more than enough, he "knew" by heart the mystery of eternal Love that is given freely, the Almighty's compassion which is never denied.

Nevertheless, despite every confirmation, Brother Francis had his doubts here and now. He thought (felt) that the sins he had accumulated outnumbered God's mercy. What was happening? How can this be explained? Francis had entire regions that had not been "visited," where Grace and Compassion had yet to enter. There were sediments that were untouched, zones that had not been redeemed. This, theologically speaking, is absurd. But this is our daily bread in the history of souls.

Despite "knowing" so much about God's infinite mercy, the following took place in Brother Francis' soul. From the unknown regions of his subconscious, areas that "had not been visited" rose to the surface of his consciousness. They took possession of those primary planes, dominating the general sphere of his personality. Brother Francis felt as though he "did not believe" in divine forgiveness; that is, that which he "knew" he did not feel. This was due to what?

This was probably due to certain negative characteristics in his personal constitution or to a religious training combined with fear and trembling... The fact is that a crisis of profound distrust took possession of him. Distrust of what? That he was sufficiently pardoned, that he was accepted by God. For this reason he repeated incessantly:

"Have pity on me, Lord, for I have greatly sinned."

And in spite of his existential knowledge of God's infinite mercy, these doubts were controlling him and he could not dispel them.

Deep down, he was lacking in hope. All despair stems from relying on oneself, from "being turned" to oneself, from trusting and distrusting oneself. In short, Brother Francis needed to come out, to come out of himself.

Every act of hope involves trusting not oneself, but rather relying on Another. Brother Francis should not have paid attention to his frivolous youth, to his past sins. He should have focused his attention on God's infinite compassion. Not look at himself, but look at Another. An exodus was lacking, a passover.

We know that, throughout his life, he was an eminently paschal man, looking outside himself and projecting himself onto the Other. But now he was suffering a crisis, that is, finding himself in an exceptional and transitory situation.

A leap occurred, a coming out took place on the high rocks of the Sabine Hills on the day the crisis was overcome.

* * *

All of this also had a lateral dimension. The lack of self-confidence, his acute awareness of his unworthiness made him distrust himself as the leader of disciples.

The work that the Lord entrusted him to do could suffer because of his unworthiness, or perhaps his inability, or both simultaneously.

If he was not accepted by God, what could be said of those disciples who were placed in his charge? How could a sinner lead the chosen?

Due to this crisis the Poor Man of Assisi, who always looked towards God, began to look at himself. The idea that he was worthless, that he lacked preparation or qualities to lead a group of disciples and, worst of all, that he was an unfaithful sinner took a firm hold. Poor Brother Francis was in dire straits.

The vital context was the following. In faithfully following God, he incited a revolution in his family and in the city, that is to say, a tremendous scandal. The Lord himself showed him the evangelical way of life, and he walked happily along that path. Certainly this way of life was fundamentally different from all existing religious institutions. He had no other intentions or projects in mind, except to live literally by the Gospel.

However, it was not long before the Lord sent him brothers, one by one. They followed the same evangelical path. They now numbered eight. Now what was to be done? What was this family of brothers? What did God want of them? Their religious life style was different from all others.

And what if the Lord continued to send him brothers? He was solely responsible.

But, who was he? And here he began his all-exclusive self-absorption. He was a poor man, a *nobody*, with no preparation, uneducated, lacking in all the vital credentials of a leader.

These disciples trusted him. But what did he have to offer them? His unworthiness and his condition as a sinner. What would become of this group of disciples after three or four years? Finally, to go to the Pope and ask for the authorization to live a particular kind of religious life? Was this a presumption? Who was he to aspire to such heights? And precisely what was he to ask this of the Pope? Could he possibly form a group attempting heroics? And if he were to fail? In the final analysis, wasn't he a trickster, impudent, and, above all, a sinner?

There was no way out. Francis was so self-absorbed that he found himself rolling down the slopes of insecurity, doubt, and distrust. His anguish was overflowing its banks like a river, drowning his entire being.

* * *

There was only one solution: to come out.

And, once more, the Lord made the supreme gesture and led him out. In the deepest sense of the word, to come out means to forget oneself and to think of Another. To focus one's complete attention on Another—to the point that one forgets that one even exists—is the gist behind the mystery. And that is what took place in the extreme solitude of Mt. Rosatto after many days of fasting and tears.

Brother Francis of Assisi was getting a clear and vivid picture of God. It was much more than a conviction. It was something other than an idea. It was as if the Lord had said:

"Poor Francis, why worry? Why suffer so much? It is *I*. I am the dawn without end, the present without a past. I am eternity. I am immensity. I have no contours or boundaries. I *am*.

"Why be afraid, Francis, son of Assisi? I am the only Savior. I can do anything. From cold rocks I extract living, breathing children. In an instant I can resurrect generations. Since time immemorial I have been and will be forever the only Shepherd. I am the only one who can guide the nations. I am also the only Shepherd who guides the eight little orphans—and all the orphans to come—from the Porziuncola.

"Francis, son of Assisi, believe in me. Put your faith in me. Francis, take the leap. Come into my arms. I am here in the deepest fissure. Come on, jump. The only thing you need to do is to take my hand. I will do the rest. I am the founder and director of the new Order. I will be your solace and your strength, your security and your happiness, your father, your mother..."

* * *

The same thing always happens. The more intense the desolation, the more profound the consolation. The chronicles attempt with great difficulty to describe what took place: a sudden and explosive happiness or ecstasy (what can it be called?), more intense than ever.

Brother Francis emerged from the deep *speco*. It was as if the Sabine Hills had disappeared and the bosom of the world had spread out into infinity, blurring the distant galaxies...and there was no earth, mountains or stars. Only joy existed, better yet, only God existed... It was as if Brother Francis had expanded outward, grown, risen, scaled the slopes of Being to the point where he almost touched the

189

boundaries of God. And, oh what a miracle! Just at that moment the Lord was the Almighty and he, the *Poverello*, an insignificant little ant, omnipotent notwithstanding, in the hands of the Omnipotent. You are my everything, I am your nothing. Who are you, who am I?

It was difficult to imagine a more heightened sense of being. What was it? Another extremely powerful *transfiguration*? I believe so. The conscience in the "I" (Brother Francis') was completely drawn to the Other, as if he were dazed by the strength of the Other.

Brother Francis felt extended. And, as a result, Francis was completely focused on the Other. Brother Francis stopped focusing on himself. He surrendered. In surrendering, he freed himself from self-absorption. He stripped himself of his insecurities, his distrust, which were replaced by security, happiness, and peace.

After giving an in-depth narration of this episode, Celano concluded by saying: "When that light and softness finally disappeared, the other man appeared, who was transformed and spiritually renewed."

To Make You Knight of Christ

Who could possibly describe Francis' joyous re-encounter with his companion? He was in a hurry, almost anxious, to get back to the Porziuncola. His other companions were also likely to ask themselves (it was almost inevitable): What will our future be? Without a doubt this question was asked repeatedly during their fraternal conversations. The only one who could answer was Francis, but he did not have an answer.

But now that the Lord had lifted the veil from his eyes, he had a concrete answer and he felt an urgent need to communicate it to them. They would go to Rome and ask the Holy Father for permission to live their lives according to the Holy Gospel.

He was so sure of himself that he began to invite followers. Until now, the disciples had come of their own volition. The Lord Jesus also called. Following his example, Francis began to summon the young men in this new manner. They descended the mountain, and walked happily through the valley toward Rieti. They crossed the streets and gave their usual greeting: "May the peace of the Lord be with you" to the transients.

They reached the main plaza. Brother Francis' soul was overflowing with peace. A small group of people were engaged in animated conversation under the arches of a doorway. He approached them and began to speak. A river of peace flowed from his lips. It was inspirational. He spoke to them about Love, riches, poverty, and the absolute freedom of those who renounce everything for Love.

When they concluded their discussions and were disposed to leave the city, a young man who was listening in the plaza detained them. He asked them who they were and about the type of life they led.

Since Brother Francis found himself in a state of euphoria, he spoke at length about his ideals. The young man was very much impressed by what he said. His name was Angelo Tancredi. He had the look of a gentleman and was of feudal stock. Brother Francis was captivated by the youth. In fact, anything having to do with chivalry and courtly manners fascinated him.

Brother Francis saw that the young man would make an excellent knight of Christ. After further consideration, he said to him candidly:

"Young man, you have spent enough time serving the count of Rieti and the emperor. Come with me. I will arm you, knight of Christ. You will find freedom on the dusty pathways. Your tongue will be your sword and the trumpet of salvation. You will walk under the banner of peace, and Christ will be your one and only captain. March on, soldier of Christ!"

Great News

The youth said his farewells to his family, and Francis took him to the Porziuncola. During the trip back, Brother Francis wanted very much to see all his disciples upon his return.

"Please Lord," he begged God, "have them all return."

And, sure enough, all were there. Their fraternal fervor erupted like a kettle that had reached a boiling point: hugs, tears, kisses.... Emotions, impossible to control, abounded. Following the first few moments, Francis summoned his disciples to the hermitage.

After greeting Mary of the Angels and introducing the new candidate, Brother Francis, with eyes shining brightly and with jubilant words, expressed what he had suppressed for days:

"Knights of my Lord Jesus Christ, our breath will be happiness and our dress will be joy. I bring you great news. Be happy. Praised be the Lord.

"First of all, I must tell you not to fear. Don't let sadness overwhelm you nor blush at being so few. Don't blush at our insignificance. The Lord has revealed to me that he personally will make our family grow prodigiously in number, transforming it into an immense village that will spread out over the horizons of the world.

"The Lord has expressed that clearly to me," continued Brother Francis. "But he has revealed much more. I would gladly guard the secret and not tell a soul, but I think the news will do us good. Listen.

"I have seen, I have seen an innumerable multitude of men, from the east and west, of every tongue and nation. They are coming from all directions to St. Mary of the Angels in order to wear our attire and to follow our way of life. I still hear their footsteps. The French are coming. The Spanish are hurrying along. The Germans are getting closer. The English are running. When you see this, your hearts will beat with emotion. They are coming by sea, crossing mountain ranges, paths and causeways, by road and by air. The Lord's chosen are coming from every direction."

Their arteries expanded and their pupils dilated upon hearing these words. Brother Francis infused them with such confidence that all he had to say was:

"And now, onward to our Holy Father!"

And if he did not say it, he carried the decision firmly in his heart.

Within a few weeks there were three new novices among them. They were now the twelve penitents of Assisi.

In a Few Simple Words

"We need the Holy Father's backing," Brother Francis said to himself. "He is Christ's shadow here on earth. No one has ever hinted or advised me on what to do. The Lord Himself has revealed this evangelical way of life. But even so, it's wise to have it ratified by his representative here on earth. Yes, it's a good idea to prepare a small document, written in a few simple words, that synthesizes and reflects the kind of life we have lived up till now. It will be a reminder for future generations and it will also serve as the document for pontifical approval."

* * *

While the disciples went about their daily routines, Francis and Peter Cataneo, the lawyer, remained in the Porziuncola writing the document.

During that time, the disciples discovered an abandoned stable not far from the Porziuncola, in an area that was called *Rivo Torto* near a brook that zigzagged its way across the plains. Since there was not enough room in the huts of the Porziuncola for the twelve disciples, some stayed in the shepherd's hut at Rivo Torto. Sometimes Francis and Peter went there for peace and quiet, and to write the document.

They began their working day with a long prayer. Afterwards, once they began the task at hand, Francis dictated and Peter wrote the draft. They both edited the document. Francis concerned himself with the words and the spiritual emphasis, and Peter with the legal format. They were not inventing anything, rather reflecting the brothers' life style in written form.

At the end of the day, once the disciples had returned from their outings, they all gathered together in the main hut after intense prayer. Francis read them the document in draft form. The disciples asked questions and expressed any doubts. Brother Francis made clarifications. After a few days of revisions they had their document.

* * *

It was called the primitive Rule or *protoregula* (the first of subsequent Rules).

The document has not survived and its reconstruction proves impossible. But it is known that most of it was a collection of passages of the Gospels which refer to the norms Jesus gave to *followers*, and other conditions concerning renunciation and poverty. He added to this collection of evangelical citations, which were written in a more or less organized fashion, a few elements standardizing the life of the disciples. In all, the document consisted of four or five small chapters.

Brother Francis' aim went far beyond the document. He wanted to declare the Gospel to be the only inspiration and mandate in their lives. The Gospel was everything, and was to be followed to the letter.

And he knew that it was not necessary for the Holy Father to ratify the Rule. It was not necessary to approve, or rather to confirm it since it had to do with following Jesus' word. In his heart of hearts Brother Francis knew it was something like deference, a courtesy extended to the Holy See to allow its representative to give his approval.

The following is a summary.

Francis and his successors promise reverence and obedience to the Pope. The disciples will follow the teachings of the Gospel, particularly those stipulated in the document. The candidates will renounce their worldly goods and distribute them among the poor. The brothers will dress poorly and respect those in lavish attire. The last to enter will be responsible for the brotherhood and will serve the others. They will observe uncommon charity among themselves: no criticism, no anger, always respectful, and welcoming. They will welcome thieves kindly, they will attend to the sick like a mother attending her child. They will work in the same vocation they held prior to entering the brotherhood, if at all possible. They can receive food and clothing as recompense for their work, but never any money; they will ask for alms when necessary. They will take nothing with them on their journeys, and they will know the joy of living among lepers and beggars.

Chapter Four

AT THE FEET OF HOLY CHURCH

"These orphans," Francis said to himself, "are like a small unprotected sugar plantation exposed to the winds. It's always the same danger: the little one makes himself smaller before greatness, and the insecure one cowers before any symbol of authority. They are incapable of seeing the Pope as something other than an emperor whereas he is only the blessed shadow of Christ. They have not completely placed their trust in God," he declared in a loud voice. "But when they do, they will be omnipotent like God himself. Blessed be the Lord!"

For weeks rumors spread among the disciples concerning the trip to the feet of Mother Church. Brother Francis loved to clothe important events in solemnity.

One day, as dusk approached, he summoned all the disciples to the Porziuncola chapel. The first days of summer were upon them and the forest resounded with freshness. It was an important moment and Francis expressed himself with tremendous warmth.

"My dear children," he said to them. "The moment has come. Our wings have grown and are thick with plumes. Now we can fly. Our family grows day by day, and we need the blessing and seal of the Holy Father. We are embarking on the journey to the feet of our beloved Mother, the Holy Church of Rome. We'll tell the Holy Father everything: our adventures and joys, our tears and also our deeds of fidelity to Lady Poverty. We will ask his consent so that we may continue on our journey. Don't be afraid of the Pope; under his solemn vestments beats the heart of a loving father.

"At this very moment," he continued, "I'd like to be a hen and you to be my defenseless chicks; I would like to hurl you into the ocean which is God. Only then would you begin to be omnipotent and to see from the ocean that the greatness and grandeur of the world is but a puff of smoke. You are aristocrats of the Kingdom of the Father and, in being insignificant, you are his favorites. In being poor, you are the heirs and kings of the Kingdom of Heaven."

These words were very encouraging and the disciples were anxious to embark on their journey. Francis added:

"It is necessary to appoint a guide. He will be the voice of Christ. We will follow the path that he has chosen, and we will sleep where he thinks that we should rest. He will be our shepherd and the vicar of Christ."

They drew lots and Bernard was to be their guide.

* * *

Very early the next morning the penitent men left the Porziuncola. It was unnecessary to prepare the luggage. According to what is written in the Holy Gospel, they carried nothing with them, literally nothing: no bags, no provisions, no change of clothing...

How strange to see an army with no swords and no ensign! The lands they were to conquer were, first and foremost, the terrible frontiers within themselves and then the invisible kingdom of the spirit. Since the days of the Gospel when the Master sent the Apostles on their way with nothing save the Word, a spectacle such as this had not been seen on the face of the earth. There was never such a contrast: the joy at having nothing, the freedom of poverty, and the power—omnipotence—emanating from God.

They were happy. Their conversation revolved around the examples and words of Christ. Every day the disciples took turns getting food "for the table of the Lord."

They also ate *shafts* from the stubble fields, wild strawberries; they drank fresh water from the springs. There was a tremendous delight in their faces and a general satisfaction that was difficult to describe.

At times they formed small groups for sleeping accommodations: some slept in straw lofts; others on patches of threshed wheat; others in old castle ruins... Every night was an amusing adventure, and they would recount their comical adventures the following morning. They laughed. Francis told them that those were chivalric adventures on behalf of the Lady of their dreams, Poverty.

Francis was untroubled when he saw how happy they were. Nevertheless when they stopped, he would give them words of hope and consolation. Until now he had no cause for worry, but he knew that in Rome they would be tested severely.

He gave them words of encouragement:

"I dreamt last night that I was walking along *Via Flaminia* and on the side of the road rose a tree of tremendous height that was very full at the top. It dominated the landscape. I stood at a distance in order to fully appreciate its proportions. And while doing so, oh prodigy! My small stature began to grow until I stood equal to its height. I took the tree's mane in my hands and bent it to the ground without any effort whatsoever."

"Without a doubt, God has given him this dream," said the disciples.

Everyone commented on the dream as they walked, each giving his own interpretation. In general, they all understood the dream to be a good omen.

When they spied a church tower in the distance they would kneel and devoutly pray "We Adore You." It was a spectacle to behold. Often, Bernard would decide to enter solitary woods and remain at prayer for hours or the entire day. Now and then, Brother Francis would separate himself from the group, enter hamlets, and summon the townspeople to the plazas where he would speak to them about Love, Peace, and Poverty.

As they walked through Via Flaminia they crossed the high Rieti plateau. Then they walked down to the lowlands of the Roman countryside. And so, one fine day, they reached Rome.

In Search of the Pontiff

Most of them had never been to the Eternal City. Once inside its walls and on its streets, the disciples were stunned and oppressed by the murmur of the lively city. Innumerable churches, some more resplendent than others; palaces and towers; feudal lords with their entourage; elegant ladies on black or white steeds; kings and their attendants... and, in the middle of this splendid scene, we find a handful of little orphans staring at the ground, hands in their sleeves, arms crossed, each clinging to the other, an unforgettable spectacle.

They walked through the city in between the shadows cast by the crowds who looked at them, asking them who they were. The disciples barely noticed a thing; they were totally absorbed by the idea that they were stepping on sacred ground.

They crossed one of the bridges over the Tiber and quickly knelt at the tomb of the Apostles in Constantine's great basilica on Vatican Hill. As wanderers dashed here and there, our little brothers remained right there, nailed to the ground, bowed and eyes closed, forming a little bundle, as usual. What a sight!

The little group was in the grip of emotions. So many thoughts crossed Francis' mind. We are very little and worthless, thought the Poor Man of Assisi. What can we do to strengthen the columns of the Church? We cannot fight against the Saracens because we have no arms. Furthermore, what would be gained by fighting? We cannot fight the heretics because we lack dialectic reasoning and intellectual preparation. All we can offer are the arms of the insignificant, that is: love, poverty, and peace. What can we do to serve the Church? Only this: to live literally by the Gospel of the Lord.

* * *

Upon leaving the basilica, the Poor Man of Assisi approached a priest and asked where the Holy Father resided.

"In the Lateran Palaces," the other responded.

"Is it difficult to reach the pontiff?" insisted Brother Francis.

"Kings, princes, and cardinals wait entire weeks in the anteroom before being granted an audience," the priest responded.

"Let's go to the home of the Vicar of Christ," Francis said to his disciples. "Without a doubt he'll receive us with open arms because he is the blessed shadow of Christ on earth. If it was easy to speak to the Lord on the hills of Galilee, why would it be difficult to be granted an audience with His Holiness on the Roman hills? Let us go in the name of the Lord."

And, having said this, they directed their steps toward the Lateran Palaces.

Once again the little group pressed round each other as they walked through the city, passing palaces and drunkards, travelling vendors and peddlers, courtiers of foreign kings, extremely elegant and perfumed ladies, citizens of every tribe and nation.

The little brothers, between bouts of fear and amazement, never raised their eyes, and were not the least bit curious about visiting palaces or churches. They came in search of the Holy Father and the rest was of no interest to them.

First Interview

When they arrived at the grand esplanade of the pontifical palace, Francis said to them:

"Stay here, brothers. Ask the Lord to persuade the Holy Father, both in heart and mind, to put his seal on our little Rule."

He left their side and walked calmly toward the main door of the enormous building. People were everywhere. After passing the main door, he continued on his way, barefoot and wearing his strange garments.

He walked through one corridor and then another. He asked the whereabouts of the Holy Father and they gave him rough directions. He looked everywhere and at everyone. But he did so with such innocence in his eyes and with such poise that the watchmen never showed any distrust.

Francis slowly made his way to the heart of the building, coming ever nearer to the papal antechamber. And in the corridor that separated the antechamber from the chamber,

Brother Francis of Assisi suddenly found himself before the imposing figure of Pope Innocent III. Instantly, the Poor Man of Assisi threw himself at the Pope's feet, and began to speak in haste:

"Good morning, Most Holy Father. I am Francis of Assisi. I kneel at your feet to ask you to grant a privilege: the privilege of living literally by the Gospel. I want the Gospel to be the only inspiration and rule in our lives. I want neither income nor property, only to live by the labor of our hands..."

He expressed his wishes while looking at the pontiff from head to foot. He was kneeling and looked very small, while the pontiff stood, looking very imposing. Pope Innocent did not cut Francis off immediately because he saw in the Poor Man's eyes a strange transparency, and perceived in his disposition an infinite reverence, completely devoid of servility.

But after the first few sentences, the pontiff said:

"All right, all right!" as if he wanted to say *enough*!

Brother Francis quieted immediately. The pontiff was surprised by his strict obedience. All of this occurred within seconds.

During this interval of time, the pontiff was slow to regain his composure and grew silent for a brief moment. Brother Francis (interpreting it as a tacit authorization to continue) took the opportunity to say:

"The Lord himself has expressed the desire that I live according to the Holy Gospel. Two years ago I began to follow this way of life. Then the Lord gave me brothers. We are now twelve. They are outside. We have written a little Rule with a few simple words..."

And when he reached under his arm for the Rule, the pontiff made a slight movement, a gesture of sorts, as though he wanted to say: Enough is enough.

"Francis, son of Assisi, urgent and grave problems weigh upon my shoulders," said the Pope. "I am old. I cannot attend to everything personally. If you want me to listen to you, get a recommendation stating that you wish an audience, and wait your turn."

And he turned and left.

Brother Francis got up and did not remove his eyes from the pontiff until he entered his chamber. He slowly began the walk back toward the entrance. As he turned the corridor, he looked back in case he might see the pontiff one last time.

As he walked past the interminable corridors leading to the courtyard, Brother Francis thought to himself:

"He's right. The Holy Father carries the world's problems on his back. They're serious problems. Our problems are trivial. I didn't want to waste his time. I only wanted him to say 'that's fine' to our petition. Ask a recommendation of whom? I don't know anyone. We're insignificant. Tonight I'll take counsel with the Lord."

A Recommendation

Upon reuniting with his disciples, he saw their inquisitive glances and the first thing he said to them was:

"We must pray more and do penance. Let's leave the city and look for a wooded area where we can pray. The Lord himself, and only he, will remove the obstacles."

As they crossed the streets near the city walls they suddenly came upon Guido, bishop of Assisi. This came as a great and joyous surprise to everyone. Bishop Guido knew nothing of their intentions or adventures. He thought the disciples, as was their custom, were on one of their apostolic expeditions.

"Francis should not get involved behind the scenes of diplomacy," thought bishop Guido. "The Church administers eternal treasures, but its foundation is rooted in the earth. Its destiny is to transform earth into heaven; that is why its interests are celestial, but its functions and practices are terrestrial. Francis does not belong to the political. He belongs to the transparent. It would be a shame if Francis were to lose the Church for lack of political orientation, and for the Church to lose such a powerful evangelical leaven. The spirit is not enough to triumph in the Church; one needs a particular skill, insight, and circumspection. In other words, basic diplomacy," bishop Guido concluded.

The bishop decided to give Francis all of his support and to help him obtain access to the ecclesiastical hierarchy, in order to ensure that his voice reach the ears of the Holy Father.

"Stay here, brothers. I will clear the way."

All of a sudden bishop Guido remembered his great friend, Cardinal Juan de San Pablo.

"At present," thought bishop Guido, "Juan de San Pablo is the most influential Cardinal in the College of Cardinals and, above all, is most esteemed by the Holy Father."

Bishop Guido went straight to the Cardinal's home. He presented a historical background on Francis and on the movement, speaking enthusiastically about the spectacle in Assisi and about other wonderful and dramatic events.

"They are submissive and reverent with priests," he told him. "However, his life bears witness to events that, at times, challenge and confuse, and almost always oblige the clergy to examine their lives. But that is good," he added. "And I think it would be wise," he said in conclusion, "for Your Eminence to meet with them personally for a few days."

In fact, Francis and some of his companions were guests of Cardinal de San Pablo for a few days.

Attempting to Dissuade

The Cardinal had studied and practiced medicine. Later on, he had entered the Benedictine Abbey of St. Paul Outside-the-Walls. After devoting many years to penance, he was removed in order to be named Cardinal in 1193. His heart was made in the image and likeness of Christ. In the College of Cardinals, it was difficult to find a man as austere and as full of faith.

During their stay with the Cardinal, Francis and his companions practiced their way of life to the letter, as was the norm. The Cardinal studied their attitudes and words. Since he was sensitive to things concerning the spirit, it did not take him long to discover and weigh their determination.

In the days that followed, Francis underwent intense questioning. The prelate was soon captivated by the simplicity of soul and the spiritual potential of the Poor Man of God.

"One has the impression," thought the Cardinal, "that the Gospel was a mouldy, hard bound book, with golden chants, covered with dust and abandoned in the corner of a library. But thanks to the magical touch of God's little dwarf, it can now be said that the book has reclaimed all of its original splendor. Blessed be God! Now that the Church is a powerful and sacred republic with the Pope as its emperor, the time is ripe for a poor helpless soul to appear and remind us that only God is omnipotent."

* * *

But, even so, he felt that establishing a foundation was a daring venture. Although there have been several reformations, there have been very few foundations in the history of the Church. The Cardinal summoned Francis in order to dissuade him from this course of action.

"Francis, son of Assisi. A new foundation," he began very slowly, "a foundation, in the simplest terms, is a tremendous enterprise and a very rash decision in this case."

He lowered his voice as he finished his statement, so as not to hurt Brother Francis.

"Very reckless," Francis interrupted.

The Cardinal was startled by his response and did not fully comprehend the intent or meaning behind this intervention. If he had not been sympathetic to the speaker's extreme simplicity, he would have thought his reaction a bit ironic. The speakers were on two different orbits and that explains everything.

"As I was saying," continued the Cardinal, "at present, a foundation is a risky proposition."

At that moment, the Cardinal was thinking about this little group of illiterates enlisted in the Legion of Blessed Ignorance. He had firsthand knowledge of the opinions and fickleness of the ecclesiastical machine. He was well versed in the power of influence and the influence of power.

He had committed to memory all the secret ins and outs in the Lateran Palaces, as in all the palaces of the world, where political criteria prevail; where money, military victories, and the balance of power play on center court. He felt that a new foundation would fall prey, one way or another, to these maneuvers.

"A new foundation," continued the Cardinal, "requires intellectual preparation on the part of the initiators." He looked at him affectionately and said, "Francis of Assisi, a new foundation is almost like a battle and, at the very least, the initiators need to maneuver their dialectics with the skill of a soldier wielding a sword. With regard to these curiae, as with most of the world's palaces, the approval of a foundation requires a strong recommendation. A strong recommendation presupposes strong recommenders. The powerful are solely influenced by power, be it spiritual, apostolic or military. You are enlisted and swear loyalty to the Order of Holy Powerlessness. Your intentions are doomed to fail; forgive me, my dear son."

* * *

Brother Francis listened calmly and attentively.

"All of this," the Cardinal added, "was foretold when the Lord commanded that we be as prudent as serpents."

In his heart of hearts, the Cardinal was in complete agreement with Francis' ideals. However, since he knew how the Roman curiae operate, he feared that Francis' solicitation would be refused and he wanted to prepare him mentally, to help him avoid frustration.

"It would be terrible," he thought, "to see this new prophet embark on the road of rebellion.

"Moreover," continued the Cardinal, "you already know what happens in the course of human events on all levels (not only in the palaces and curiae). When embarking on a great and original enterprise (or to give approval, as in the present case), there are always more reasons to abandon a cause than to continue. We fear the uncertain and the unfamiliar; and we prefer security in the familiar rather than the uncertainty in the unknown. We want to avoid failure at all cost. For this and because of this, I recommend a solution: Why not join a strict religious Order whose way of life emulates the one you wish to follow? What do you think, my son?"

Vulnerability Is Power

There was a long yet blissful silence. The Poor Man of God stared at the ground. It was not the first time, nor would it be the last time, that this proposal was intimated. After a moment, he repeated in a low and natural voice: "Very reckless."

"We have nothing," he began to say calmly. "We're not intellectuals and we lack formal education. We have no homes, no possessions. We lack political influence. We lack support for a proper recommendation. We won't impress since we lack a sonorous and apostolic vocabulary. We're the peculiar Order of Holy Ignorance and Holy Powerlessness...."

The intensity of his voice reached a crescendo.

"We can't," he continued, "offer the Church universities that would prepare combatants to defend the truth. We're not a compact squadron of dialecticians out to confuse the Albigensians. We don't have large monastic stronghold to shelter the men who wish to dedicate themselves to God. We have nothing, can do nothing, are worth nothing..."

And, as the Poor Man of God reached the climactic moment, he rose to his feet, raised his arms and his voice and added:

"For this reason, because we're powerless and weak like the Crucified Christ, because we replicate the uselessness of Christ on the cross, for this reason the Omnipotent will clothe our powerlessness with omnipotence. From our uselessness the Almighty will extract the immortal energies of redemption. Through us, through our unworthiness, uselessness, ignorance and sins, only our God and Savior will rule on the face of the earth, rather than power, organization or science. God will reign victorious rather than diplomacy."

The Cardinal rose without saying a word and walked away so that Francis would not see the tears in his eyes. Deep within he sensed a reawakening of old, dormant ideals. He entered the room once again and said:

"Francis of Assisi, go to the chapel and pray."

As for His Eminence, he took the Cardinal's coach and rode quickly to the Lateran Palaces.

He asked for an immediate audience with the Pope.

"Holy Father," the Cardinal said. "God has witnessed how faithfully we have labored all these years to sanctify the Church. We have been waiting for a *messenger* from the Lord who would restore ruins and resurrect the dead. Holy Father, the one we have been *waiting* for has arrived. Blessed be God. I have observed him carefully and scrutinized his soul. He is a man who is forged into the mountain of the Beatitudes, and his chords vibrate in unison with those of Christ."

The pontiff was absolutely overjoyed with the news and ordered that all meetings scheduled for the following day be cancelled. He asked that this man and his companions be summoned, and that the cardinals attend the conference.

A Stormy Debate

The next day the Poor Man of Assisi and Pope Innocent III were face to face once again. When the latter took his throne, the Poor Man approached and threw himself with infinite reverence at his feet and slowly kissed them, saying:

"Bless me, Holy Father."

It seemed as though Francis had thrown himself "reverently and submissively" at the feet of the entire Church. It was one of the most thrilling moments of his life. Pope Innocent III recognized him immediately, and he smiled sympathetically and with great pleasure.

When Brother Francis was given permission to speak, he began in this way:

"Most Holy Father, I bow at your feet to ask for the privilege of literally living by the Holy Gospel of our Lord Jesus Christ. We desire neither remuneration nor possessions. We want to live by the sweat of our brow. We will walk the earth without provisions, bags, money, only to preach the word of the Lord..."

There was not the slightest hint of nervousness in his voice. His look was sincere as he spoke to the Pope and the Cardinal. He had the look of confidence that was enough to disarm an enemy. The eyes and ears of the Pope and the Cardinal were fixed on his lips. It can be said that they were more anxious than Brother Francis of Assisi.

"Today, in the presence of His Holiness," continued Francis, "we want to celebrate our divorce from money and our marriage to Lady Poverty. We want to dress poorly and not defame those who dress extravagantly. In the eyes of the world, we want to love one another and care for one another as a mother loves and cares for her precious child. We will not show resistance to those who resist us. We will turn the other cheek to those who hurt us and we will forgive those who offend. We will kindly welcome thieves, and the beggars and lepers will be our princes."

* * *

"You are dreaming," one of the cardinals said out loud.

The Poor Man of Assisi looked in the direction of the speaker.

"My son," the Cardinal continued, "our backs break with the weight of such disillusion. Golden dreams make their way to this chamber every year. Time buries these dreams, one by one, in the grave of frustration. We have reached the point where we no longer believe in words. We are accustomed to wait quite skeptically for results."

Francis looked at him and said:

"Everything that I have just stated, prince of the Church, we have put into practice, thanks to God's infinite mercy."

"Now you are but a few," responded the Cardinal. "Few and idealistic. You have just begun. Things always look promising at the beginning. Many of us, when we were young, had idealistic dreams. Only the young dream because they have not lived. Life obliges us to put our feet firmly on the ground. We are not defeatists, rather realists. Rather than wings, we have feet made of clay. Man is clay, full of limitations. Francis, son of Assisi, can you tell me, for example, how you intend to feed two thousand disciples?"

The Poor Man of Assisi listened attentively and was touched by his words. He had been clairvoyant from an early age and his idealism did not cloud his vision of frail humanity, beginning with his own life.

"It's true, Lord Cardinal," said Brother Francis. "We have the hearts of eagles and the wings of sparrows. We're as fragile as a vessel made of clay. My own experiences can attest to this. No one in this chamber," he said as he looked around the semicircular room, "has sinned as much as I have; few have been treated as I have had the privileged to be treated by Grace," he said almost inaudibly. "What would become of us if it weren't for God's infinite mercy?"

However, he was asked a very specific question that he could not neglect to answer. And with incredible certainty he said:

"Lord Cardinal, in reference to your question: If until this point in time the hand of the Lord has fed twelve little orphans, why not two hundred? Why not two thousand? How many millions of birds are there in the world? Isn't the Lord the one who feeds them? Are there limits to what the Almighty can do? How many millions of flowers bloom all over the world? Doesn't the Lord open their petals every morning? How many millions of stars illumine the heavens? Isn't it the Almighty who lights them every night? If a sparrow doesn't die of hunger, would he let an immortal son die of hunger? Holy Father and my Lord Cardinal: you are learned and I'm ignorant; forgive me for saying these things."

And, raising his voice he said:

"If the Almighty's compassion is deeper than the chasms and higher than the mountains, his omnipotence and richness exceeds all imaginable boundaries. We only need to do one thing: jump."

* * *

Pope Innocent III had fought many battles and won many victories, and he had suffered only one defeat: the reformation of the Church. From a very young age, his idealism and compassion were his unique characteristics. At thirty-nine years of age, he was elected to the papacy and his *Christian Republic* penetrated even the highest ranks with astounding speed; at present he was practically the emperor of the world. Never had theocracy spread over such vast spaces. His brilliant pontificate operated through diplomatic channels and pitched battles, always keeping priorities in mind.

At this moment, as he listened to the Poor Man of Assisi, he felt as if he were shedding his pontifical demeanor and breathing life into his old passions. The pontiff felt a strange enchantment that he could not explain.

He was feeling profound sympathy for Brother Francis. He wanted to tell him at that precise moment: You have my blessing; begin. However, he thought it wise to allow the Cardinals to subject the prophet to intense scrutiny and to screen his plans. The intriguing debate continued.

* * *

In fact, there was a group of cardinals that did not fall under the spell of this divine and captivating individual, and they analyzed his plans unsympathetically.

"It is impossible," they said. "A flock is manageable. But this is an overly ambitious project. Francis of Assisi and perhaps one other individual could very well live strictly by the letter. But this has to do with the approval or rejection of a Rule that affects many. It is impossible."

At this point, the venerable figure of Cardinal de San Pablo could be seen rising to his feet. He said:

"Brothers of the Sacred College of Cardinals. I am pleased to see you arbitrate so judiciously. I consider it your responsibility to do so. Flights of fancy must be put in check. We must take care," he paused, "to always be consistent. If Your Eminences are under the opinion that this way of life should not receive approval because you fail to see its practicality, I ask you: Is this Poor Little Soul of God proposing anything other than to live strictly by the Gospel of the Lord Jesus? If this endeavor is impractical, let us be consistent! Thus, the Gospel is also a utopia and its author a dreamer. Now, if the Gospel is nonsense, what is the Church? What is the point and significance of the College of Cardinals and the Pope? Then, what are we doing here? The answer: We are a bunch of imposters."

Nothing could have compared with those earth-shattering words. The Cardinal fell silent and stared at the ground. It was obvious; from that moment on, the person to raise his voice in protest of the Rule would be accused of trickery. Not even the most audacious dialectician could put his hand on this hot iron. The debate was self-defeating. The only thing left to do was to call an end to the meeting.

* * *

Despite the fact that Pope Innocent III was accustomed to such stormy disputes, this time he was uneasy. He was afraid. He feared that this spiritual renewal would disintegrate at the very doors of the Church. He was accustomed to the Cardinals' candor and stubbornness, and he knew that they were perfectly capable of hindering the triumph of the spirit in the name of common sense.

"That would be a shame," he thought, "even a tragedy."

Furthermore, the meeting had reached scalding temperatures. The pontiff was accustomed to maneuvering with skill. And if Francis were to exercise caution, he would gain an advantage, which would be much better than to collide with controversy. Therefore, he decided to suspend the meeting.

He rose and approached Francis, held him affectionately by the shoulders and said:

"Courage, my son; let us humbly seek God's will. Pray that the Lord himself will show us the way."

Consolation

They all left the chamber. The disciples felt a mixture of fear and anguish. In truth, the meeting stood on shaky ground, ending tensely and clouded by uncertainty.

Francis asked to be alone. In fact, his disciples needed him now more than ever. But at that moment, Francis could not give them what they were needing most: consolation, certainty and peace. He first had to recover those gifts for himself.

He was also hurt. He felt like a soldier wounded in battle but numb to the pain while in the heat of battle. As the hours passed, Brother Francis began to feel the pain.

* * *

When he found himself alone, the black wings of despair began to hover over his soul.

"I don't understand," he said to himself. "The word of the Lord is as solid as a rock: why all the vacillation? It's a simple matter. Why all the complications? It's so easy. Why all the delay?"

Having been so accustomed to putting inspiration immediately into practice, the delay was incomprehensible to him.

"Why doesn't the Holy Father personally settle this matter and give me authorization?"

He was surprised to hear himself complain about the Pope and he instantly interrupted his reflections.

"None of that," he said in a loud voice, not wanting to think about it any longer.

He took his usual position for prayer: kneeling, forehead on the floor. But it took terrific effort to give himself to God. It took him a while to relax and regain his sense of peace, and much more effort to *truly* give himself to God.

He had to leap once again, just as he had done on the rocks of Mt. Rossatto. Time and again, he denied himself and let the Lord enter his soul. Over and over again, he heard the words of days gone by:

"Come, my son. Jump into my arms. My hands hold the key. I lock and unlock the papal and cardinal doors. Take my hand, surrender and have faith. I will do the rest."

And he was consumed with the peace of a shadow at dusk, when mountains cover the valleys below with their shadows. Very slowly, little by little, peace began to fill his soul. Now he was able to console his disciples.

Le Jongleur de Dieu

A third meeting was called. The ease with which Francis won authorization presupposes consultations among the pope and the cardinals some time between the second and third meetings. In view of his personal charm, they decided to grant the man of Assisi verbal authorization.

"Maybe," thought the Poor Man of Assisi, "I'm no good at generating issues based on ideas. Perhaps that's why the manner in which I presented the project failed to convince the Cardinals. I lack the heart and soul of a scholar. Furthermore, my Lord Jesus, I addressed them more like a rhapsodist spewing parables and making comparisons. I've always dreamed of instituting the Order of Jongleurs de Dieu. This would be a good time to describe the new minstrel profession to the Holy Father. After all, this profession suits me, since I'm a knight of Christ and ambassador to Lady Poverty."

* * *

When Brother Francis arrived in the papal chamber, he said the following when he was given permission to speak:

"Once there was a woman who lived in the desert. She had no home, no garden. She was very poor. The emeralds in the earth and the stars in the sky gathered together, and said: 'Let us give the woman in the desert some of our radiance.' And that is what they did. She was so beautiful that no poet felt worthy enough to honor her, and rhapsodists were speechless in her presence.

"One day, a king crossed the desert in his royal coach. Upon seeing the woman, an arrow pierced his heart and he was blinded by her beauty. The king and the woman fell in love and had many children. The children were nurtured by their mother and they soon grew into adulthood. One day, the mother called them and said: 'You are poor but do not be ashamed. Walk with your head held high for I bring you great news: You are children of a great king. Go to his court and say what it is you need.' They were overjoyed when they heard the news.

"They went to the king's court and asked for an audience. Upon seeing them, the king's heart began to beat loudly and he knew not why. 'Who are these children who are the mirrors of my soul?' he said. Then, as he looked at them he said: 'Who are you and where is your mother?' They responded, 'Our mother is a poor woman who lives in the desert.'

"When the king realized that they were his children, he was overcome with emotion. Once he regained his composure, he said to them: 'You are princes and heirs to my kingdom. Strangers sit at my table, but you have precedence and will be seated at my right and at my left. Be happy.'"

* * *

A troubadour in the papal chamber! There had never been anything like it. All he needed was to play a lute and to twirl about. Pope Innocent III had seen many things throughout his papacy, but never had he seen a penitent with the soul of a minstrel. No clarification was needed after this rhapsodic narration.

Nevertheless, the Poor Man of Assisi added humbly with a certain air of satisfaction:

"I am that poor woman, Your Holiness."

Everything else was very clear. One must be poor to enter the Kingdom. Only the poor are God's heirs. The poor belong to God and God belongs to the poor. Those that have embraced absolute poverty are aristocrats of the Kingdom.

Francis' followers were those that had no home, no country, no money, and who carried in their hands the scroll (poverty) that identified them as crown princes of the Kingdom of Heaven.

Blessings and a Farewell

Pope Innocent III rose to his feet and approached Francis. He motioned for all to come closer, forming that familiar group. He placed his hands affectionately on Francis' shoulders and said to him:

"I am old, my son. Look at all that has occurred in the last fifteen years. Kings acquiesced. Crusaders have reached the Holy Sepulchre. The world does as we command. But not every endeavor has resulted in victory. Here inside, I have wounds that do not heal. I wanted to be saintly. I am mediocre. I have fought hard for the men of the Church to become holy. Instead, I have seen avarice and ambition plague the cities. Instead of the reformation of the Church, I have seen heresy, protests and the rebellion rear their ugly heads. I organized crusades in order to eradicate the rebels. They were destroyed on the battlefields but, as by magic, they have sprouted everywhere else. In time, I realized it is better to light a candle than to curse the darkness. I have spent many a sleepless night, and there were nights," he said lowering his voice, "where I just cried. It is awful being the Pope. There is nothing lonelier on the face of the earth. Everyone comes to me. But who can I turn to? Unhappy is the Pope who does not turn to God!"

* * *

He went too far. He was accustomed to protocol and formalities, but with this little group he felt very much at home. The disciples looked at him with sincerity, making him feel welcomed and loved. He lost his inhibitions.

"In the solitude of night," he continued, "I have begged God ardently and repeatedly to send his *anointed* one. From Rome's watchtower, I have been the sentinel looking in every direction for the *chosen one* who will restore the Church. It seems that my prayers have been answered; blessed be the Lord. Francis, son of Assisi, I have been thinking of you and your disciples for many days. I asked God: My Lord, is this Poor Man of Assisi the one? And last night," he paused at length, "last night I received God's response."

His voice cracked as soon as he said these words. He paused once again. Some of the disciples were frightened, and all eyes were wide with anticipation.

"Last night I had a dream, and it is as clear as the midday sun... These sturdy towers of St. John Lateran began to sway like palm trees. The entire edifice began to creak, and when it looked as though the church walls would come crashing down, a little poor man put his shoulders to the wall and saved the church from destruction. That tattered individual, and I still see it very clearly, is you; it was you, Francis, son of Assisi and minstrel of God."

Some of his disciples broke down and cried; others screamed. Francis did not even blink an eye as he stared at the pontiff.

"I am old," the Pope said in conclusion. "But now I can die in peace. My sons, go out into the world with torches in your hands. Hang lamps on the walls of night. Put fountains where you see fires. Plant roses where swords are forged. Transform battlefields into gardens. Dig furrows and sow love. Place flags of freedom in the homeland of Poverty. And announce the arrival of Love, Happiness, and Peace. After some time, before I die, come and recount your adventures and soothe my soul."

He blessed them. He hugged them, one by one. And the disciples left the city and returned to Assisi.

The Golden Age

They reached Assisi and settled in Rivo Torto. Doubts, fears, and distrust were thrown to the four winds.

They were radiant. They did not look like men of flesh and blood. The spirit took possession of the body and reduced it to ashes. It appeared as though all that remained was the spirit.

"We are a strange race of men," Brother Francis said to himself. "We are married but have no wife, drunk without wine, satiated with hunger and rich with poverty. We are the freest men in the world because we are the poorest in the world," he said in a loud voice. "We lack nothing. This is paradise!"

The dwelling was terribly scant. Long ago, it had been a den for migrating animals. Occasionally it served as a shed for fodder. It was standard lodging for beggars. It had been neglected for years. Drafts entered through the breaches in the walls, and the rain seeped through the holes in the roof. Very tall nettles surrounded the hut and clinging vines climbed the cracked walls. The only solid structures were wooden beams that firmly supported the shack's framework.

* * *

The Franciscan movement's golden age transpired in this strange palace. It was a tight squeeze for the twelve disciples. In order to avoid confusion at the hour of prayer

221

and when they retired to rest, Francis took a piece of slate and wrote each brother's name on a different beam. That way, each had a designated area. He placed a wooden cross on one of the lateral walls. The hut was a dormitory, chapel, and refectory. It was difficult to imagine a more fitting throne for Lady Poverty.

Rivo Torto offered the disciples other advantages. A leper colony was a short distance away. A main pathway was nearby where they often saw their friends, the beggars.

The foothills of Mt. Subasio were just a few miles away. After passing the rough gorges, which look like scorched areas left by a bolt of lightning, one reaches the caverns or *cells* carved by nature. They were ideal places to foster the contemplative life. To top it all off, Rivo Torto was one angle of a triangle, with St. Damian and the Porziuncola chapel forming the other two angles. They spent the autumn, winter, and spring months here.

Betrothal to Lady Poverty

It is an allegory. The author and date of the composition are unknown. The following is a brief transcription of the poem:

Francis asked passersby in the streets and plazas:

"Have you seen the Lady of my dreams in the mountains or in the valleys?"

"We don't know what you're talking about," they responded.

Then Francis called on the physicians and magnates of the city, and asked them:

"Would you know the whereabouts of my Lady Poverty?"

"We only know this," they replied. "Life is short. Eat, drink and be merry for tomorrow we will die."

Francis said to himself:

"Surely my Lady does not reside in the city."

He went to the countryside and met two ancients sitting on a rock. The sun kept them warm while they talked about the transitory nature of life.

Brother Francis approached them and asked:

"Please tell me, honorable ancients: Where does my Lady Poverty reside? wander? rest?"

"We know her," they responded. "She has walked this way several times. She would go accompanied by another; she would return alone. Very often she would cry and say: 'Everyone has abandoned me.' We consoled her by saying: 'Don't let this distress you, great lady; many love you.' She lives high in the solitary mountains. But no one knows exactly where, so it is useless to ask; not even the eagles know. However, we know that there is a secret to reaching her retreat: first, you must renounce everything, absolutely everything. Only by not carrying the extra load can one expect to reach those lofty heights. Since she loves those that love her in return and lets them find her, she will soon appear before you. And at that very moment you will no longer be troubled. There is no greater joy than this."

* * *

Brother Francis took several of his companions and they were soon at the foot of the frightful mountain. But some were stunned when they saw the steep incline, and they said:

"It's impossible. We can't do it."

"We can do it," Francis replied. "That is, you must first lighten your load, throwing away any dead weight with regard to your will and the burden of sins. Never look back. Always look to Christ who walks barefoot in front of us. It's a wonderful adventure. It's the march of freedom."

The disciples were encouraged and began the climb.

As they climbed, Lady Poverty peered down the harrowing slope. When she saw the intrepid men scaling the side of the mountain with such enthusiasm, she exclaimed:

"Who are these men who are rising like a cloud?"

And she heard a voice from on high saying:

"They are royal stock of the chosen."

And she asked them this question:

"Brothers, what are you looking for on this mountain of light? Are you by chance looking for me? Can't you see I'm only an abandoned cottage ravaged by tempests?"

"Lady and Queen," Francis said to her, "we come for you. We have been told that you are majestic and beautiful. Our ears knew that; now our eyes confirm it. We kneel before you, Lady of our dreams, and we say to you: Walk ahead of us. Take us by the hand and lead us to the Kingdom. Save us from fear. Free us from agony of soul. Bury anguish deep within the ground. Let sadness blow in the wind like funeral ashes. Raise the flag of freedom, march on, and guide us to the threshold of Salvation. Look kindly on us and mark us with the seal of predilection. Stay with us forever."

* * *

Lady Poverty was profoundly moved by his words. She gave each of them a warm embrace and said:

"I will stay with you forever. Today we seal our eternal union."

Brother Francis was radiant with joy and he intoned a hymn in gratitude. They all descended the mountain together and went directly to their shack. It was midday.

"It's time to eat," they said to her. "Oh, Great Lady, you are welcome to sit at our table."

She replied:

"Before I do, I would like to look at your chapter house, chapel, and cloisters."

"There is no monastery; this shack is all we have," they responded.

"Yes," said the Lady, "you have nothing. Yet, you are radiant and full of peace. What a paradox!"

"Lady and Queen," they said to her, "You must be exhausted after such a long walk. You need to get your strength back. If you like, you can sit at our table."

"Yes, I would like that," she replied. "But first, bring me water so I can wash my hands and a towel to dry them."

They brought her water in a piece of earthenware (they did not have a proper vessel). As they poured the water over her hands, they looked in all directions for a towel. They did not find one, naturally. One of the disciples offered her the tip of his tunic. The Lady appreciated the gesture.

They walked over to the table, or what they referred to as the table. Actually, there was no table, only green grass on firm ground. They all sat on the ground, Lady Poverty observed carefully and noticed that there were no more than three or four crusts of bread on the grass. She exclaimed admiringly:

"Never have I seen such a spectacle as this. Blessed be You, Lord Jesus Christ! Friends, I would like to eat cooked food."

Instantly, they brought her a bowl of fresh water in which to dip the bread.

"I would like to eat some spiced vegetables," said the queen.

"Madame," they replied, " we don't have a garden, nor a gardener."

But this did not discourage them. They went quickly into the woods and grabbed handfuls of wild herbs to take to their Lady.

She persisted:

"Pass me some salt for these bitter herbs."

"Have patience, our Lady, while we go to the city to get some salt."

"In the meantime," Lady Poverty continued, "give me a knife so I can cut this bread that is as hard as a rock."

"A thousand pardons, Lady and Queen," they said. "There isn't a blacksmith among us, nor do we have utensils for cutting; you will have to use your teeth. We beg your pardon, Madame."

"That is fine," she replied. "But, would you have some wine?"

"Great Lady, our sustenance is bread and water. Besides, wine is unworthy of the wife of Christ; a thousand pardons, Madame."

They were satiated and happy. The queen was tired and went to lie down on the ground. She asked for a pillow. They brought her a rock.

After resting for a while, she asked them:

"Friends, where are your cloisters and quarters?"

Francis took the queen politely by the hand and escorted her to Mt. Subasio, and he pointed to the snowy peaks of the Apennines, and responded:

"Our Lady, these are our cloisters and our possessions."

Tempted by Nostalgia

Poverty was exacting in Rivo Torto. The autumn and winter months were upon them. They protected themselves against the cold and torrential downpours with great difficulty. They lit bonfires to keep warm and to dry themselves.

At times they had nothing to eat. They went through open country looking for beetroots and turnips. They did not worry about trespassing on private property.

It was not harvest time. They could not find steady work in the fields. On certain days, weather permitting, they would work with the peasants in the sown fields. The majority of the disciples attended to the lepers in the leper colonies. Some repaired shoes or made furniture. They all took turns going to the *cells* to spend time in personal reflection with God.

"This is the novitiate of the new order of the knights of Christ," Francis said to himself. "With the Lord's understanding, we shall abandon the apostolic expeditions for a few months," he told his disciples. "We need to grow in prayer, in obedience, and, above all, in brotherhood. Oh, the heart of man! You can throw your body into the flames, but nostalgia can bend it like a bamboo shoot in no time at all."

Francis was afraid, afraid that the tempter would come dressed in the finery of nostalgia.

"It's the worst temptation because it's the most elusive."

There were days when the rain seemed endless. Many times they were snowed in and could not leave the hut. They spent idle hours with their arms crossed, drenched in dampness, while winds and rain crept through every crack and crevice, staring at muddy waters in the wake of torrential rains, and they had nothing to eat...

During these moments Francis could feel temptation drifting dangerously near the dwelling and saying:

"This is an absurd life. It makes no sense. Life is much better up in the city, in comfortable homes with warm hearths, to be next to a loving wife and affectionate children, enjoying the harvest from a year's labor..."

Brother Francis was familiar with vulnerability, and spoke to his disciples everyday, repeating the following words:

"My beloved brothers, God is our wife. God is our hearth. God is our banquet. God is our festival. With God in our souls, the snows give warmth and the winters become springs. Where would we be without the Lord's help? We would be pulled by the currents of temptation like a rushing stream."

Francis, like a skilful mentor, showed his disciples how to plunge into God's abyss. After plunging into such immeasurable depths, frost, snow and nostalgia would no longer be insurmountable obstacles.

From Poverty to Brotherhood

Two interdependent trees grew very tall in Rivo Torto: poverty and brotherhood. But there was a flower that had its own individual sparkle: happiness. Penance dressed in happiness!

"We are the happiest men on earth," Francis said to himself, "because we have nothing."

Throughout those months, Francis repeated what would become sealed in the rule of life:

"Be happy with the Lord, and show joy and kindness wherever you roam."

Franciscan happiness stems from Franciscan poverty, just as roses originate from seeds, and the Resurrection from the death of Jesus.

"Brother," said Francis to one of his companions, "it's a nice day; go to the 'Lord's table' and ask for alms."

After several hours the brother returned with very little alms, but singing joyfully. When Francis heard his singing from a distance, he ran outside to greet him. He helped him with his bundle, gave him a warm embrace, kissed both of his shoulders, and took him by the hand, and said:

"Blessed be our brother who has gone out asking for alms but without begging, and is full of gaiety upon his return."

* * *

Once, when all had fallen asleep, one brother began to moan.

"What's wrong?" asked Francis.

"I'm dying," the other replied.

Brother Francis jumped up, lit the lamp and began to make his way among the disciples, while asking:

"Who is it? Where are you?"

"Here I am, it's me, Brother Francis," responded the other.

Francis brought the lamp closer and asked:

"What's wrong?"

"Hunger, Brother Francis, I'm dying of hunger."

Francis felt his heart breaking and the sympathy only a mother can feel consumed him.

He wanted to disguise the pain in his heart with joy and good humor.

"Dear brothers, get up. Let's celebrate. Bring everything there is to eat."

What did they have? Some nuts and olives? They ate everything there was to eat. Everyone sang. This poor and happy family was a sight to behold! The nocturnal feast filled Francis with warmth. Deep within, however, his happiness was nothing more than a pious mask. He felt as if a serpent had curled itself up inside his heart: Could all of this be too much for them to bear? Was it insensitive of him to subject them to a life of poverty? He suffered. He was afraid.

At that moment, priorities were not the issue, not even poverty. The brother who suffered was the only thing that mattered. It did not matter that it was a day of rigorous fasting. Silence did not matter, nor did other formalities.

The brother was the only thing that mattered. This was a family. Every brother was as important as the family, the Order or the city. There was nothing more valuable than a brother. When one suffered, all suffered.

Once again, they all fell asleep in the midst of jokes and merriment, all except for Francis. He thought about each one of them. And he placed each of them, one by one, in the hands of the Lord God.

* * *

And this was the beginning of the great leap: from poverty to brotherhood. Where members of a community are self-sufficient and want for naught, brotherhood is difficult, almost impossible. The life itself, more than its principles, begins to open fraternal channels. Where there is a need, another comes to help. Poverty creates needs, and needs open brothers, one to the other.

Firstly, this way of life was lived on a daily basis; and Brother Francis codified it during his last years.

Francis began by saying that "the brothers had no possessions, no home, no place to call their own, nothing." Possessions give a man a sense of security. When a brother has nothing, he is like a bird without feathers, a toy at the mercy of the winds, and feels orphaned and completely vulnerable.

Man needs a sense of security. Otherwise, he collapses under the weight of desolation. Where can he find it? In the arms of brotherhood.

Francis said to his disciples who had no monastery, no home, who were orphaned and totally defenseless, out in the open country, "wherever you are or when you find yourselves in each other's company, be familial with one another."

The idea and the word are brilliant: *familial*; that is, the brotherhood is a substitute for the home. Being understanding and cordial with one another, the warmth of the brotherhood, would be a substitute for the home. The sense of security, that others feels in a comfortable home, will be evident in a hut in the form of fraternal warmth.

What else? At this point, very few issues had been resolved. Many needs and crises remained with respect to clothes, food, illness. Francis was aware of this: How do we solve these problems? Money is the answer to many things. The disciples did not and could not have money at their disposal. Then, what could be done?

Once again, Brother Francis responded with words of wisdom: "Express your needs openly to one another." Here, poverty and brotherhood are intertwined in a harmonious relationship. Break down barriers that inhibit the expression of kinship! That is, brothers who are *open* to one another, some giving, others receiving, some expressing needs, others addressing those needs. Francis incited the paschal exodus with simplicity. It was the great fraternal *ascent,* the source of all freedom and maturity.

What if there are too many needs or problems that are impossible to solve? What can be done? Once again, Brother Francis raised the *maternal* flag which transforms the impossible into what is possible: "Do as a mother would do for her precious child."

* * *

Without postulating theological or psychological concepts, Francis launched his disciples on a grand fraternal adventure out in the open country of poverty. Chapter VI of the Rule is an inspired treatment on their way of life.

Let us suppose that four disciples go out into the world. One of them hurts his foot. The other three "turn" to help him. One fetches warm water. Another asks for strips of gauze. Meanwhile, the third brother provides treatment and care. All three are *turned* to help the injured brother.

One day, another brother comes down with a fever. They postpone the pilgrimage and assist the ailing brother for three days and three nights. One goes out into the countryside to look for medicinal herbs. Another brother enters a village to ask for lodging for his sick companion. The third stays with his ailing brother. They alternate duties. The three live *for* the sick brother, just as a mother would for her child. At night, they lend him a cloak to keep him warm. They are happy when the fever subsides. They continue on their journey once again. As the brother convalesces, they watch him and check his strength and endurance, and modify their pace accordingly. In short, each is *disposed* and *inclined* toward the other.

Another brother feels depressed and confides in the others. They feel his pain and suffering and pray for him. They console him and give him strength. There is no "mine" and "yours." Everything is communal: health, sickness, sadness, happiness. Everything is out in the open and communicated.

Francis imagined the worst: one of the disciples falls deathly ill during their pilgrimage. What hospital or infirmary will treat him? They have no home, hospital or infirmary. What can be done? Francis has the answer: The brotherhood will be (substitute for) the infirmary: "The other disciples are to attend to him as he would attend to his brothers." Fraternal care "is" the hospital.

They need one another since they are poor. In needing one another, they help and love one another. In loving one another, they are happy and attest before the world that Jesus is the Agent of God.

Dearest Mother

This is what Brother Pacifico, "king of verse" and provincial of France, called Francis: "mater carissima," dearest Mother.

A few days before, a brother had taken ill. The others were not aware of this. Brother Francis knew, and had been watching him for days and was worried.

"What do I do?" he asked himself.

One day he replied:

"If he were to eat very ripe grapes instead of fasting, he could soon recover."

Without thinking twice, he awoke the sick brother early the next morning while the rest slumbered. He took him by the hand and stopped at the first vineyard they saw (trespassing was not a concern). They sat on the ground and ate heartily. Francis looked for large and ripe clusters. They did this for several days. The brother had a healthy aspect at the end of one week.

The concept of private property was not annulled, rather transcended. Nothing mattered more than a brother. This was unequivocal and all other things were relative to this fact.

Moreover, this was one of the many virtualities emanating from poverty: *lordship.* Francis and his companions not only affected an air of chivalry and aristocracy, but also walked like lords and masters of the world.

All great mysteries are rooted in one source: Jesus' nobility emanating from his position as *servant*, according to the early catecheses. With reverent submission to death, a death on the cross in obedience to the Father, *ipso facto* the universal lordship of Jesus is also fulfilled in heaven, as well as on earth. In short, the Lord is born of the Servant.

Likewise, the Poor Man of Assisi in renouncing everything became the Lord of everything. Since he had nothing, he felt he had the right to everything, when the need arose. When pointing to the endless horizon, Francis said to Lady Poverty: "These are our cloisters and our possessions." In other words, to be poor is to be a lord.

* * *

On one occasion, Francis and Leo took a long walk. They were both exhausted and Brother Leo was hungry.

"Sit here, my son, and rest," Francis said to him.

Brother Francis walked off the road and went into the countryside. He directed his steps toward a vineyard. He cut the best clusters and took them to Brother Leo.

"Here, eat," he said to Leo. "And while you eat, I'll go and gather a few more for our journey."

And while Francis was happily gathering the ripest grapes, the owner appeared with a rod in his hand and hit Francis several times on the back.

As they walked home, they had a hearty laugh about the tragicomical incident. It inspired a song and Francis sang it to Leo every now and then:

Brother Leo's gift made him happy and gay;
Brother Francis was the one who had to pay;
the treat was a feast for Leo;

Francis took his beatings with brio.

They were full of merriment as they walked home. All the disciples joined in the revelry when they heard about their adventure.

* * *

Francis was well aware of the temptations and doubts that troubled his disciples, and he suffered more than they did. He would spend sleepless nights thinking about the vicissitudes each had experienced. If they worried, he worried. If they were happy, he was happy. He asked the Lord repeatedly to keep them in his heart.

"This is absolute poverty," Brother Francis said to himself. "To do as a mother would do in denying herself and showing concern for another."

Francis was an extremely sensitive man, a characteristic apparent since birth. However, if he had kept that abundance within, he would have been an extremely vulnerable, hypersensitive, egocentric individual. Poverty had unleashed his richness. Man must forget himself before remembering the other.

To Brother Francis, there was nothing worse than ownership. In the open country, in the sands of combat, man acquires strength. For this reason, he never detained his disciples for long. He would release his disciples to the challenges awaiting them because he knew that battles foster strength, and maturity is the fruit of many wounds.

Every parting and reunion was a wonderful display of brotherhood. The chroniclers give several descriptions of each parting: Francis felt the heartbreak only a mother could feel and emotions that were difficult for him to disguise. He hugged them tenderly and placed them in God's hands. He would often accompany them for miles, with tears streaming down his face.

He thought about them constantly during their absence. How is Brother So-and-so? What about what's-his-name's state of mind? When will they come back? Francis soon found himself in the world of a mother longing for the return of her sons.

Each time the small group made its appearance on the horizon, the chroniclers say that the reunion was beyond description: Francis would leave the hut, walk quickly toward his disciples, eyes filled with tears, hug them, bless them, treat them like valiant knights, take them by the hand as they walked toward the hut, break vows of silence, put aside the work for the day, and other daily observances, and prepare a great celebration. It is difficult to imagine a happier family.

A person can love a child, a lover, a special friend in this manner. But in order to express that kind of love to each individual in a group, one must be in a total state of *passover.* Poverty is paschal strength.

* * *

As in any family, Brother Francis concerned himself primarily with the weakest members. When kind persons brought them a special treat, Brother Francis would save it especially for his ill brothers, even if it were a day devoted to fasting. Francis would calmly take the first bite, then pass it to his ailing brothers. That way, they would not feel guilty.

He had no qualms about begging for meat for his ill brothers during the season of Lent, much to the surprise of the townspeople. The brotherhood took precedence above all other obligations.

* * *

Brother Rizzerio suffered from a persecution complex, as it is called today. He was the kind of person who would weave gratuitous suspicions in his head: this one doesn't love me; I don't like the way he is staring at me; that one no longer gives me the time of day; they are conspiring against me...

So somehow Brother Rizzerio got the notion in his head that Francis did not love him, and, to Brother Rizzerio, that was a terrible sign that God no longer loved him. As is common among these types of individuals, he was melancholy day and night, slowly sinking into the abyss, reaching the point of no return.

Francis was informed of the matter and immediately put pen to paper and wrote him a *little love letter*:

"My son: Please, I beg you to rid yourself of these thoughts that are haunting you. The truth is this: I love you very much. What is more, I love you more than all the rest. If it is true that I love all of you very much, then you deserve to be my favorite. Come to me when you wish, and when you look into my eyes, you will see my sincerity with absolute clarity, and the love I feel for you."

This little letter was the magic talisman that finally liberated the brother from darkness and suspicions, transforming him into what he would soon become: Blessed Rizzerio.

"The lack of love is at the root of all melancholy," Brother Francis said to himself.

On the days that Brother Francis received the wounds on Mt. Alvernia, he was living in another world and, as a consequence, was less attentive to Brother Leo. The latter, being a sensitive soul, gave in to temptation and was saddened by the notion that Francis no longer loved him. Brother Francis soon realized what was happening.

"Brother Leo, beloved lamb of God," he said to him, "I have not forgotten you. No, on the contrary, now I love you more than ever. Bring me pen and paper and I will give you proof of my predilection."

And he wrote the famous blessing that Brother Leo treasured until the end of his days.

* * *

"Even the smallest piece of a toenail can console a person when it is given with kindness," thought Francis to himself.

Once, a brother was experiencing a trying time while battling a series of personal crises, and he said to himself:

"Oh, if I had just a little piece of Francis' toenail, these temptations would disappear in an instant. Where is Francis?" he asked.

"He's in Rieti, and he's very ill," they responded.

Without giving it another thought, the weary brother went to Rieti, making plain his desire to have a piece of Francis' toenail. Those attending Francis found the idea utterly ridiculous and barred his entrance.

Francis got word of this and immediately demanded that they allow him to enter. Francis extended his foot very tenderly and consoled him as he cut a piece of his toenail. Afterwards, he blessed him affectionately. There was not a happier man alive than the weary brother, with his piece of Francis' toenail and affection.

"It's so easy to make someone happy," Francis said to himself.

* * *

For months, things did not go well for that particular brother.

"It's an endless chain," Francis would say. "Simply one test after another. It's the human condition. If the Lord, in his infinite mercy, did not test us with rigorous yet liberating tribulations, man would be forever self-absorbed. It's the worst form of bondage!" he exclaimed out loud.

One day, Francis called the weary brother and they took a stroll through the forest. As they walked, Francis repeated several times:

"Remember, my son: The greater the tribulation, the greater my love for you."

The magic of love! He reflected during their walk:

"No one can truly serve God without having suffered trials and tribulations. A trial accepted in peace is the ring that unites a person to the Lord. The Lord only tests the strong."

* * *

Francis had many experiences in a short period of time. From the moment the Lord gave him brothers, he never left the battlefield called human relationships. He had learned many things about that field of endeavor.

"We walk a very fine line between discord and order," Francis thought to himself. "Order demands that waywardness yield. Societies do not tolerate widespread dissension. The very foundations of a society would collapse. Nevertheless, when that fine line is too taut, it snaps. What can be done?

"Order must be safeguarded. Reprimands and admonitions are necessary, not to mention an occasional masked threat, all done with patience and tenderness. But which is more important? The Order? The brother? And what if, to assure order, we oppress the brother? And what if, in order to respect the brother, we encourage disorder? A society cannot exist without order. But aren't societies established for the brother?"

However, Francis never allowed himself to get carried away with such reasoning. He always believed that love is the greatest force in the world.

Francis went further, much further than order, society, discipline, reproach, daily observance. He was dealing with the problem of *redemption.*

"A wayward brother," Francis would say, "without a doubt will yield to a threat, such as an ultimatum. But will he redeem himself? Certainly not. On the contrary, he will be resentful, melancholy, obstinate."

Life taught him that reprimands are necessary and assure order. But only love redeems. There is no substitute.

He spent many years exploring human behavior and came to the conclusion that an affective problem lies at the heart of all rebellion. An ill-tempered individual is ill-tempered because he feels rejected. He also knew how difficult it is to love someone who is unlovable. The reason they are unloved is precisely because they are unlovable, and the less they are loved, the more unlovable they become. If there is anything in this world that can cure and lift the spirit of a wayward individual, it is love.

He always came to the same conclusion: "Love is salvation!"

During his final years, when the Brotherhood numbered in the thousands, ill-tempered brothers among them, Francis countered with the love offensive. He wrote the following cherished letter, truly the *magna carta* of compassion to a provincial minister who complained of being mistreated by some of the disciples:

"Love those who mistreat you. Love them precisely for this reason...

"We are two who serve you and I will know you love the Lord and that you love me if you proceed in this manner: Never allow a brother to distance himself from you, no matter his sins, after he has looked into your eyes and seen your compassion, that is, if he cares to see it. And if he is not looking for your compassion, ask him if he desires it.

"And if a brother were to sin a thousand times before your very eyes, love him more than you love me, and you'll bring him closer to the Lord. And always sympathize with his troubles."

Mother House

One day at dusk, all the disciples were at prayer in their dwelling in Rivo Torto. An ill-tempered peasant, who was pulling a donkey by the reins, approached with the intention of spending the night. The man got furious when he saw that the hut was occupied.

Thinking that it was a resting place for passersby and that the wanderers might possibly stop there indefinitely, the unpleasant yokel took affirmative action and behaved as if he had every right to enter, tripping over the others in an insolent manner.

He began to yell, wanting his vulgar words to be taken as a personal affront. Pushing the donkey, he screamed:

"Inside, inside. It's nice and cozy in there."

Francis could stomach any insult with ease. But profanity hurt him to the core. He was always so sensitive about courteous and discourteous behavior! What should he do? Resist?

"We are God's poor," he said to himself, "and we have no rights. God's will is manifested in the errant peregrination of heavenly bodies. Would it not also manifest itself in the grotesque language of a repulsive muledriver?"

Brother Francis was completely calm, assuring himself that God could conceal his will even in this brusque scene.

He turned to his disciples, saying:

"Beloved brothers, what is the Lord's intention here? Surely he wants to liberate us from the temptation to claim that something is ours. Don't we say everyday that we are pilgrims and strangers in this world? Remember: Where there is ownership, there is security, and where there is security, there is no room for poverty. Let's go, brothers, and rejoice. We have nothing in this world save the Almighty's infinite mercy."

And without another word, they abandoned the dwelling, the precious cradle of the Franciscan movement. More importantly, the freedom of poverty was worth more than a cradle made of gold. And at nightfall, the brotherhood found itself errant once again, drifting, not knowing where they would spend the night. They decided to go to the Porziuncola chapel. However, it could not accommodate all of them, so some had to go to the public kilns, something they were already accustomed to doing.

* * *

The next morning, Francis went to the Benedictine monks of Mt. Subasio to ask for authorization to occupy the Porziuncola chapel and the surrounding forest. In light of the accelerated pace at which the Franciscan movement was growing, the Benedictine monks gladly acceded to the petition. Also, they manifested the desire to hand over the property on the condition that it be recognized as the cradle of the great movement that was destined to appear.

Brother Francis responded by saying:

"We do not want possessions, not now, not ever. We want to live as the Lord Jesus lived, without a permanent dwelling, in little huts made of clay and straw, to remind ourselves that we are strangers to this world and citizens of another."

But Brother Francis was not content. He knew very well how easily man puts down roots and grows attached to his home, first emotionally than legally. And to make certain that this would not occur with the *Mother House* of the Franciscan movement, Francis decreed that every year the Brotherhood of the Porziuncola chapel would take a basket of fish as payment to the Benedictine monks of Mt. Subasio.

And every year, during the first days of summer, we would find the little brothers of the Porziuncola wading in the waters of the Chiaggio River until they filled their basket with fish.

Afterwards, they covered it with aromatic leaves from the forest and carried it, with a certain liturgical aura about them, to the monastery at Mt. Subasio. What a spectacle! There was an air of simplicity and drama in everything that Brother Francis did. It was a protest: they were not proprietors. It was an affirmation: they were passing only.

The abbot responded to this act of courtesy by sending a large pitcher of oil to the Brotherhood of the Porziuncola, as a kind of receipt. This exchange went on for centuries until the abbey was destroyed.

A Sermon for the Flock

During that period, Brother Francis called upon Brother Maseo and said to him:

"Brother Maseo, I've been in a muddle for days and I don't see a way out. What do I do, do I fold my wings, settle at God's feet and stay there forever? Do I extend my wings, fly all over the world and proclaim the Word? At times I fear that as I walk the earth I'll get covered with the dust on the road. But when I think about our blessed Christ who renounced paradise to save our souls, I just want to jump on top of the world and never stop. What do I do?"

"Brother Francis," replied Brother Maseo. "I have always heard it said that God manifests his will to highly prayerful souls. Why not consult with one of them?"

"Brother Maseo, tomorrow morning you will go to St. Damian to speak with Sister Clare. She resides in the Lord's most secret chamber: she has knowledge of all the divine mysteries. You will tell her that Francis would like to know if he should dedicate his life to contemplative or evangelical pursuits, or both. But tell her that prior to giving me a response, she must consult with the simplest, most innocent, and most unlearned sister in the convent. Then, my dear Maseo, you will climb the deep gorge of Mt. Subasio until you reach the *cells*, where you will find our Brother Rufinus in deep meditation, and you'll ask him the same question."

The next day, before sunrise, Brother Maseo set out to fulfill Brother Francis' wishes, following his instructions to the letter.

Francis, in his turn, spent most of the morning asking the Lord to manifest his will unequivocally. The hours passed and Maseo did not return. Actually, it was a very long and arduous journey. Francis was anxious to know what the two great worshipers would reply.

* * *

Brother Maseo returned at midday. Francis was overjoyed when he saw him. However, he did not ask him about the outcome of his errand. First, he gave him a warm embrace. Then he took him by the hand to one of the little huts where he had a basin with warm water. He washed Brother Maseo's feet with reverence and affection. Then he dried them and kissed them lovingly. They walked to the large hut where he had prepared a meal of olives, dried figs, bread and fresh water.

Afterwards, he took him once again by the hand and walked deep into the forest. Francis knelt before him like a knight-errant. He took off his hood reverently and extended his arms outward in the shape of a cross. In a loud voice he asked:

"What does the Lord Jesus Christ command?"

"It has been revealed not only to Sister Clare but also to Brother Rufinus," replied Maseo, "that you are to go out into the world and proclaim God's love."

The Poor Man of Assisi felt profound exaltation upon hearing the response. He got up, raised his arms and said:

"Onward, in the name of the Lord!"

And, without returning to the hermitage, he set out for the countryside with Angelo and Maseo at his side, in the direction of Spoleto. They were driven by the Spirit and were simply drunk with happiness. They soon arrived at a small town called Cannara.

A small group of people gathered and he began to speak about Eternal Love, Peace, and Poverty. But a multitude of swallows and swifts kept chirping and gliding in all directions and made it impossible for Francis to be heard. As he modulated his voice ineffably, Francis begged the swallows to keep still and to stop their incessant chirping, in the name of Love.

And the swallows did as he asked. The people stared in amazement, wanting to abandon everything and follow Brother Francis of Assisi. He said to them:

"Calm down, do not act in haste; your time will come. I will not forget you."

The townspeople were comforted by his words and the miracle of the swallows. The disciples walked toward another hamlet called Bevagna. Francis was full of joy and enthusiasm. He was the happiest man alive.

* * *

At a distance, to the right of the road, there were several tall, full trees. Francis focused his attention on them, but as he approached he began to hear a spirited and polyphonic clamor. Brother Francis stared with his eyes wide open. He could barely believe what he was witnessing: a multitude of birds of every size and plumage imaginable filled the trees.

"Brothers," Francis said to his companions, "stay where you are. The Lord has summoned this marvelous audience. Birds will also enter paradise. Who's to say that at least one in a hundred does not have a contrite heart?"

Francis advanced very slowly, barely touching the ground. He kept a certain distance as he began to preach to the birds that were pecking at the ground. It is difficult to believe what was taking place. The birds fidgeted as they went about pecking tiny seeds. As soon as they heard Francis' voice they quieted down and arranged themselves in a semicircle. They stood absolutely still as they looked and listened to Francis.

He continued to speak. And, oh what a miracle! Millions of birds flew down from the tangled branches and arranged themselves in order in front of Francis: the smallest ones up front, those of medium height next, and the largest in the back. During the entire sermon, not one could be heard chirping, not one pecked at the ground. They remained absolutely still until the end of the sermon. But instead of flying away, they waited patiently for Francis' blessing. As he preached, Francis moved among them. And even when the hem of his raiment brushed up against them they remained calm and motionless.

This phenomenon would not have been believed if it were not for Brother Maseo recounting it to Brother James of la Massa.

* * *

These were the words that Brother Francis addressed to the birds:

"Birds, my dear sisters: You possess creation's greatest gift: the ability to fly. God's children should not feel envious. But I must confess: I envy your ability to fly. At this very minute how I would love to fly to the top of this tree, to that inaccessible cliff. For you nothing is inaccessible. What a panorama you must see from those heights!

"Your precious songs, your resounding whistles, all do little to praise the love and the wisdom of our Creator. From dusk till dawn you will part the winds announcing that the Almighty is none other than our Creator. Even if no one will listen, fly all over the earth singing the praises of the Lord.

"In his infinite imagination, the Creator has dressed you in double and triple layers of plumage to protect you from the cold, the hot rays of the sun, and to make you beautiful. The Lord has given you feathers that repel the rain, giving you the ability to fly even in torrential downpours. Your feathers cover a spectrum of colors, more than in the rain-

bow: green-black, black-blue, red-white, green-yellow...
You're very colorful, my sisters, the birds. All by the Grace
of God.

"Your Father was careful to include you in Noah's ark
in order to save your kind from total annihilation. And when
the waters receded, one of your species was the first to leave
the ark to ascertain whether the earth was inhabitable. You
are the only species that can fly above the waters. Also, the
Lord has given you blue skies and open spaces so that you
can joyfully flap your wings and sing. You are never sad. On
the contrary, I have always seen you happy. You are the most
privileged creatures in all creation. All by the Grace of God.

"Furthermore, your Father has filled the earth with
springs and rivers to quench your thirst and for you to bathe
in during hot weather. He has also raised tall mountains and
spread wide, spacious valleys for you to glide through
freely. And God's greatest invention, his most precious gift
to you, are the trees. I will forego mentioning their attributes
since you are more familiar with them than I. I only wish to
point out that trees are tall so that you can build your nests
in springtime without fear. In this way, children—who like
to play with nests—cannot reach them and destroy them. All
by the Grace of God.

"Finally, your food is prepared for you everyday. Man
has to go out into the fields and sow in the winter, weed in
the spring, and reap in the summer; and he has to build
numerous factories and shops in order to put clothes on his
back. You need none of that. All you need to do is jump from
your nests and the Father dresses you for life. Moreover,
never have I seen a bird die of hunger. All by the Grace of
God.

"Actually, you are the favored creatures of the Almighty
Father. Your only sin is ingratitude. Watch out for that vice,

my sisters. And praise, bless, and be eternally grateful for the love of our Lord."

* * *

While Francis spoke to them, all the birds began to open their beaks and sing, stretch their necks, extend their wings, and bow their heads respectfully as a way of expressing their happiness for his words of admiration.

Brother Francis of Assisi cheered and took pleasure in their delight as he continued to marvel at the multitude and spectacular variety of birds, their undivided attention, and their affable manner. For all of this he devoutly praised the Creator.

Finally, when he finished his sermon, Francis made the sign of the Cross over them and gave them permission to leave. Then, all of the birds took flight, singing harmoniously. They divided into four groups, following the cross Francis had traced in the air. One group flew eastward. Another toward the west. The third flew south, and the fourth travelled north. And each group flew away singing beautiful harmonies.

The minor brothers, as with the little birds, go around the world with no belongings, putting their trust in God's hands.

The Outlaws of Montecasale

Up a steep incline, a few kilometers from Borgo San Sepolcro, is a place called Montecasale. A rock of extraordinary dimensions projected (*speco*) from the ravine. It looked like a roof that could span the earth.

Francis always searched for places such as this to cultivate a relationship with God. The disciples were protected from sun, rain, snow, and they also had running water nearby. Above and on one side of the ravine, Brother Francis built a hut of clay, branches and dried leaves. It was called the *hermitage of Montecasale.*

Brother Angelo Tarlati stood before the hermits who, just like his namesake Angelo Tancredi, was a gentleman and a man-at-arms. Three famous bandits, who made it their business to rob transients, prowled these secluded areas. Since they were famished and there was no one around to assault, they approached the hut with malicious intentions in mind.

Upon seeing them, the old soldier became enraged and severely reprimanded them:

"You lazy-good-for-nothing assassins; no, you're not content with just robbing respectable people. Now you want to gobble up the last of our olives? You're old enough to work. Why don't you go out and get contracts as laborers?"

The bandits seemed unperturbed by these words. On the contrary, their cold stares betrayed their persistence to carry on with their less than honorable intentions.

"I think you should know," said Brother Angelo threateningly, "that I used to be a soldier and I've cut swines like you down to size many times. I may no longer wield a sword, but I do have a club which I'll use to break your backs."

And he grabbed his club and began to hit them as they made their escape. It was one more victory for the former soldier. The disciples were thoroughly entertained and raised a storm of laughter.

* * *

Francis returned later that afternoon. He had been out asking for alms. His disciples laughed and cheered as they recounted the incident.

As they related the episode, not the slightest smile materialized on Brother Francis' face. They concluded that he failed to see the humor in what they considered a funny story, so they also stopped laughing. Brother Francis did not say a word when his disciples finished their narration. He left them in silence and went into the forest. He was upset and needed to calm down.

"A soldier!" he said to himself. "We all carry a soldier within; and the soldier is always escaping, wounding or killing. Military victory! When has a military victory ever erected a home or a village? A sword has never sown a square meter of wheat or hope."

Francis was extremely upset. However, he was careful not to direct his anger toward Angelo Tarlati, because it seemed to him that it would be the same as striking the bandits with a club.

"My Lord, please remove this sword of ire and calm the tempest inside my soul," said Brother Francis in a loud voice.

When he was composed and decided to speak with his disciples, he said to himself:

"Francis, son of Assisi, remember: If you reprimand your brothers with ire and vexation, it will be worse than clubbing the outlaws."

* * *

He summoned his disciples and began to speak to them calmly. They were frightened at first, but when they saw his serenity, their fear subsided.

"I believe," he began, "that if the thief of Calvary had had a piece of bread when he first felt hunger, a wool tunic when he was cold or a kind friend when he first felt temptation, he would never have committed the crime for which he was crucified."

Francis spoke in a low voice, did not accuse anyone, and stared at the ground as if he were talking to himself.

"None of the executioners," he continued, "had a loving mother to guide them. What if the opposite were true in every case? How many times has the rising sun hid behind the mountain! No one is bad. Fragile is more like it. The more accurate term is *sick*. We have promised to defend the Holy Gospel. And the Gospel tells us that we have been sent to help the sick, not the healthy. What are they suffering from? Love. Therein lies the secret: The bandit is lovesick. Share a little piece of bread, a little bit of kindness and we would have no more need for prisons. Oh love, invincible fire, divine spark, immortal son of the Immortal God! Who can resist love? Are there any obstacles that love cannot overcome or injustices that cannot be remedied?"

Francis then intoned a hymn in honor of Love, Son of God.

"And now," he said slowly, lowering his voice, "I will walk along these foothills in search of those bandits to ask for their forgiveness, give them bread and show them kindness."

Brother Angelo jumped up when he heard those words:

"Brother Francis, it's my fault; I should be the one to go."

"We are all guilty, my dear Angelo," replied Brother Francis. "Together we sin, together we sanctify ourselves, together we save ourselves."

Brother Angelo knelt and said:

"For the love of Love, Brother Francis, I am asking to do this penance."

Francis was touched by his words, and he said to him:

"Very well, my dear brother, but you will do exactly as I say. You will climb mountains and comb the lowlands until you find the bandits. They can't be very far. When you see them you will say: 'Come bandits, my brothers, come and eat the meal Brother Francis was kind enough to prepare for you.' If they see serenity in your eyes, they will approach you immediately. Then, you will ask them to sit on the ground. They will obey you. Place a tablecloth on the ground. Take bread, wine, eggs, and cheese. You will serve them with kindness and extend every courtesy. When they finish the meal, you will go down on your knees and implore them to never assault anyone again. The rest you leave to God and his infinite mercy."

And that is how it happened. Every day the ex-outlaws went up to the hermitage carrying wood on their shoulders. Francis would frequently wash their feet and speak with them at length. A slow and complete transformation was taking place within their souls.

Why You?

At that time, Brother Francis was accompanied by Brother Maseo during his apostolic journeys. Brother Maseo was one of the most beloved disciples in the early years of the Brotherhood: a man of prayer, gallant, and courteous to a fault. The other disciples knew that when Brother Maseo went out asking for alms, a good harvest would be had that day. People were drawn to his natural charm and friendly manner.

Brother Francis of Assisi was now known and admired throughout all of Umbria and part of Tuscany. It was not rare to hear church bells ringing as he approached the villages. Whole towns would come to see, hear, and touch him.

Brother Maseo had been watching him for days and was intrigued. He could not understand why the populace rushed to his companion. And one day, as they walked in silence, he asked this critical question for the first time:

"Why you?"

Francis did not understand the question and continued in silence. After a while, he raised his voice and asked him once again:

"Why you and not someone else?"

"What do you mean by that, Brother Maseo?" Francis asked.

"Francis of Assisi, I don't understand anything."

"What don't you understand, Brother Maseo?"

"Look," he replied, "according to worldly standards, there is no reason why you, Francis of Assisi, should attract so much attention. You're not handsome: Why does everyone want to look at you? You're not eloquent: Why does everyone want to hear you? You're not educated: Why does everyone seek your advice? Why then does the entire world turn to you when there is absolutely no reason why they should? What's your secret? What makes you so fascinating?"

Francis was visibly moved upon hearing his words.

"Never have such words of wisdom been pronounced on the face of the earth," said Brother Francis. "Tell me, Brother Maseo, where did you acquire so much knowledge? Who inspired those astute observations?"

He knelt on the ground, wanting to kiss Brother Maseo's feet, but the brother did not permit Francis to do so. Brother Francis lifted his eyes to the heavens and said:

"Thank you, Almighty Father, for revealing great truths to transparent souls."

And then he directed his words to Brother Maseo:

"You want to know why everyone comes to me? I'll tell you: to *confuse*. Oh Brother Maseo! The Almighty Father, who is Love and Mercy, has a thousand eyes with which to penetrate all the cracks in the human soul. He looks beyond the surface. Where there is darkness he will see the light. Well, those almighty eyes have circled the earth and have failed to find a more incompetent, useless, ignorant fool. This is the reason why he chose me, to manifest to everyone on the face of the earth that the only Marvelous one is the Lord. If Francis of Assisi were handsome, eloquent beyond compare, schooled in the classrooms of Bologna, possessed the wisdom of angels, people would say: 'It is his beauty, it is his wisdom, it is his eloquence.' But when he is lacking in these qualities, people are obliged to come to the following conclusion: 'It is the Lord.'

"Brother Maseo," continued Brother Francis, "do you recall the sublime words of our blessed Mother, the Virgin Mary? She said: 'I work wonders, but they are not mine. Since I am *insignificant*, I was chosen to bear witness that the Marvelous one is the Lord.' Why was I chosen? How can I say it, Brother Maseo? I repeat: to confuse, my brother, to confuse. In order that it be known, evident, strident to the entire world that wisdom, education and charisma do not *save* souls. God is the only one who can save, redeem, and resurrect. There is no Almighty God other than the Lord. In short, I was chosen to confuse the nobility, the great, the strong, the beautiful, and the wise of the world."

The one who was thoroughly confused was Brother Maseo. They walked in silence for a while, reflecting on these thoughts. For days, Brother Francis spoke to Brother Maseo about humility of heart.

"Oh Brother Maseo!" Francis said to him one day. "How I would love to be a shadow in the presence of the Light. We have nothing. Better yet, whatever we do have is borrowed.

God frees us from the temptation to steal. Yes, Brother Maseo. The person who takes God's gifts is a thief. The brother who is conceited about his virtues (which do not belong to him) is a vulgar charlatan. Oh Brother Maseo, I've sinned more than anyone in the world! And this is neither a lie nor an exaggeration. If any other individual were privileged enough to receive the sympathy I have received, he would be a true servant of God."

A Woman Called Clare

Very few secrets have been so carefully guarded among women as what transpired on that day. It was Palm Sunday, 1212. Clare, an aristocrat, daughter of Scifi, was obsessed with some capricious notion which her mother and two sisters failed to understand. It was totally incomprehensible. No one knew why she chose the most luxurious dress from her trousseau. Her mother, Ortolana, and her two sisters, Agnes and Beatrice, found her to be overly enthusiastic and even whimsical.

Clare, turning a deaf ear to their criticism, began to adorn herself with layers of silk, numerous bracelets, and her most precious jewels. She looked like a princess bride on her wedding day. The four ladies entered the cathedral of St. Rufinus amidst the cheerful clanging of bells, averting the gaze of passersby.

It was to be a solemn farewell, the last adieu. No one knew this, with the exception of her cousin Buona and perhaps Bishop Guido. The aromatic fragrance of laurel, palms, and olive branches filled the cathedral.

The Mass began. When the congregation advanced toward the presbytery to take the palms that had been blessed, Clare remained glued to her seat at the back of the cathedral. She no longer knew where she was, she was totally unconscious of her surroundings. She found herself at the turning point of the battle, tangled up inside herself in the final assault: surrender or retreat. Now or never.

She had shown determination throughout her life. And if she had one outstanding quality, it was this: her unfailing faith. It would be difficult to find a better example of the *devout woman* of the Bible.

The step she was about to take was a mortal leap over the abyss. She had spent her eighteen years in the loving home of a wealthy family, beside caring parents, and among five affectionate siblings. She was a beautiful young lady, full of charms and lovely qualities, admired, adored by almost everyone in Assisi.

In the blink of an eye, her dream castle crumbled to the ground. She was not blind to the fact that her eminent plans would attract the wrath of the city. At best, no one would understand or, at the very least, approve her decision. She came to her decision in the grip of absolute solitude, and to have it come to fruition was a reality both admirable and terrible. It almost had the characteristics of a conspiracy.

A strong-willed and determined individual, Clare, at that very moment, was taking her turn at the game of *all or nothing*. And so, it was not strange to picture her fortitude as solid as the foundation of St. Rufinus.

Something extraordinary happened at that moment. Bishop Guido withdrew from the presbytery, walked up the central nave to where Clare was seated and weeping, with great sympathy. To everyone's amazement, he handed her an olive branch. God had undoubtedly accepted Clare's offering. The bishop's predilection was the sign.

Clare no longer suffered. She left the cathedral with her family. She left her doubts behind those doors, burning forever like golden incense before the Lord. The die was cast. Clare was calm. She went about her day as if nothing had happened. She joined in the family festivities, and attended to her guests with courtesy and kindness.

The Nocturnal Escape

Night was falling. One by one, the lights were extinguished, the voices hushed. Clare said her good nights to her sisters and mother before retiring to her bedroom. It was a daily ritual for them. For Clare, it was to be her last good night to the family. The world was wrapped in silence. It was a favorable hour for a conspiracy.

In literature we find countless narratives about women who risk their lives in order to meet with their lovers, even dying for that impossible love. History is full of lovers who perform heroic deeds. Nevertheless, it is difficult to imagine a woman who would organize and execute a plan, as Clare had done, in order to be with her Lover.

Clare and her cousin were astute, detail-oriented women who anticipated thousands of obstacles and explored every possible solution. It would be difficult to leave the castle without arousing suspicion. It was even more of a challenge to leave a fortified enclosure. The armored gates were lowered every night. They needed to fool the sentinels in order to escape into the valley. More than likely, they spent the previous days examining the perimeter of the fortified walls in search of a narrow opening. It is also very difficult to imagine a woman lying in wait on the corner of a dark street, in the middle of the night.

It is written that when a woman is in love with Jesus Christ, nothing can deter her, not road blocks, nor rough terrain, nor the shadows of the night. The escape had all the marks of a conspiracy, a holy conspiracy. And the two women put their plan into action, with cold, calibrated maneuvers, an ardent heart, and with perfect timing.

* * *

That night, Clare did not retire to bed. At midnight, she
left her room wearing her lavish gown. She was careful not
to make the slightest sound and, barely touching the floor,
she made her way down the stone stairway toward a secret
passage she had discovered in the palace just a few days
before.

But her escape route was obstructed by a pile of debris:
wood, branches, rocks. Anyone else would have immediately abandoned the mission. She, on the other hand, tena-
ciously and patiently removed the barriers, one by one. Her
thoughts were focused on Jesus, giving her the energy to
persevere. She removed the last impediment and the old
door was finally within reach. She slowly unbolted the door
to prevent it from creaking. In no time at all, she joined her
cousin who was waiting on a street corner. Everything went
according to plan. Blessed be the Lord!

Like two fleeting shadows, they silently wended their
way through the streets and quickly reached the opening
they had discovered a few days earlier. They descended the
rocky banks trying desperately not to arouse suspicion, and
headed toward the valley below. Two fugitives? Two exiles?
No. Two wanderers in search of a better homeland, in search
of complete freedom.

Clare set out on the solitary and rocky path traversed by
history's *chosen* few, a precarious, lonely and uncertain
path. But she walked without fear, with the brazen bliss of
those in love. It was a cold and starry night, the last winter
days in the year 1212. That night, Clare's heaven was also
full of stars.

The disciples prayed all night for Clare, hoping that she would not suffer setbacks; they prayed for an outcome that would fulfill her desires.

"Clare is a sweet, pliable, unbreakable willow plant," Francis said to his disciples. "She has enough fire in her heart to burn all obstacles in her way."

"Brother Francis," his disciples said to him, "Clare is a woman, and women are afraid of shadows and fear the dark."

"But a light in Clare's heart illumines her path. It's the veiled light of her Lover's face. At any rate, it's best that we go out and meet her."

Clare and her cousin took a familiar route, five kilometers in length. They soon saw lights in the distance. It was Francis and his disciples coming out to greet her. They lit logs they had found in the forest and used them as torches.

* * *

From the dark reaches of the night, Clare's fair, slender, and radiant figure slowly began to materialize before the light of the torches and the brothers' dark, smiling eyes. Francis smiled as he walked ahead of them to greet her, and said:

"Welcome, courageous fiancée of the Immortal King."

Clare smiled. She was elated. All her fears were dissipated. Her dreams were fulfilled.

In between two rows of torches that pierced the darkness of the midnight hour, the fair figure walked in the direction of the hermitage amidst joyous singing. Possibly, never in the history of the spirit has man witnessed a comparable nuptial procession. It has been written in the pages of

Francis' life that his would have an air of fantasy and romance.

Clare approached the altar and knelt before the portrait of the Virgin. The disciples remained standing, their torches held high.

Francis turned to the congregation and said:

"Sister Clare, it is your wedding night, a night as clear as your name. The wings of the world are folded and the wings of your spirit are extended, ready to embrace your Fiancé. The angels of St. Mary have arrived and flit nearby, waiting to attest to the betrothal of eternal bonds. Everything is ready. Christ is the Husband; St. Mary is the celebrant; the angels will be the witnesses. But I must inform you, Sister Clare, that you are marrying a widower. His first wife was Poverty; she is now a dethroned and exiled queen. His new wife must resemble the first. Here is your wedding gown."

Everything had been meticulously prepared. Her cousin had made the earth-colored habit, following the same pattern used in designing dresses for the nobility, as would normally be done in the best dress shops in town. At this point in the ceremony, Clare left the hermitage with her cousin. And with her help, she removed her overskirts and underskirts, one by one, and put on the earth-colored dress.

Clare entered the hermitage once again. It was incredible. Under the torch lights, Clare looked radiant, even more so than she had in her luxurious gown. She wore sandals made of wood. All that was left of the old Clare Scifi was the mass of golden locks tumbling over her shoulders. What a spectacle!

* * *

Clare knelt before the altar, her words surfacing from deep within her heart:

"My Lord, open the golden coffer, for within it I wish to place my heart. Tonight, I light this eternal flame over the world's censer. I want this flame to flicker forever in the wind, long after the stars fade and disappear.

"My Lord, my one and only master, stretch your wings over the horizons of my world. I will walk barefoot with you until all the torches of the world are extinguished. For me, there is only one voice, one face. Nothing will come between us, save the sword of fidelity.

"I am young. I know very few things about life. They have spoken to me about autumns. There are no autumns in your spheres. I have heard that love is threatened by the poisons of tedium and routine. They even speak of desertion and indifference, things that are unimaginable to me. I know that the flag of faith will always flutter in your bell tower, and that you will carefully guard my gift in your golden coffer until the end of time."

She raised her arms and said:

"My Lord Jesus Christ, place your seal on my words and graciously accept my consecration."

Francis could not control his emotions. Tears streamed down his face. His disciples were sobbing. Clare was incredibly serene. Buona Guelfuci also wept.

* * *

In keeping with the precepts of the ritual, Francis took a pair of scissors and, without uttering a word, approached the newlywed and cut a clump of her hair. Then another. Francis performed the ritual delicately, almost reverently. He looked as though it saddened him to cut those golden locks that adorned Clare's shoulders. He placed the clumps of hair on the altar.

Then he placed a white veil on her head, and over it he placed a black one. Clare of Assisi was born to the history of the Spirit. Francis uttered his final words to her and with that, the ceremony came to an end, but not the night.

As with any perfect plan, the protagonists fussed over every last detail. They anticipated having to form a chain of familial strength in order to protect the noble lady. And in doing so, they searched for a safe haven.

That same night, Francis, Buona and a few of the disciples escorted Clare to the Benedictine convent of St. Paul, approximately five kilometers from the Porziuncola chapel. They arrived at daybreak. Clare of Assisi, exhausted but happy, was finally able to rest in a tiny room in the convent.

A dizzying twenty-four hours had elapsed. The young woman's mind buzzed with recent memories. In the recesses of her imagination, the events unfolded, superimposing themselves, creating a tangle of thoughts in waves of emotions. Her vacillations, her fears, vanished completely. Every obstacle was happily overcome. It turned out to be a successful holy conspiracy. Praise be to God! A few hours of sleep were surely welcome.

The Rescue Attempt

That morning, Ortolana realized what had happened: her eldest daughter had run away. Within minutes, she had the entire family up and in no time at all they discovered the whereabouts of their girl. They planned the rescue operation strategy in rapid succession: first, compassion, then promises, later threats, and, if necessary, action. Ortolana was the only one who did not indulge in wishful thinking. She took her daughter's tenacity very seriously.

It was time to proceed with the rescue operation. Family and friends marched to the doors of the convent. Clare had anticipated their assault and was psychologically prepared. She received them with open arms. They told her of the uproar in Assisi, the family's disappointment, and the tears Ortolana has shed as a consequence of her decision. It was an insult: the most intelligent girl in the city had donned tattered garments, adopted the life of a vagabond, an existence that held no promise for her or her future.

In the first round, the noble lady took the blows without flinching. In light of their thwarted efforts, the family continued with the second offensive. As calmly as they could, they told her that if she wished to dedicate her life to God, they would give her absolute freedom: no more talk of marriage, limitless time with the lepers. She graciously acknowledged their offer, but declined to accept, adding that her fate was sealed.

Her voice was serene. The family members, in total exasperation, turned to threats.

They raised their voices and told her that her plans were absolutely ridiculous and capricious in nature, that she had disgraced the family, the most patrician family in Assisi, that her behavior was intolerable, and that they were going to put an end to this folly by fair means or by force. As the threats mounted, so did Clare's serenity.

There was nothing more they could do; they tried to exercise restraint. They raised themselves off their chairs in a threatening manner, ready for the attack. Clare also got up, stared at them with indignation in her eyes, and unleashed the following phrase spoken by St. Paul:

"Who in this world would dare separate me from the arms of my Lord Jesus Christ?"

As they rushed at her, Clare slipped through their fingers and ran into the church.

Everything had been premeditated: she knew very well that the altar was an inviolable haven even for criminals, and her short or tonsured hair signified that she no longer belonged to the natural world, rather to the ecclesiastical dominion, and only the Church could pass judgment on her.

In a spectacle bordering on the grotesque, the family succumbed to persecution, chasing Clare around the altar. With quick reflexes, Clare grabbed the altar cloth with one hand and she removed her veil with the other. Her tonsured head was visible to all. Her family finally understood and stopped dead in their tracks. If they had come one step closer, they would have risked excommunication and adjudication by the Church. Clare of Assisi was victorious once again.

* * *

Brother Francis of Assisi schemed like a cunning eagle to defend the virgin of Assisi in her first attempts at flight. When he received word of what had happened, Brother Francis searched and found a safer sanctuary, fearing that her family might plan successive assaults. It was the Benedictine convent of Sant'Angelo di Panzo, which was situated on the southern slopes of Mt. Subasio. The convent was fortified by thick walls and solid wooden doors fixed with a double grating.

Ten years had passed since Brother Francis had first embarked on his solitary journey, a journey which no one else had made before. Amidst uncertainty, the most complete in a successive chain of events, the Lord had guided his footsteps from the revelation of an evangelical life to the approval of this new way of life by the Pope. It was a decade full of novelty and wonder.

And here, once again, we find Brother Francis of Assisi contemplating an uncertain path, not his path but Clare's. What did the Lord want in this new situation? It was the prophet's destiny: to walk unknown paths and expand the world's horizons.

Anyone else would have taken Clare to one of a number of convents in the Umbrian valley. It was the easiest and most likely solution to this problem. But his intuition and the simplicity of his faith told him otherwise. The Lord wanted something else for Clare. But what?

This tremendous audacity, this willingness to immerse oneself in the unknown, meeting challenges day after day, can be endured only by those who are endowed with a faith that is simple and absolute. And they walked on together.

Clare's Intention and Its Significance

At first, it seemed that Clare's intention was to imitate the life initiated by Francis: living poorly, attending to the lepers, and probably living an itinerant, apostolic life.

In October of 1216, Jacob of Vitry, in a letter written to the canons of Lyon, expressed his thoughts in such a way as to establish similitude between the life of the Brothers and that of the "Poor Clares." It said:

"I have had the good fortune of seeing many men and women renounce their possessions and go out into the world in the name of the Lord: They are called 'Friars Minor' and 'Minoresses'...

"During the day, the Friars go to the cities and towns, devoting themselves to apostolic works. At night, they return to their hermitages or retire to a solitary place where they can devote time to contemplation. With respect to the women, they live in various hospices and shelters near the cities, and do manual work for which they do not accept anything in return."

This addendum to the Franciscan rule of life communicates information of extreme importance and gives reason to believe that Clare's original intention was to live an evangelical life, imitating Francis and his disciples.

Later on, the "Sisters of St. Damian" followed the rule of monasticism, at the request of the Holy See. During the Middle Ages, no other religious life was even remotely imaginable for women. They could not envision the existence of an active order for nuns.

Nevertheless, it seems that these monastic principles have a significance that transcends the usual stipulations of the Holy See.

* * *

Without question, Clare was definitely drawn to the contemplative life, a quality Francis never fully developed. We know very well that Brother Francis of Assisi felt an irresistible attraction to the hermitic life early in his conversion. Even today, the sacred sites of the Franciscan movement are carved high in the central mountains of Italy, like silent testaments to Francis' frequent and prolonged solitary retreats. No one would fail to acknowledge that Francis is "the man of the caves."

Brother Francis' life was one of seclusion and inclusion, from the mountains to the pathways, from the multitude to solitude. His three final years, now marked by the *stigmata*, were hermitic pilgrimages. He vacillated many times during his lifetime, not knowing whether to live the contemplative life as something inclusive or exclusive.

It seems that Francis was always dissatisfied with his unquenchable thirst for God, and part of his soul felt empty and frustrated. If it were up to him, he would have been content living as an anchorite on any crag of the Apennines. But it was the Gospel that released Francis from solitude.

Clare filled in that part which was incomplete. I dare say that Clare, with her *eremitic* existence, fulfilled Francis' most private and personal dreams, his unconscious desires, that corner of his soul which he simply adored: the longing to wear the Visage of the Lord and to devote himself exclusively to fulfilling God's will.

Without Clare, the Franciscan movement would be a plant without flowers, a score without music.

* * *

To adore! That was Francis' dream. Everything else was simply an embellishment. He told his disciples countless times:

"Care for the lepers, help the peasants or fishermen, do what you can to assist the oarsmen and those who bury the dead, go where you wish or do as you wish, 'so long as you keep the spirit of prayer and devotion.'"

To Adore! That is the principal occupation: to proclaim that God is paramount.

Supreme adoration is a holocaust. In ancient times, there were sacrifices and holocausts. In a sacrifice, the animal was immolated and given to God as an offering. But its meat was taken by the Levites and assistants of the Temple.

In holocausts, on the other hand, the victims were *completely burned* or incinerated after immolation. That way, the flavorful meat could not be consumed by anyone. This "uselessness" was the most profound expression of adoration because it verified God's supremacy. That is, any expression of adoration is done only for the sake of worshipping God, and not because it provides an added benefit.

This was the meaning behind Clare's actions at St. Damian's. She did not catechize, she did not attend to the lepers, she did not preach the Word, nor did she teach in institutions. It was a "useless," unproductive life. It is precisely for this reason that her contemplative life was the ultimate expression of adoration. It illustrates the fact that God is great and is worth the sacrifice. In order to honor him, any other type of existence is superfluous.

Within the walls of St. Damian, Clare was like a candle of no practical use, a candle consumed by the flame. She lived her life without "doing" anything, save adoring God. Her existence was as "useless" as burning incense or as an accessory that highlights a person's natural beauty. In short, Clare fulfilled the most profound dream sealed in Francis' soul: adoration.

Agnes

Clare stayed a few weeks in the convent of Sant'Angelo di Panzo. Agnes visited her sister almost everyday. She was an enchanting girl of fifteen. Agnes, just like her sister Clare, had a striking spiritual sensitivity within her soul. After her sister's escape, the family depended on Agnes to fulfill their dreams of posterity, and they soon had her promised in marriage.

"My dear Agnes," said her sister. "I'm not mistaken. There is no more intoxicating wine than the Lord. It's better to live one day in the Lord's vestibule than a millennium outside its walls. Youth is a passing breeze; beauty dissipates like smoke; love ages like a dress in a wardrobe; life expires in one breath. Nothing is left. Oh, my dear sister! If you would only taste the height and breadth of the Lord's love. I assure you that there isn't an ocean that contains as much solace as the Lord. Agnes, my sister, we need a spouse that knows neither age nor death."

Clare was on her honeymoon. She needed a confidante, someone with whom she could share her ardent, mystical experiences. The fire in her heart rapidly inflamed Agnes' sensitive heart.

After seven visits, Agnes also escaped from the Scifi palace and asked Clare to protect and hide her in a safe place. She was more than certain that her decision would ignite a fresh persecution.

They were not mistaken. Once again, a rescue operation was put into effect. The Scifi family appointed Monaldo, a family member, who was in the military, to plan and execute a rescue operation to save their daughter, no matter what the cost. Monaldo, a man-at-arms, was violent and impetuous. He arrived at the convent with a band of soldiers, demanding that they open the doors. Seeing that the Benedictine nuns refused to obey his orders, he and his soldiers forced the doors open, and they marched into the convent with their swords held high.

Upon finding themselves face to face with the edge of a blade, the frightened Benedictine nuns promised them their fugitive. The soldiers reached the room where Agnes was staying and instructed her to return home. Agnes adopted her sister's attitude and refused to heed their warning.

The commander had strict orders to use brutal force if necessary, as a means of intimidation. So they rushed at her amidst savage screams emanating in all directions. They grabbed her by the hair and dragged her to the main door, pushing and shoving their way through while Agnes valiantly resisted. Neither Clare nor the Benedictine nuns could do anything to fend off the armored barbarians.

Monaldo's soldiers dragged her outside the convent walls and down rocky slopes. Clumps of her hair were yanked from her head. Her dress became tattered rags as they continued to drag her across rough terrain.

All of a sudden, the girl weighed more than lead and it became impossible for the twelve soldiers to move her. They were frightened and abandoned the cause. Monaldo, in a fit of anger, raised his arm, and was about to strike her when it froze in mid air, leaving him in excruciating pain.

At that moment, Clare ran from the cloister, intent on fighting to the death to save her sister. She confronted the soldiers, and without averting her gaze, said: "Miserable cowards! Don't you fear God's verdict? Don't you see the miracle? Neither you nor an entire battalion could possibly move this creature." Crestfallen, they rode back to the city.

Clare very affectionately took Agnes in her arms and carried her back to the convent. They were both profoundly moved by God's miraculous intervention. She used salt, vinegar and medicinal herbs to treat her sister's wounds.

Francis went to the convent once he received word of what had taken place. He praised Agnes' courage and gave her the veil and the religious habit.

After the two sisters had been lodging in the church of St. Damian for a few years, Beatrice joined them without opposition from her family. Years later, the mother Ortolana, now widowed, also joined the "Poor Clares" of St. Damian, along with her three daughters. In so doing, the mother, who had infused her daughters with unbending faith, finally fulfilled an adolescent desire that had been interrupted only by her marriage: to dedicate her life to God.

Their Way of Life

The two sisters who were rooming in the Benedictine convent could not stay there indefinitely. But what did the Lord desire of them? God's will manifests itself in the course of daily life. They were to meet the challenge of one unforeseeable event after another. There was no other alternative.

Francis found them a permanent dwelling. The Benedictine monks of Mt. Subasio offered the hermitage of St. Damian, completely restored with Francis' own hands. The sisters went to their new retreat.

Later on, more young women, who wished to emulate their way of life arrived. At first they were called "Sisters of St. Damian." Then Clare changed it to Minoresses, replicating the form of the Friars Minor. However, Francis, who loved to refer to everything in chivalric terms, called them the Poor Ladies. Years later, when convents were founded around the world, they were called the Poor Clares, in honor of their foundress.

When the sisters numbered in the hundreds, Clare asked Francis to help her organize a *rule of life*, transferring the Franciscan ideals to a cloistered situation.

Among monastic institutions, poverty was the outstanding characteristic of the Poor Clares. The women who entered the order had to renounce all their possessions and give them to the poor. This simple clause was a novelty in a time where princesses, while adopting the religious life, kept their grand estates. Clare's convent simply did not permit candidates to hold property, a revolutionary idea in the monastic way of life. The monastic community lived by the labor of their hands. If this alone could not provide their sustenance, they could ask for alms.

However, the most important innovation—practically a revolutionary concept—was to be found in the Rule that Clare wrote a year before her death, which made reference to fraternity. Clare made an end of the vertical use of authority, basing herself on the origin and use of "power." Fraternity, with its commanding and resonating presence, was the primary value that emerged from this legislation.

And so, in this way, Clare's religious life began unimpressively, yet extraordinarily rich in spirituality and fraternal love in the tiny retreat of St. Damian. Those were thirty-eight years in a radiant and isolated existence.

Solace for Francis

Since birth, Clare had carried a spiritual appetite within, an insatiable thirst for God, which is the sustenance of every contemplative woman. Throughout her life, she probed deeper and deeper into the successive layers of her soul. The chronicles record not a word of this decisive history. We only know that her heart raced when pronouncing Jesus' name, all at once transporting her to another world.

Throughout her life, Clare's aristocratic mien did not hide her cordial manner. In her thirty-eight years of cloistered existence she demonstrated a mother's instinct, a woman's tenderness, and a Franciscan's heart. Every night she walked several times about the dormitories, lovingly covering the girls with their blankets. If, at the hour of Matins, one of the sisters happened to oversleep, the chronicles state that Clare would awaken her lovingly and affectionately.

* * *

She possessed a quality that Francis lacked: a certain something, a sort of equanimity, an invulnerable serenity. Francis, on the other hand, was impressionable. And Clare's strength was a precious haven to him in those moments when he felt despair. Francis, in his final years, "wounded" many times on the battlefield of his ideals, sought and found consolation and security in Clare.

It was a stunning spectacle. Francis was Clare's inspiration. Francis introduced Clare to the great Franciscan adventure. She was a faithful disciple, the most beautiful plant in the garden. Nevertheless, very frequently Francis found himself needing Clare's affirmation, her validation of his ideals. Time and again, she was like an invincible mother whose courage gave him encouragement during those difficult years.

As a whole, Clare had a personality that was very clearly defined. She was an absolutely enchanting individual.

Tremendous Faith

However, the most impressive facet of her life was her tremendous faith. It was a sublime and sorrowful life, a life that is referred to as the *privilege of poverty*. In the Middle Ages, they could not conceive of a convent without income and properties. Clare promised Francis to live her life without ever holding property. This promise was ratified by the Holy See, which specified that those living in the convent would live by the labor of their hands, not with the help of a dowry or income of any kind.

Clare outlived Francis by twenty-seven years. In those three decades, the popes and Cardinals did all they could to persuade Clare to abandon this ideal which they considered unrealizable. Furthermore, of the twenty-four monasteries established for women known as the Poor Clares, only the one at Monticelli followed the privilege of poverty to the letter.

On the other hand, in the twenty-seven years after Francis' death, the original ideal of Franciscan poverty began to collapse before her helpless eyes, until it was no more than a conventual concept.

And so, under these circumstances, it is incredible to find Clare holding fast and true to the rigorous ideal. But that was not enough: before her death, she requested that the Holy Father ratify this "privilege" for future generations. The final offensive was an honorable victory for this invincible warrior.

* * *

It occurred in the final year of her life. Clare had written a Rule which included the privilege of poverty but approval was refused.

Clare's health was deteriorating day by day, and at times the pain was agonizing. In September of 1252, Cardinal Reinaldo went to see her. Clare considered the Cardinal's visit purely providential. While lying on her sickbed, she used every argument and means of persuasion at her disposal. Finally, the Cardinal yielded to her demands and, in his capacity as representative of the Pope, finally approved the Rule. Nevertheless, Clare insisted that the Pope himself approve it. But Innocent IV considered the Rule too rigorous and he refused.

Clare was now at death's door. At that time, the papacy was in Perugia, twenty kilometers from Assisi. Innocent IV went to St. Damian when he received word of Clare's condition. Clare was under the impression that the Holy Father had arrived with the papal bull of approval. She asked the pontiff whether the purpose of his visit was to give consent. His answer was evasive. For Clare this meant a negative answer.

She was like a wounded animal on a bed of thorns. And, a few hours before taking her final breath, pure faith ignited one of the most emotional battles imaginable.

Where did she find the strength to speak? What arguments did she use? The fact remains that in those minutes Clare must have displayed such powers of persuasion and such emotional force, that Innocent IV soon found himself in the papacy writing the official document of approval. The ink was still fresh when the document arrived at St. Damian. Clare kissed it; they read it to her over and over again; she was moved to tears as she listened and... she died that same night.

The Death of the Lady of Light

From another perspective, her final hours took on the peaceful colors of a late afternoon. Clare was like a golden wheat field, an apple tree full of golden apples. She was ripe and ready for her harvest.

She went without nourishment for three weeks. However, she was lucid and had her usual strength of mind. Her sister Agnes arrived from Monticelli and was crying at the foot of her bed. Clare put her hand over her head and said:

"Dear sister, there is no need to cry. Our separation will last but a moment in time. Very soon we will be together once again."

In fact, Agnes would die three months later.

Her old and loyal friends, Leo, Angelo, and Juniper were with her in her final hours. She asked them to read the Passion one last time. Juniper read the Gospel and shared very comforting words describing God's love. Meanwhile, Leo, with tears in his eyes, knelt at the foot of the deathbed, silently kissing the straw on which she lay. Angelo tried to console the other poor ladies who were weeping. What a spectacle!

Clare, like a meteor in the heavens, began to slowly and sweetly lose her brilliant light as she travelled further and further into the far reaches of eternity.

She opened her mouth, making the effort to speak. They all came closer to hear her last words. With an almost inaudible voice she said: "Thank you so much, dear God, for creating me!" And, as she firmly held the papal bull between her fingers, she gave her soul to God.

This was the passing of the Lady of Light, "a woman called Clare, all the brighter for her life," according to Thomas of Celano's expression.

Chapter Five

GREAT DESOLATION

Like a Bird in Flight

There is a period in Francis' life that is shrouded in obscurity due to the lack of information and chronological accuracy. This period extends approximately from 1211 to 1218.

It was a time of apostolic journeys to Christian lands and excursions to non-Christian territories. In the autumn of 1212, Francis embarked on a journey to Syria. Severe winds prevented a safe disembarking on the Dalmatian coast, so they travelled back to Ancona.

Later on, he made another attempt to reach Morocco, this time by way of Spain, with the intention of converting the sultan Almohad. Francis was accompanied by Bernard. But again he suffered disappointment, for somewhere in Spain he was taken ill. He took advantage of this opportunity and traveled to St. James of Compostela.

During this time, he embarked on another apostolic excursion through Tuscany with a number of new disciples who had entered the Brotherhood. The following year, he spent the Lenten season fasting on the principal island of Lake Trasimeno. He celebrated Easter in the hermitage of Le Celle. It was during this period that two men of opposing dispositions entered the Order: the blessed Guido and

Brother Elias. Brother Francis was absolutely captivated by Guido's courteous manner, commenting to his companion:

"My brother, courtesy is one God's most marvelous attributes. It is charity's sister. It extinguishes hate and ignites fraternal love."

The Brotherhood spread rapidly over the lands of Christianity. Before 1216, it had spread through northern and central Italy, through France and Spain.

Directing his attention to the Romans, he stopped at the Montefeltro fortress. He spoke to the knights about Poverty, Peace and Love. Count Orlando was moved by his words. He wished to lavish attentions on him, and offered the solitary mountain of Casentino. What a strange gift! Francis accepted the gift with the object of establishing a hermitage for penance and contemplation. It was Mt. Alvernia.

Several hermitages were founded during these years, like spiritual nests high up in the mountains: Sarteano, Cetona, Montecasale, San Urbano de Narni, Foresta, Greccio, Fonte Colombo, Poggio Bustone...

In November of 1215, he attended the fourth Lateran Council. Here Francis learned that, according to the prophet Ezekiel, only those marked with the letter *Tau* would be saved. From that moment, this sign was to be his countersign. It was probably during this same Council that Francis of Assisi met Dominic Guzman.

During these years Francis obtained the indulgence of the Porziuncola for God's mercy and the salvation of souls.

During the Chapter of 1217, he made the resolution to send groups of missionaries to Christian lands. The Order was therefore divided into provinces. During the Chapter of 1219, he decided to send expeditions to non-Christian countries particularly to territories governed by the Saracens.

By the end of the first ten years, the brothers in the Order numbered in the thousands.

The Source of Conflict

The Brotherhood took hold and spread like a pure breeze, like a spark blowing from a burning log. The disciples followed the Gospel as their one and only law of life; the Gospel followed to the letter, without easy interpretations or rationalizations. It was a formidable spiritual program, but an indelible law for a group of men!

Until this very moment, Francis was not only the father and model for all the disciples, he was also *their law*. In short, he was the *book of life* for all of them. Given a few exceptions, Francis was the source of inspiration and a guiding light to all his disciples.

The disciples saw everything through Francis' eyes with respect to priorities, personal objectives, course of conduct, and mental health in general. Whether the disciples lived in Lombardy or in Tuscany, they breathed the Porziuncola perfume.

* * *

The Brotherhood grew at an amazing rate. Events and experiences succeeded one another with an accelerated speed.

At the beginning they were few in number and heroic. Almost all of them were former citizens of Assisi, or, at the very least, from the Umbrian valley. They were all friends or acquaintances. The unifying factors were their language and certain behavioral characteristics unique to their group. But, above all, they were all cut from the same mold: the soul of Francis of Assisi.

Within a few years there were Germans, Hungarians, English, Spaniards...the bourgeois next to the humble craftsman, renowned clergymen next to the humble layman, the doctor, schooled at the best universities, next to the ignorant peasant. Not one common denominator, not even an alma mater, united this terribly heterogeneous group of men.

The norms governing their way of life were inadequate. How could they solve such complex issues without compromising the primitive rule, but, at the same time, maintain some semblance of order within this enormous congregation of brothers?

* * *

The first disciples at Rivo Torto and the Porziuncola, forged in the likeness of Francis, found themselves in contact with an enormous band of brothers. The *penitent men* of the city of Assisi who were under Francis' care were not especially influential with regard to public opinion. Of the thousands of brothers, the majority did not receive direct instruction from Francis; many of them were not even acquainted with him.

The leading figures of the Brotherhood were mainly distinguished and influential members of the clergy, men who joined forces with Brother Francis. For the most part, they were good men with honest intentions and true vocations. All of them loved and admired their founder.

They believed that Francis of Assisi was God's *chosen*, the disciple who would engender a great movement toward the reformation of the Church. But once having initiated the movement, they found him to be incapable of organizing, directing, and guiding that great multitude of followers. He was ignorant and a "partisan" of ignorance.

He was not an organizer at heart. And, what was worse, they felt that he was the type of individual who did not appreciate the importance or the need for organization.

In short, at this stage, Francis posed a *threat* to the Franciscan movement. If discipline and order were not enforced, the movement initiated by Brother Francis of Assisi would be in danger of overflowing its banks, going off course, leaving chaos in its wake and being consumed by total frustration.

* * *

As we have seen, Brother Francis respected the aptitudes and inclinations of each disciple. They exercised their freedom, some living as hermits, others contracting daily work or going out on pilgrimages; some were nurses and there were those who were also itinerant preachers.

In the beginning, they all obeyed Francis; he was the center that united them. The concept and exercise of authority was relative and limited. The group leaders were provisionally named for each missionary expedition. They were chosen democratically or sometimes by taking lots. They were not so much the guiding light of society as they were domestic servants caring for the needs of the disciples. Today an illiterate layman; tomorrow an erudite clergyman.

Without a doubt, it was an ideal way of governing a group of penitent heroes. Under the auspices of Grace and a free spirit, these penitents scaled the tallest peaks of spiritual maturity. But an Order with thousands of disciples, not all with true vocations, lacking a solid formation was a different matter altogether...

In short, the Brotherhood was not prepared to receive this torrent of disciples. It lacked educational guidelines, a system of government, courses of action and a mainstay with regard to sustenance. The only driving force was its magnetic appeal, its tremendous ability to attract followers.

The Wager

The need to restructure was apparent to all the disciples. But reorganization might damage the roots and wound the primitive ideals. This was the raw battlefield on which the dispute was waged between the intellectuals of the Order and Brother Francis of Assisi.

As the following pages will illustrate, the ministers and intellectuals maneuvered from the perspective of supporting the need for reorganization. For Francis, on the other hand, it was a matter of a *wager*. Brother Francis had bet his life on the Gospel. They were opposite points of view.

At the core of this *suffering*, which we will witness, the Gospel itself was being called into question. This was Francis' eye on the world. That tempestuous scene between the Cardinals and Innocent III was still ringing in his ears. If Francis' evangelical program was not feasible, then the Gospel itself was nothing but a utopian ideal, and its author a dreamer.

If the ministers claimed victory in this approaching battle, then Francis would lose the bet; that is, life would contradict the Gospel. Life itself would proclaim the Gospel as nothing more than fantasy. In short, the battle for Francis was in defense of the evangelical ideal.

* * *

The author who devotes time and energy to St. Francis must identify in some way with the soul of the Poor Man of Assisi. Otherwise he would not write. In the painful battle that was fast approaching, the author runs the risk of presenting the opposing side as something of an aggressor, the cause of Brother Francis' suffering.

But this would be unjust. From the outset, the author must make it clear that the attackers were motivated by honest and just intentions.

The Spirit's Darkest Night

The historian perceives the phenomenon, but the profound mystery remains inaccessible. Chroniclers use antiquated words to describe Francis' desolation as poignantly as they can. Brother Leo, his confidante and inseparable friend, qualified the crisis as a "severe spiritual temptation." Using the terminology of St. John of the Cross, it is clear that the Lord subjected Francis to the painful yet purifying test which is called the dark night of the *spirit*. It was much more than just a dispute about organization.

It was agonizing. Brother Francis walked into a starless night. For more than four years, Francis ceased being the Brother Francis of Assisi that we all know. He succumbed to the worst temptation: distress. He allowed the most dangerous weed to grow in his garden: violence.

This was the deep-seated problem: What is God's will?

What was worse: Where is God?

At the very core: Does God *exist*?

Let us show sympathy and affection as we accompany Brother Francis of Assisi on this mysterious, painful, and transfiguring pilgrimage. It is, without a doubt, one of the most difficult periods that touches upon the mystery of Francis of Assisi.

* * *

All crises present a contradiction. Historical factors (guided by the hand of the Father) have mistakenly placed

God's *chosen* at a crossroads: two forces pulling him in opposite directions. The result? Disintegration.

"The Lord has revealed to me that I must live the Gospel, in poverty and humility." This was to Francis as clear as a blue sky: clouds of doubt never appeared in that sky, it was a personal revelation. Now, the papal deputy and the intellectuals argued that we should structure our lives in an orderly, disciplined and efficient manner. Whom do I obey?

For Francis, there was nothing more satisfying than following the will of God. But where was it? Was it in the voice of the Porziuncola that commanded him to go around the world as a pilgrim and stranger to this world, to work with his hands, never to carry pontifical documents, to place daily worries in the hands of God? Or was it in the voice of the papal representative who wished to make the Brotherhood into an efficient and productive establishment to meet the needs of the Church? Can these two voices contradict each other? And if this is so, which voice is mistaken? Where is the will of God?

Had not Francis always said that his brothers were and wished to be "submissive and obedient to all?" If they want to be submissive to everyone, all the more, then, to the authorities of the Church! Did not Francis of Assisi always demonstrate "reverence and obedience" to the Holy Father? Did he not request a Cardinal protector for his Order, assuring him the same obedience one shows the Pope? Furthermore, could anyone deny that Ugolino was his best friend, defender of the Franciscan movement, who challenged hostile cardinals?

The Franciscan program is a magnificent testimony to humility. Why not do what is honorable, forsake his point of view and adhere to the opinion of persons in authority? Brother Francis of Assisi believed in obedience to God. The Church is the voice of God, is it not? The Church manifests

God's will, does it not? If the Church or Francis were to be mistaken, it is only natural to assume that Francis had erred. The Church, with all its universal knowledge and experience, would know much more about the world's needs and concerns than Francis of Assisi, would it not? Christ said: "Those who obey you, obey Me." Francis wanted very much to be an apostolic man. Why not begin by obeying Peter's successor?

* * *

This cloud of interrogation threw a dark shadow on Francis' soul. At this terrible hour, when he needed to hear the voice of God, God did not speak a word. If God was silent, were not his representatives the voice of authority? The questions bombarded him incessantly.

The Pope's representative and the ministers also condoned poverty and humility; but a rigid framework was needed to control the large group of wandering friars and place them in the service of the Church. For centuries this model had been put into practice by the Church. Could the Church have made a mistake? In face of this structure, Francis announced that a new way of life had been revealed to him, an itinerant and penitent life, in poverty and humility. Can God himself forge such divergent paths? Where is God?

It was agonizing. Francis was not an administrator, nor a dialectician, nor a fighter. He used to be so happy with just his God and his lepers! Then the Lord placed him in the middle of an innumerable mass of disciples. At that moment, Francis resembled a shipwrecked sailor caught in the epicenter of a whirlpool. He looked to the skies, but no one responded. He lost his calm demeanor. He was moody, menacing, tense, and somber. He began to curse. He was no longer Brother Francis of Assisi. He was another person entirely.

But it was much more than that. The *chosen one* had placed himself unconditionally into the hands of God. All that the Eternal Father desires is to liberate man and to make him holy, thus, hurling the *chosen one* into the most inexplicable abyss, into depths that surpass psychological suffering. Hence, the *dark night of the spirit* begins. I will endeavor to elaborate.

* * *

The ship is lost at sea. Menacing waves pound the ship from all directions. It is pitch black. Is it pitch black or is something out there?

The Lord has revealed to me that I must live my life according to the Holy Gospel. And what if it were someone other than the Lord? What if what I heard was my own voice? Could it be that these are nothing but fanciful notions of my own device to compensate for failing on the battlefields of life?

To be adored by millions and to envision oneself as merely an empty mask. From the very first moment, the disciples held on to Francis. And Francis, whom did he hold on to? To champion an ideal, and to discover in the end that it was simply a delusion of grandeur.

To discover in the end that one has been deceived is painful, to say nothing of dragging a multitude into the same delirium. But what do you do when you realize that it is utter madness, and, in spite of this, that others continue to believe? Is there any reason to wake them?

The *dark night of the spirit* is a squall that drags everything in its path into the abyss.

How can I describe this? It is similar to suddenly discovering for yourself that you are living a lie, that you are playing this game with yourself, like a game played by children who know that they are lying to each other.

How can I describe this? It is something resembling an individual with a split personality who suddenly discovers that one side has deceived the other (that other is the same person), and the other is deceiving himself, and the two know they deceive and are being deceived.

Comparisons only touch upon absurdity and tragedy. Words like disappointment, disillusion, etc., are empty and superfluous and mean nothing in comparison to this kind of agony.

"A horrible and tempestuous night," says Saint John of the Cross.

To make matters worse, faith lies intact under all the absurdity and darkness, as cold as an invincible sword. It seems ironic, but there is a new and tragic split personality at play between the *knowledge* of and *feeling* faith: *feeling* is bent on convincing and deceiving *knowledge*, and *knowledge*, knowing that the other wishes to be deceived, attempts to convince and delude *feeling* in a vicious yet amazing cycle. Feeling says: Everything is a lie. Knowledge says: Everything is true.

It is total darkness. To die! It is the only way out.

Jesus' "feeling of mortal sadness" in Gethsemane can be interpreted as: *I wish to die*. Jesus also lived momentarily the *dark night of the spirit*. It is, in short, a crisis of absurdity and contradiction. It is agony. Francis lived this kind of night.

Nevertheless, mysteriously enough, souls that are subjected to this terrible catharsis never yield. I do not know of anyone who has burned in this inferno. It is an extremely purifying trial by fire, and God our Father only subjects those souls that he knows will not break with the weight of his hand.

On the contrary, they emerge from the night transformed into luminous stars. They are completely naked and free. Francis of Assisi, in his last three years of life, was an almost hallowed figure of a man, a prelude to the man in paradise.

Encounter with Ugolino

As previously mentioned, the Brotherhood had grown at a rapid pace. Brother Francis no longer had direct contact with his disciples due to their increasing numbers. Therefore, he decided to have an annual celebration when the entire Brotherhood would convene. It moved him to tears to think that King Arthur did exactly the same thing with his knights of the Round Table.

They traveled from all corners of the globe and gathered in the Porziuncola. They arrived at the break of day like neophytes newly admitted to the Order. Francis approached each one, expressing words of encouragement. He presented a general overview of their way of life.

There was no definitive Rule. Nevertheless, the rapidity with which the Brotherhood was growing necessitated organization of some kind. Every year, new principles were added that were practiced during that year. The Rule that was documented only codified those norms *lived* during that year. For this reason, it was named the *Rule of Life of the Friars Minor*. The assemblies or chapters were celebrated at Pentecost.

* * *

In the Chapter of 1217, Francis said to them:

"My dear brothers, our family has grown enormously, thanks be to God. We're like an impatient brood waiting to leave the nest. Let's go then and move mountains, sow and plant in faraway lands. Keep in mind the valiant knights of King Arthur who waded across tempestuous rivers, traversed snowy peaks, and penetrated forests seized by the enemy. Our blessed captain, Christ, walks ahead of us, barefoot, holding the colors of Poverty, Peace, and Love."

Every *send-off* made Francis emotional. He suffered privately and tried to conceal it as best he could. He knew what awaited them. It would have made him extremely happy to subject himself to all their trials and tribulations and save them from suffering, but he knew that this was impossible.

"I can't protect you from danger. You're the brave knights of our valiant captain Christ, and I know that the words I'm about to say will frighten you. No one has asked you to come. No one waits for you. You are unfamiliar with the language and customs of foreign lands. You can't preach like Christ, but you can suffer in silence as Christ has done, and this will be our contribution to the Redemption. Don't carry money or bags with provisions. Some may think you are heretics and persecute you. It goes without saying that you are forbidden to request letters of recommendation or ecclesiastical documents specifying that you are Catholics. Our blessed Christ did not ask for letters to protect him from persecution. Happy are those who are persecuted for following Christ's example. Be glad, for you will be saved along with him.

"How many of those present wish to go on this apostolic expedition?" asked Brother Francis.

Several hundred brothers stepped forward.

"It would not be chivalrous," he continued, "to send you off into combat while I remain here in this quiet retreat. I will also go with you."

The news filled the volunteers with enthusiasm.

The following day, Francis gathered his volunteers and said to them:

"You will go two by two, walking humbly, praying constantly and avoiding frivolous words. During the day you will conduct yourselves as if you were in the hermitages, carrying your cell with you, which will accompany you wherever you roam. And the hermit that inhabits the cell is our soul, which should live united with God."

He imparted his benediction and embraced each disciple. It was difficult for him to contain his tears. He said to each of them:

"My son, cast your worries into the lap of our Father, and walk on."

And, in the company of Brother Maseo, he took the route to France. He enjoyed that country because of the special attention it gave to the Blessed Sacrament.

* * *

Upon arriving in Florence he met Cardinal Ugolino, who at that time concerned himself with the crusades in Tuscany.

He had many reasons for befriending Francis. Cardinal Ugolino was, among other things, a man devoted to God. Mystical currents ran through his veins and deep-rooted forces lured him toward God. In this respect, his soul was one with Francis'.

Moreover, since he was a true man of the Church, Ugolino was extremely enthusiastic about the ecclesiastical reformation. The secret force that guided his political maneuvers was the Glory of God. In this respect, Ugolino looked upon Francis as a providential man for the good of the Church. For this reason, he was very curious about Francis.

Finally, he enjoyed Francis' personality and admired his charisma, without compromising his stance with regard to a few of Francis' ideals.

Firstly, there was a unique spiritual harmony between them. And secondly, owing to his posture before those in authority in the Church, Francis looked upon Ugolino "with reverence and adoration."

He might have also regarded the Cardinal as a vital cornerstone protecting him from the Curia. Francis' views with respect to the interpretation of the evangelical ideal also differed considerably from those professed by the Cardinal.

* * *

One day Ugolino did not have pressing engagements and he summoned Francis. He was anxious to converse with him and exchange ideas. The conversation began in a formal palace chamber, but they soon found themselves walking through the gardens. After a few comments of no immediate import, the Cardinal went straight to the point.

"Francis, my son. In the Curia, there is a group of influential cardinals who still look upon you and the Brotherhood with some degree of skepticism. They have not forgotten the impression you made on Innocent III. They call you a dreamer. This is nothing new to you, I am sure. But there is more: now they call you a dangerous dreamer."

Brother Francis lowered his eyes. He felt the blow.

"My son, the most wonderful gift among friends is honesty," said the Cardinal. "It hurts me to say these things to you, but we all have the Church's best interests at heart. From all over Italy, news about your disciples has reached the Curia. And not all of it is good. You know what happens: we receive thirty positive reports and three that are negative, and, for some unknown reason, the negative accounts carry more weight. And for those who are skeptical, all reality is reduced until there is nothing left to discern but three unfavorable reports.

"I, and a few other Cardinals, will do everything that can be done to defend you. But you have to help us. I advise you not to cross the Alps. Do not go anywhere. Your flock is in danger. Christ kept watch over his flock and took care of them. He was a good shepherd. If you go away to foreign lands, the most guileless of the Curia will accuse you of behaving irresponsibly. And they would have just cause to voice such an opinion."

A shadow veiled Francis' eyes. It was a prelude to sadness. However, the shadow that crossed his eyes lasted but a minute. Brother Francis quickly "awakened" and composed himself.

"Lord Cardinal," said Francis. "My brothers are lambs and they walk among wolves. Experience tells me what awaits them: sarcastic remarks, dogs, rocks, and curses. It would not be chivalrous of me to push them into the middle of a storm, and for me to remain quietly behind, next to a warm hearth."

"Between the audacious knight," responded the Cardinal, "and the fainthearted there lies a middle ground: recklessness. Permit me to say the following: you have acted carelessly, my son. You made a rash decision in sending your defenseless brothers out into remote regions of the world, subjecting them to all kinds of criticism. Circumspection, my son! Wisdom! In other words, weigh strengths and weaknesses and understand human nature."

* * *

Instantly, the Gospel and the example of Christ came to mind. Francis, his eyes shining bright with joy, raised his voice and said:

"Forgive me for speaking, Lord Cardinal, but I'm an ignorant fool. My Lord Jesus Christ did not send for an army to defend himself against those countless assaults. He did not shield himself with his omnipotence when he felt powerless. He relinquished the advantages of being God and subjected himself to the disadvantages of being man. He turned the other cheek, did not offer proof of his identity, nor letters of recommendation..."

"Enough!" exclaimed the Cardinal, in an impatient tone of voice.

He weighed his words before speaking and, lowering his voice as if he were speaking to himself, said:

"How can a man compare himself to God? What man would dare state that he emulates Christ? This goes beyond recklessness. This borders on defiance. No, utter foolishness."

He pronounced these words almost in a whisper. He looked at him affectionately and added:

"Francis, we are made of dust. There is no reason to be ashamed."

A somber shadow covered Francis' face. It was sadness. Brother Francis bowed his head in silence. He could not recall the last time he had been overcome with such feelings of dejection.

Thousands of thoughts crossed his mind during that moment of silence.

"The Cardinal is right," Francis said to himself. It was so obvious, and yet it had never crossed his mind. "It's utter defiance to compare oneself to Christ. Yet, all my life I've done nothing else but imitate Christ, follow in his footsteps, do as he had done. In short, live by his standards. And that is, without a doubt, defiance, and what's more, it's foolish, or plain impertinence with respect to reality."

For the first time in his life Brother Francis was unsure of himself. And, what was worse, he was letting the joy of living slip from his fingers.

* * *

Cardinal Ugolino was a sophisticated individual. He was a prudent man of uncommon ability, and extremely ambitious. He was kin to Innocent III and clearly shared his ideals. He would become the Cardinal protector of the Franciscan Order, and, later on, Pope Gregory IX for fourteen years of his life. As Pope, he would canonize Francis.

He was distinguished for his austere life. His favorite "pastimes" included communicating with the monks and men of God. He always put the interests of the Church before his own.

He lived to be almost one hundred years old. And at this time, he had already reached the venerable age of seventy. He was a master in the art of governing, a realist who always tackled the fundamental issues expediently.

* * *

Ugolino realized that sadness had taken complete possession of Francis' soul, and this caused him great pain. But he knew it was the only way to shatter that stubborn streak in Francis.

The ministers and intellectuals of the Order did not dare confront Brother Francis directly, and asked the Cardinal to use his influence and wear down the armor that kept Francis from contemplating even the slightest modification in his position. No one could possibly imagine the pain this caused the honorable prelate. But he knew it was for the good of the Church.

"Francis, my son," he said to him as they walked in the garden, "the Church, by its very existence, is the master of life. The archives in Rome tell of a number of crusades for reform that began as protests and ended in ashes. Spirit and freedom are good things, but if they fail to flow through proper channels, they lose control, overflow their banks, drag everything in their path, and finally disappear leaving absolutely nothing in their wake. I fear that something similar has happened to the Brotherhood."

* * *

There was a long silence. It could not get any worse: Francis had lost the will to fight. Instinctively, life comes to its own defense. When life no longer defends itself, it is a sign that it is no longer a life to live. Since Brother Francis did not say a word, the Cardinal continued:

"My son, have you ever seen a windmill? When the winds are channeled properly and serve a definitive purpose, what efficiency! But, on the other hand, if the winds are not channeled properly, and left to their own devices, they cannot serve any purpose and are ultimately dangerous. The Order is the wind. Francis, do you understand what I am trying to say? Three thousand men walking the face of this earth with no home, no monastery. It is impossible! Why not build some small structures? Some simple yet sturdy monasteries? What about intellectual pursuits geared toward the service of the Church? Some degree of monastic stability...?"

At this moment Brother Francis would have taken up arms, but he lacked the strength to do so. He felt incapable of clenching a sword and marching into battle. He and the Cardinal were turning on completely different orbits; they were so distant from one another that a battle was pointless. Why say anything?

Brother Francis' silence prompted the Cardinal to speak once again:

"Say something, my dear Francis."

Brother Francis lacked enthusiasm and his words lacked conviction. But soon the warmth of inspiration began to fill his heart:

"Lord Cardinal, everything has a surface and a core, an obverse and a reverse. I'm familiar with the language of the intellectuals of the Order: a small group, they say, well educated and well disciplined, at the service of the Church; life has its rhythm, they say, and it's called evolution; the program at Rivo Torto isn't geared to present-day reality; they insist on strict organization and discipline... Lord Cardinal," he said, lowering his voice, "it's the language of those who serve in battle: Power! Conquest! I use other words: Crib! Nativity! Calvary!"

Francis did not say another word and waited for the speaker to respond. This time the Cardinal stared in stunned silence. He did not know what to say. Brother Francis continued:

"The ministers' phraseology is quite fascinating. But it only touches the surface, Lord Cardinal; a mask, if you don't mind my saying so. Reality is something else entirely: no one wants to be insignificant; no one wants to appear weak on the throne or in the Church. Instinctively, we are all enemies of the Cross and the Nativity, beginning with the men of the Church. We can shed tears before the Nativity and be proud to raise the cross, even on the battlefields as crusaders often do, but we're ashamed of the Cross. I wouldn't dare call anyone a fraud, but that is utter deceit, almost blasphemous. My God, forgive me!"

* * *

Frightened, the Cardinal replied:

"My son, you have gone too far."

"Forgive me, my lord," Francis quickly replied. "In all the world, no one has sinned as much as I have sinned; I'm not passing judgment, only analyzing the facts. Delusion lives in the subconscious. No one is bad, but we live in deception. Ugly things need pretty masks. The world that revolves deep inside our hearts needs lavish costumes. The old man, the soldier that we carry inside wants to dominate us, rise to the surface, take possession of our being. That ugly instinct dons sacred vestments, and we say: baffle the Albigensian natives, annihilate the Saracens, conquer the Holy Sepulchre... At the very core lies the primitive instinct to dominate and to prevail.

"We go around saying: We must build great monasteries in which order and discipline reign. Deep down" continued Francis, "no one wants to live in huts. They say: serving the Church effectively necessitates knowledge of science. Basically, they are ashamed of appearing ignorant. They say the Church needs powerful representatives. Deep down, no one wants to appear weak. We say that God predominates and rules all things. But in reality, we want to predominate and we swell with pride, in the name of God. God is never looking down from above. He is always beside his children, ready to wash their feet, attend to their needs, or nailed to the cross, mute and powerless. We are the ones who shake the dust off old dreams of power and confuse them with the powers of God, projecting them onto him.

"They say: Bringing souls to God requires intellectual preparation. What God? To really praise God, it would be better to appear before the pulpit baaing like sheep. We shout: Men of the Order, the interests of the Church, the Glory of God! And we identify ourselves with the name of the Order, with the interests of the Church, with the Glory of God. But the truth is something else entirely: no one wants to appear small and weak. Despite lovely phrases, we're ashamed of the Crib in the manger and of the Cross on Calvary.

"Lord Cardinal, there are too many preachers in the Church who elucidate quite splendidly on the theology of the Cross. The Lord did not call upon us to preach the mystery of the Cross with brilliant words, rather to live it humbly. Roland, Olivier and other great knights did not go around singing the praises of other men. They went out and lived these adventures for themselves."

Ugolino did not say a word. He was defeated, but had yet to be totally convinced. He weighed the truth of what had been expressed and began to accept it all indiscriminately. So many things would have to change at the very foundation of the Church! It was astonishing. It was thrilling to have such charismatic individuals in the Church, but other elements were just as important.

Francis Hits the Roof

Francis returned to Assisi. Brother Pacifico directed the expedition and, in such a capacity, the "king of verse" had the honor of founding the Order in France.

In every country, the disciples were considered either heretics or lunatics, and they were treated as such. This new predicament was a formidable weapon in the hands of the opposition. Blow after blow, their experience was proof enough: Francis was incapable of governing his brothers; their very experiences proved the program to be a complete disaster. The Brotherhood could not go on like this. The disciples needed formal training, they needed to learn languages, and acquire papal documents for purposes of protection. The majority of his brothers were saddened by the outcome of the missionary expeditions, and many began to feel ashamed of their founder's naiveté and incompetence.

* * *

In 1219, a new general assembly convened at Pentecost. The opposition was gaining ground, and they conducted the gathering as they saw fit, in view of their lack of respect for Francis.

When Brother Francis arrived at the Porziuncola, he came face to face with a formidable challenge. In a few day's time, as if overnight, the dissidents had erected a chapter house next to the hermitage of St. Mary.

It was as if, in a temple of peace, someone had shouted: War! It was as if a statue in praise of Mammon had been erected in the cradle of poverty. What sacrilege! What blasphemy! On the other hand, it was also a signal that the opposition was taking the offensive and that the battle was becoming a war waged with heavy artillery.

Francis of Assisi did not say a word. At first he was overcome with sadness. But that sorrow quickly ripened into fury. At the first opportunity, he went in search of his first companions and said to them:

"To the roof."

Time had run out. Words were not enough and it was time to take action.

They climbed to the roof. Francis and his companions began to tear down the edifice. One by one, the tiles went

301

flying. The dissidents were under the impression that it was simply theatrics on their part. But when they realized that the disciples were serious about demolishing that structure, the opposition called upon residents of Assisi with whom they had spoken previously.

"Brother Francis," the citizens screamed, "the property you are destroying belongs to the municipality and the disciples have no business going near it."

Francis was perplexed. He had no knowledge of these legal matters. He realized that they were deceiving him, but he lacked the resources for a persuasive counterattack.

The Chapter opened under these somber conditions. In the first general assemblies, Francis, with his inspirational words and spontaneity, had been the heart and soul of these meetings. Joy reigned as the brothers breathed the confidence and enchantment that pervaded the assemblies.

It was no longer that way. A program was introduced along with concrete ideas; and subtle political schemes taking place behind the scenes dominated the plenary sessions. Brother Francis found it difficult to function in such an atmosphere. But what could he do? God appointed him the *father* of this group.

One More Fool in the World

On the Chapter's second day, the intellectuals launched their first premeditated offensive. It was common knowledge among the disciples that a Rule was in order and that Francis was going to write it. Therefore, the intellectuals asked for an audience with Cardinal Ugolino, who shared some of their views, and they said to him:

"Lord Cardinal, we are unwilling to accept Francis' norms for the new Rule, for we believe they are absolutely impractical. A baby speaks a particular language, wears suitable clothing, and demonstrates behavior befitting his age. Simplicity, ignorance, and ingenuity were fine for the Brotherhood of Rivo Torto. But now we are many. This immense group of brothers is also drifting. Yes, Lord Cardinal, we still are orphans with neither home nor homeland. There is only one solution: to create a solid foundation of subsistence, taking advantage of the knowledge gained from the proven experiences of the Benedictine, the Cistercian, and the Augustinian Orders; and to have the brothers dwell under those eaves. We will not accept Francis' Rule if our expert advisors are denied entrance during the drafting phase."

* * *

Ugolino summoned Francis for a meeting deep within the forest.

"My dear Francis," said the Cardinal, "a group of qualified disciples wish to consult during the drafting of the new Rule. They want you to follow the main principles of monastic observance and prescribed asceticism with regard to the reorganization of the Brotherhood."

Francis listened as the Cardinal expounded on the advantages specified in the Rules of St. Augustine and St. Benedict.

"Those rules offer solutions to the majority of the problems at hand," concluded the Cardinal.

"My brothers, my brothers. The chosen path is silence." Without saying a word, he took the prelate by the hand and they walked toward the assembly. Francis climbed onto a stump of a dead tree and began to speak. He was visibly moved, and his face betrayed a strange mixture of anger, happiness, confidence, and fear. His posture was one of a panther fiercely guarding his cubs. He raised his arms and literally exclaimed:

"My brothers, my brothers. I've taken the path of humility and simplicity.

"If this program is something new to you, let me remind you that God himself showed it to me, and by no account will I follow another.

"Don't talk to me of other Rules, nor mention St. Benedict, nor St. Augustine, nor St. Bernard, nor any other way of life, save the one that the Lord has shown me and given to me in all his mercy.

"And the Lord said that he wanted me to be one more fool walking on the face of the earth; and he had no desire to put us on another path, save this 'scientific' path.

"With regard to your wisdom and your science, may God confound you. And I hope that the Lord, in the guise of a cruel master, punishes you if you ever sway from your vocation, obliging you to turn once again onto this path."

Never before had he expressed himself in this way. This was not Francis of Assisi. A new personality, with the fires of Sinai, took possession of Brother Francis.

He was that mother who found that last ounce of energy needed to defend her children from those who wish to abduct them.

The Cardinal was flabbergasted as he stared at the ground, paralyzed, defeated. He would have given anything to be on the highest peak of the Apennines. The intellectuals and ministers did not know where to look. The first disciples composed themselves and thought:

"Finally Brother Francis has taken a firm stand!"

The intellectuals' offensive strategy fell to pieces before their very eyes. Ugolino and the ministers thought it best not to insist any further, at least for the moment. The Chapter directed their attention to other matters and issues of import.

The general chapter's greatest innovative idea was the missionary march to non-Christian lands. And what was most surprising was Francis' own decision to visit Moslem territories.

Francis assigned two trusted vicars to represent him in his absence, Matthew of Narni and Gregory of Naples. The former would reside at the Porziuncola and admit novices to the Order; and the latter would "visit the Orders and console and comfort his brothers."

One morning in June, Francis, surrounded by his brothers, embarked on the trip to Ancona, and from there he set sail to the East. When they arrived at Ancona, all his companions wanted to travel with Francis. Brother Francis said to them:

"The mariners say there isn't enough room for everyone. I can't choose because I love you all equally. Let us then allow God to manifest his will."

They called a boy who was playing nearby and Francis asked him to choose twelve brothers, pointing to each of them with his finger. Francis embarked with those brothers the boy had chosen.

Why Did He Leave?

At this point, several questions must be asked. The Brotherhood was like an active volcano. With regard to the Order, never was Francis' presence as vital as it was at this very moment. Why did he leave? To escape? Was he being unrealistic? Did he fail to see that he was acting irresponsibly?

Another question comes to mind. Two years before, in Florence, Ugolino, had told Francis that it would be unwise to leave the country in view of the threats against the Brotherhood. Given the present circumstances, the crisis had reached its most critical point. So why did the Cardinal give Francis permission to leave and journey to foreign territories, non-Christian lands no less, where his life would undoubtedly be in danger? There are many who would maliciously presume that Ugolino did so for selfish reasons: with Francis out of the way, he would be free to put things in order. In any case, to devise a satisfactory answer is almost impossible, and of no great value. On the other hand, we can adequately respond to the first question.

* * *

Francis' absence during one of the most delicate periods in the movement made him bigger than life, almost super-human. Not only was it not an escape, it was a statement that confirmed his attitude in the context of his life and his convictions.

Francis was not born to be a dialectician. Such a vocation made him feel ill at ease. He was a nonentity in the hands of subtle mental maneuvers. He saw the terrible dangers in rationalization. Francis perceived the intellectual as a skillful manipulator of words and theories (and also "theologies"), manipulating words for his own selfish interests, and doing so shamelessly and, at times, even frivolous-ly. It is called sophism or "prostitution" of the word.

Brother Francis, on the other hand, was plain and direct. Discussions made him uncomfortable. He was never "aggressive" with words, only with facts. It is interesting to note that in his final years he was not full of exhortations, but rather devoted to simple statements: "I wish to live poorly and humbly"; "I wish to obey all demands put before me"; "Now I must give good example and pray." This is called a *protestation*: to publicly express an intention. Francis illustrated this point many times and in many ways: The Lord has not called us to preach, but mainly to live.

It is in this context that we need to examine and interpret the issue of Francis' absence at a critical time in the Order's existence. What would he gain by staying at the Porziuncola, arguing incessantly with the intellectuals and the ministers?

"It's a waste of time," he said to himself.

Moreover, he would quickly lose his patience. He did not respond well to controversy.

He defended his ideals by living them, not by talking about them. Instead of getting tangled up in dialectic battles, he travelled afar to suffer for Christ and, eventually, to die for Christ in poverty and humility. He suffered persecution in peace. His ideals were reinforced and solidified by his interminable faith in them. The Franciscan program would gain respect and credibility much more in this way than it would with words and brilliant arguments. This is why he travelled to the East.

The Vicars' Revolution

Francis spent eighteen months in the East. He travelled to Damietta, intending to wage Love's battle in all camps, even before the presence of Malek al-Kamil. Actually, even the battle of truth itself was not his main concern.

"Truth does not need combat in order to gain ground," Brother Francis said to himself. "Does light need to assault darkness in order to defeat it? Light needs only to appear and darkness scatters."

Forcefully and boldly, the ministers made their presence known as soon as Francis left Ancona. They directed their attention to issues regarding scholarly preparation, reinforced disciplinary measures, and stricter standards for fasting and abstinence. Large buildings were erected everywhere.

They established a University in Bologna. Papal bulls from the Holy See assured more productive apostolates. In short, the very nature of the primitive Brotherhood was undergoing extensive alterations in the brief period of one and a half years. It was worse than Francis had imagined.

The original disciples of the Order protested these drastic innovations. The timing could not have been worse. The protesters were severely punished. Some were expelled from the Brotherhood. Others were flogged and forced to remain in conventual prisons. And some travelled to faraway lands like sad shadows, grieving the absence of their guide and shepherd.

* * *

Rumor had it that Francis had died. It is the same old story. One coward starts a rumor, and the lie or malicious story becomes the ball of snow that gathers speed as it rolls down the hill. Within a few months, the original brothers were beside themselves with grief when they heard of Brother Francis' alleged death. The Brotherhood had lost its orientation, caught in chaos and anarchy.

However, not everyone believed the malicious lie about his death. At the very least, they thought it best to ascertain its veracity.

The original disciples appointed a Brother Stephen to travel to the East, to find Francis and inform him of the Brotherhood's present situation, that is, if he was still alive. Without seeking permission from the Vicars, Stephen set sail and traversed the oceans, and after many months he found Francis in Saint John of Acre.

He gave Francis a detailed account of the Brotherhood's critical situation and showed him examples of the new constitutions. They prepared a small feast in celebration of their reunion. There was meat on the table, even if meat was strictly prohibited in accordance with the new constitutions. Francis turned to Peter Cataneo and asked:

"Peter, what do we do?"

"You are the authority here, Brother Francis," Peter replied.

And Francis said:

"According to the Gospel, we are free to eat whatever is placed on the table. So, let's eat the meat!"

Francis and four of his brothers returned immediately to Italy, arriving in Venice at the end of July.

Science and Its Domain

When he left Venice and passed through Bologna, he saw with his own eyes the revolution that had altered the Brotherhood during his absence. Lombardy's provincial, John Staccia, had erected a school, similar to a medieval College, in the heart of the city. The exact proportions of this University are not known, but its size and grandeur were extremely impressive in comparison to the disciples' modest huts.

Francis surmised intuitively what had taken place. Basically, it had to do with pride, the number one enemy of evangelical simplicity. The provincial of Lombardy established a College as a dare, modelled after the Friars Preachers' colleges.

During the Middle Ages, Bologna was the intellectual center of Italy and of Christianity. From the very beginning, the Dominican friars had secured a position of power in this intellectual city. Here, their founding saint, Dominic Guzman, was to die the following year. From their inception, the Order of Preachers had established general quarters in Bologna, and the Friars Preachers were renowned throughout

309

Italy. In 1219, in keeping with the object for which they were founded, the Friars Preachers had built and organized a splendid University of theology, in order to create a balance with the University which focused primarily on liberal arts studies and underrated the significance of the sacred sciences.

Compared to the stature of the Dominican friars, the Friars Minor were more or less eclipsed and "did not look like much." Francis had proclaimed a thousand times: our purpose in the Church is to live like the poor and the insignificant. Countless times, he had perceived the scorn his brothers would feel in appearing so inferior.

"How difficult it is to follow our vocation!" Francis would say to himself. "Our purpose in the Church is to imitate the Poor and Humble Christ. But there will be those who will find just cause to imitate the Doctor and Scholar Christ. The Lord did not call upon us to summon an intellectual following or to defend the reputation of the Church. In order to defend the Church, one must prepare brilliant arguments, and that in turn necessitates a solid intellectual preparation. But we have not been called to defend the Gospel, rather to live it. Many of our brothers look with envy at institutions that have more ambitious goals in mind. They fail to understand the essence of our vocation. They talk about efficacy. But deep down, they're ashamed of our insignificance and ignorance."

* * *

Francis was indignant but he was also hurt. He decided not to enter the University of the Friars Minors and instead chose to seek lodging in the monastery of the Preaching Friars. There, he composed himself and thought about the attitude he must adopt.

"I can't show weakness," he thought to himself. "They're liable to confuse mercy with complacency. One must learn from one's mistakes. Our brothers are in Oxford, Paris, Copenhagen, in the most important cities in the Christian world. If I fail to show them vigor and enthusiasm, the spirit of the Porziuncola will die out in less than a year."

He decided to call on the provincial of Lombardy.

"Brother," he said to him, "how could you destroy a way of life that the Lord himself has revealed to me, that prayer is more important to my brothers than intellectual pursuits?"

Afterwards, in the name of blessed obedience, he obliged all the brothers, including the sick, to vacate the intellectual establishments. As if that were not enough, he called on high to *curse* the principal protagonist, John Staccia. Never before had Francis taken such a cruel stance. No one suffered more than he at this moment, and his lips burned as he called for the chastisement of heaven. He was aware that some considered kindness to be weakness and that the most effective measure was aggressive action. He betrayed every fiber of his being with this dramatic display of force.

There was more. Some time later, when friends of Lombardy's provincial asked Francis to remove the *curse*, he said it was too late because it had already been confirmed by Christ himself.

This reaction is typical of a soul that has had a premonition of death. It is called a spasm. Life progresses in this manner. When any kind of life "smells" a lethal agent in the air, all defenses are set in motion and act aggressively to arrest it.

* * *

Francis realized intuitively that just one University could destroy his ideals since only one event is needed to

311

set off a chain reaction of comparable events. Francis thought:

"We need only to live in temporary huts. Because ministers seek efficacy, they need to live in solid, sturdy mansions. Very soon they'll need libraries with volumes and volumes of books. Later on, they'll concentrate on subtle intellectual maneuvers to demonstrate the rationale behind this efficacy, all the while losing sight of simplicity and therefore complicating their lives more and more. And if they're told to make any kind of modification, they'll argue every case in point until their position is seen as the only feasible one. They'll conjure up brilliant arguments to justify the unjustifiable, always making sure that they're one step ahead of the game. And they'll try to balance various theories on the head of a pin. They'll be praised for their knowledge, and they'll challenge those who are recognized for greater accomplishments. Knowledge will make them feel powerful and they'll use all sorts of power tactics to dominate their brothers. They'll forget to serve at table and wash their brother's feet.

"The ideal binomial would be the sanctity-science relationship. But it's so difficult! It parallels this thought: Can the wealthy 'enter' the Kingdom? Yes, they can; but it's very difficult."

Brother Francis was not opposed to learning. He said "theologians communicate spirit and life and we should honor them." Among his first companions, some had received degrees in Bologna and, at the same time, they were excellent Friars Minor.

On the other hand, he had seen many brothers who opposed scholarship outright, not as a conscious choice but due to pure laziness. These particular disciples would gladly pay homage to the goddess "Dolce Far Niente." He had seen too many brothers lead a mediocre existence, lashing out abusively against scholarship.

"A conceited scholar is bad enough," he thought to himself, "but an illiterate without a soul is worse."

Without Entering the Porziuncola

The news that Francis was alive and back in Italy filled his followers with delight. Those first disciples, persecuted by the Vicars, came out of hiding from their mountain retreats and a tremendous furor gripped the Brotherhoods all over Italy. Loyal supporters thought that Brother Francis would immediately denounce the Vicars, take charge of the Brotherhood, and that everything would simply go back to normal.

Francis, on the other hand, thought something else entirely. His intuition never failed him. The revolution that had ensued during his absence gave a clear indication that he faced a strong opposition from the powerful and influential papal Curia. The Brotherhood was enormous, dispersed, and, above all, divided. It was in urgent need of someone in authority, an ecclesiastical figure who could build bridges between enemy territories.

Francis of Assisi was not the kind of person who could direct them. He was born to inspire and to love, but not to direct. Love can engender a town, but it cannot direct its path. And Brother Francis began to concede, abdicating his position. He was also a natural born fighter, but he was tired of fighting.

During that time, he had had a dream. There was a small, ugly hen, no larger than a dove. It was surrounded by defenseless, black chicks. The hen could not shelter the mass of chicks under her protective wings. That was the dream.

Upon awakening, he related the dream to his disciples and said:

"The hen in that dream is me. As you can see, I'm small, not at all attractive, and I have black hair. I'm nothing: I'm incompetent and uneducated. The dove as represented by the hen's size is symbolic of evangelical simplicity, the foundation of our establishment. The chicks are the brothers the Lord has given me. There are just too many! Being who I am—nothing special—I can't protect you nor defend you. I know now what I have to do: I will go to the feet of Holy Mother Church and she will protect my brothers."

And they left for Rome. As they came in contact with the various Brotherhoods, Francis began to realize that the Vicars' iniquities were greater than he had suspected. Everywhere he went, Brother Francis' divine presence was the spark that rekindled the ashes left in the wake of the Vicars' devastating exploits.

He crossed the Umbrian valley and was only a few kilometers from the Porziuncola but he refused to enter the beloved retreat. He wanted to avoid any encounter with the Vicars. He had learned how to deal with confrontations, but he feared losing his composure.

He learned that the Holy Father, Pope Honorius III, was residing at that time in Orvieto, so he walked in that direction.

* * *

He was granted an audience with the Pope and, kneeling reverently and affectionately at his feet, he said:

"May the peace of the Lord be with you, Most Holy Father."

"God bless you, my son," responded the Pope.

Suddenly, Brother Francis felt safe and secure. It felt very strange. For years his soul had endured the weight of oppression. But now, as he found himself before the Holy Father, the heartache disappeared.

Despite the fact that his eyes were ailing him, they recovered their transparency and, as he looked at the Pope, he said confidently:

"Holy Father, the Lord God has placed us on a very high throne, a throne that is too high for us poor little men. Most Holy Father, I'm aware of your responsibilities: everyday you're faced with grave and urgent problems. How important can our problems be? They may lack urgency, but nonetheless, they are extremely important to us. We have tried everything to no avail. Where else can we turn but to the Father?"

"My son," Pope Honorius III replied, "there are many Cardinals here in the Curia who can assist you in my place and help find solutions to your problems."

"We beseech you," Francis responded. "Assign someone specific to this task who will be our 'pope.' We will be submissive and reverent, as though we were in the presence of the Holy Father. We will relate our problems to him, consult with him, and follow his advice. He will be the 'protector, governor, and supervisor of the Brotherhood.'"

"My son, whom do you suggest that we appoint?" inquired the Pope.

"There is one person in particular," Francis replied, "who is extremely sympathetic to our cause. He is much more than a friend. He is almost a father to all of us. He cares for the Brotherhood very much, even to the point of denying himself. He's extremely intelligent and quite capable. But what is most captivating is his faith. I'm speaking about Cardinal Ugolino."

From that moment on, Ugolino was the representative of the Holy See for Francis and for the Brotherhood. Francis addressed him as "my apostolic lord." He was an experienced man of affairs and advised them on all matters; he was the supreme arbitrator between rival parties. With patience and perseverance he accomplished the impossible: he bridged the intellectual gap which divided the founder and the ministers. Ugolino transformed many of Francis' idealistic notions into the possible and the practical. At his insistence, Francis set himself to revise the rule.

His Resignation

Francis had contracted a mysterious illness in the East that had damaged his eyes. The sun's brightness made him squint in pain. He needed someone at his side to lead him by the hand.

He went to the East in search of martyrdom, and the Lord showed him the martyrdom of a soul that was burning ever so slowly. Nothing compares to the martyrdom of a lost soul. He was tormented by feelings of failure, crucified by feelings of incompetence. At times he adopted the conscience of a sinner. How could he possibly look onto the world and speak of love if love did not reign in his soul? How could he be a messenger of peace if he himself was not at peace?

He felt the irresistible desire to return to the hermitages and curl up beside God, lay at his feet, and in this way reclaim the peace he had lost. But the Lord had given him a host of brothers. Francis had not chosen them. He simply had accepted them from the hands of God. He had accepted them as they were, with their virtues, their vices, and he could not abandon them. To abandon them would be to abandon the Lord.

Day by day, the reason for his agony was becoming more apparent. There was no doubt that he was obsessed with something. But what? His soul was gripped with terror, and peace took flight like a frightened bird. But it wanted to come back. He perceived that the road back to peace was one of total surrender, needing to make himself smaller and smaller, to divest himself of everything. As the poorest of the poor, to take refuge in the arms of God and to lay all his failures, even his sins, in God's lap. Peace would return when absolutely nothing "belonged to him."

* * *

They returned to the Porziuncola. Francis could not remain as the active director. A few years before, just a look, a loving word was enough, and the disciples would intuitively understand Francis' ideals and put them into practice. But now, they needed a director, and Francis could no longer serve in that function.

Moreover, events that had transpired during the latter part of his life filled him with doubts. If, during the course of many years, a sensitive man like Francis constantly hears: You are no good, that idea is worthless, we must revise the program, etc., that man begins to lose his sense of security and self-worth, blow after blow. The prophet vacillates. Inspiration no longer blooms with any sense of joy or spontaneity. Convictions begin to crumble. The *chosen one* is consumed by feelings of insecurity: Could I possibly be seeking myself? I must suffer and be joyful if I am to be a humble brother. Sabatier says that the most humble of men are always in danger of losing sight of their convictions in their struggle to avoid *affirmation*.

* * *

He decided then to resign. It would be another chapter in the steady movement toward total surrender. He followed his heart and appointed the man who would direct the Order in his place: Peter Cataneo, his first companion together with Brother Bernard. Now more than ever, Peter Cataneo was the best choice for minister general of the Order.

The Chapter's change in command took place on September 29, 1220. Francis found himself in a particularly sensitive mood, a depression that robbed him of his energies. On that day, the man who had always walked in sunshine saw nothing but dark clouds on the horizon. Chroniclers indicate that it was a very dark moment in his life. He said:

"Brothers, I'm dead to you from this day forward. Here's Peter Cataneo, whom we will obey, including myself, from now on."

He was accustomed to dramatizing most of the events in his life. But here, tragedy had mixed with melodrama.

He knelt humbly at the feet of the new minister, and promised him solemn obedience and reverence. The disciples could not contain their tears. They cried openly and were not ashamed to do so. The scene is hard to explain: his brothers were overcome with feelings of abandonment, as if Brother Francis had truly passed away.

Francis was a sensitive man. He sensed immediately their reaction to his words. He got up, stood before his brothers, raised his arms and his eyes to heaven, and said:

"Lord God, I place this family in your hands, the family you have entrusted to me. My sweet Jesus, as you know, due to my illness, I'm in no condition to continue as head of this family. Therefore, I'm placing them in the hands of the ministers. They will answer to you on the day of judgment if they fail in their promise, due to negligence, poor example or disposition."

* * *

Brother Francis did not sleep that night. He was overcome with an ambiguous feeling that was impossible to decipher. He felt as if he had been stripped of his own clothes or robbed of his own skin. It was similar to that feeling of relief when a weight is finally lifted from one's shoulders, or something akin to what parents feel when their adult children leave home. It was like stealing the soul and leaving nothing behind except the clothes on one's back. It was like losing control of one's own destiny, not knowing what tomorrow may bring. The multitude would take on his name: *Franciscans*. He belonged to them, but they no longer belonged to him.

That night, when all the various emotions had dissipated, Francis of Assisi began to feel light and free. He waded into God's ocean completely naked, and was able to say:

"You are my Good. You are my Comfort. You are my Security."

It had been quite a long time since he had felt such peace. But the dark night was not yet over.

* * *

During the autumn and winter of 1220, Francis dedicated his time to drafting another Rule. On March 10, 1221, Brother Francis faced a new and troubling crisis: Peter Cataneo had failed miserably in his office as minister general. It was an irreparable loss, the consequences of which were dire because the individual who succeeded such a *Franciscan* was one who had very little of Francis in him, Brother Elias Bombarone.

He was minister for three years, the most delicate time in the development of the Franciscans. All writers, ancient and modern, violently attack Brother Elias. I am not certain whether such animosity is justified. He was a controversial and mysterious figure. Before he wrote his major work, he was a prisoner of his own contradictory beliefs: on the one hand, he regarded as high treason the tribute in memory of Brother Francis of Assisi, and, on the other hand, he was glad that the world would want to pay homage to such a man.

We are under the impression that during the time that Francis lived, Elias did not openly oppose the founder whom he apparently respected, admired, and loved. Francis respected him and placed him in his confidence. How could a man as perceptive as Francis be blind to Elias' true personality? The writer is tempted to think that Elias was an excellent politician and very cunning, always advertising his best qualities with self-promotion in mind. But to scrutinize him in this manner presupposes a deliberate aim which should not be pursued under any circumstances.

He was a notary by profession, an intellectual, and a graduate of the University of Bologna. He had that human touch, that amicable way with people, and personal charm. His sympathizers praised him and his adversaries attacked him without mercy. After Francis' death, Brother Elias raised the banners of greatness and efficacy. During his life, the Order had been divided into seventy-two provinces around the world. His political tactics fell under scrutiny and he was forced to resign. He antagonized the Pope and was excommunicated. He did penance and died reconciled to the Church.

Rule of 1221

Although Francis had resigned his office as minister general, he was still the father and legislator of the Brotherhood. Moreover, it seems that, as a result of having left office, he grew in moral and spiritual stature and the disciples venerated him more than ever.

Accompanied by Caesar Spira, a man well versed in the Scriptures, Francis retired to a hermitage in order to translate his ideals into law. Until now, he had been a man of words and of good works. Nevertheless, he knew that the spoken word was at the mercy of the winds and that committing the word to paper gave it permanence. Since he was free of the obligations imposed by his former office, he now had the time to deliberate on his ideas and put them into words.

The intellectuals were hoping that the Rule would be a legislation, a formal transaction. They thought Brother Francis had learned his lesson and that the blows he had withstood during the course of his life had taken the rough edges off his stubborn nature.

They were wrong. In the extensive Rule of 1221, Brother Francis poured his soul without any inhibitions. It was not a legislative document. It was an impassioned and provocative appeal for a response to Love.

He who wrote it was not a legislator: he was a father who was making an appeal, touching the most sensitive chords to ensure a chivalric and unconditional following of Jesus Christ. Here and there, he probed deeply in order to awaken and free energies for a proper response to Love.

The Rule was composed of twenty-three long chapters and more than one hundred excerpts from the Bible. Like an electric storm, it was full of primitive and opposing energies where all of his ideals were clearly manifested with neither reticence nor circumspection, even those that had been preserved and nourished within the fibers of his soul since the night in Spoleto.

He insisted, persuaded, begged, sobbed. He exalted and went down on his hands and knees to implore. He reached out his arms in order to convince. The tone was sustained at its sharpest pitch. There was too much monotony and repetition. He adopted a careless and indifferent tone with respect to grammatical rules and elements of style. He completely ignored ministerial conventions, and nowhere does it resemble a legislative document. It is the outpouring of St. Francis' soul.

* * *

In the final days of May, 1221, the Chapter assembled, the principal object being the approval of the Rule before submitting it to the Holy See for consideration. More than three thousand disciples gathered, including the novices.

Expectation filled the air. The intellectuals maintained their belligerent attitudes. But this time, since they were captained by Brother Elias, they decided to adopt a more moderate stance and, above all, to keep their emotions in check, exhibiting only a cold, political posture.

But Francis was not a politician. The months he had spent in prayer in his mountain retreat helped to reawaken his bold, forthright manner, and he had regained his serenity while submerged in God's ocean. He descended the slopes ready for the final assault on the open battlefield. These aggressive words were his preamble to the debate: "Blessed be the Lord who has prepared my hands for battle."

* * *

Several copies of the Rule were distributed among those present, particularly among the ministers.

In the new manuscript, the primitive Rule remained intact. The new document reflected the spirit of Rivo Torto. Holding corporate property was prohibited. The precept of manual labor remained intact. If the disciples worked in foreign residences they were not to perform the duties of a secretary nor of an overseer. Instead, they would take on *minor* work (labor). They were to be kind even to common criminals. They should never be sad, rather happy and congenial. They were not to mount horses, nor own beasts of burden. There were norms for missionaries travelling to lands of the infidel. They could eat whatever was served at table. And the most controversial mandate: if a minister gives orders that go against our ideals, the disciples are not obliged to obey. And more controversial still: if the ministers deviate from the spirit of our word, the disciples should correct them, and if they should fail to abide by the rule, they were to be denounced in the General Chapter.

* * *

Clearly, the document was not an "armistice," nor did it resemble a peace treaty. On the contrary, it was a direct challenge to those who wished to alter the spirit of the Brotherhood.

The last two items in particular were dangerous weapons in the hands of the disciples directed at possible innovations. But such weapons could also detonate in the hands of the disciples themselves. There was a massive amount of virtual explosives in the last two articles that could very well become the seed of anarchy and chaos. Francis was clearly aware of these possibilities but he decided to take the risk despite the consequences. He believed it was the only way to arrest the ministers' effrontery.

The learned and legalists proceeded with extreme sagacity. Their tactic was to *stall*. They knew that so long as the Holy See did not officially sanction the Rule, they were under no obligation to concede, and Francis did not have the authority to impose the law.

The intellectuals did not lose sight of the fact that the majority of the disciples present had been received into the Brotherhood by Francis himself. Never was Brother Francis held in such high esteem as he was at this moment, and not until this moment had the Brotherhood imparted so much love and affection. The intellectuals knew this very well.

To wage a battle under these circumstances was self-defeating. Francis needed only to open his mouth, to express a few impassioned words, and the majority of those in attendance would not have hesitated to defend his cause to the bitter end. The intellectuals also took this into account. What were they to do?

Do not get impatient. Put the notion of confrontation aside. Maintain a cold and calculated stance, and do not provoke the idealists. Let a few days pass with minimal regard to the matter at hand, and distract the assembly with other pressing issues. Treat Francis with reverence and affection at all times. With regard to the Rule, deal with the issues in a surreptitious manner, persuading the Cardinal protector to enter into private negotiations with Francis.

And they proceeded in this manner. Francis of Assisi, the man given to transparency and not to politics, fell for the scheme and was putty in the hands of the ministers.

* * *

What occurred behind the scenes went on for months. The work was done patiently and extensively. Some of the ministers, in collaboration with Cardinal Ugolino, expressed the following in the course of several private conversations:

"Brother Francis, the spirit of Rivo Torto is not what is being called into question. An adequate framework is precisely what is needed in order to preserve that ideal. The Rule will be examined in Rome. Approval or reprobation will depend on their judgment.

"The Rule that you have drawn up is an excellent spiritual program, but it needs a practical set of rules for normal men, not heroes. In addition, it lacks what all legislative documents require: it needs to be concise and precise, without which characteristics the jurists for the Holy See will never grant the papal bull of approval."

The Agony at Fonte Colombo

After many months of deliberation, Francis took Brother Leo and the jurist, Brother Bonitus, to the Rieti Valley.

"Mountain air is good for me, Brother Leo," said Francis. "There you inhale peace, and God is so tangible that you can almost touch his hand. At times I feel I've taken the wrong route. I should have just tucked myself into the cracks and crevices of the Apennines. But the Lord took my hand and placed me in the middle of this numerous group of people. Who can resist God? In the heavens or on earth, there is nothing more sacrosanct than his will. God and the lepers give me the most joy. But that Will has decided something else for me. It's fine, whatever it is."

Francis had his ups and downs. At times he recovered his normal emotional state. During those moments, it was like walking in the country on a summer day: the earth was clean, fresh and bathed in peace. Francis was like an angel who had just taken flight from the hands of God.

On other occasions, the atmosphere was charged with electrical energy and bolts of lightning, especially when he received word of various maneuvers unfolding within the intellectual circle. But this kind of capriciousness hurt him deeply and he suffered greatly due to his reactions. He would lie prostrate on the bare earth and ask God for forgiveness:

"Accept me as I am."

* * *

Francis was overcome with joy when they reached the Rieti Valley. They walked the open road to the right of the valley and, bordering the sides of the mountain, they crossed the plain. Near the summit of Mt. Rainerio there was a dwelling belonging to a pious woman called Columba who gave Francis nourishment and solitude. The mountain was covered with ash trees, evergreens, oaks, fir trees, and beech trees. It was called Fonte Colombo.

They descended about one hundred meters alongside a sharp and dangerous slope and came to a rocky area with a natural cavern nearby. A waterfall cascaded to the right, and in the distance the majestic peaks of Mt. Terminillo, which are snowcapped for many months of the year, stood bare and tall. Francis wrote the definitive Rule amidst the natural wonders that surrounded them.

He began the task at hand. He had received precise instructions from the Cardinal protector, and some of the ministers gave him spiritual guidance with respect to cutting some of the clauses, trimming the lyrical phraseology, weeding out the biblical references, and adopting a legal style that focused on brevity and precision.

Very few people in the world are as useless as Brother Francis was with regard to drafting a legislative document. He was a poet and a prophet, his words needed limitless space. And now they were confining him within the narrow borders of legislation. It was like bottling the wind.

It was one of the most agonizing months of his life. He felt as if his ideals were being ripped apart. It was an extremely painful relinquishment. He did not understand laws, nor canons, nor clauses. He only understood the spirit. For Francis, the Word of God had more force than one hundred canons. For Francis, the expression to "exhort in Jesus Christ" had infinitely more power than a "command out of obedience." Every biblical reference that was eliminated hurt him like an open wound. He experienced an almost agonizing pain when told to eliminate Jesus' "commands" which had been the body and blood of his life since the days at the Porziuncola; for example: "take nothing with you on your journey..."

The agonies he suffered reached a climax and his soul fell into the darkest chasms of the night. God was depriving him of all consolations, and poor Francis was walking the thin line between life and death. Between fasts and penances, Brother Francis pounded on God's door, but God only answered with silence.

Normally, the world around him was invigorating and inviting. Robins were everywhere, nightingales and blackbirds performed an indescribable ballet as they flew from thickets to brooms, from chestnut trees to junipers, all under a radiant blue sky with perfumed gusts of thyme and rosemary blowing in the wind. But Brother Francis was impervious to it all. He was like one in agony, insensitive to any stimulus.

Something even more agonizing was gnawing at his soul. Cutting, modifying or eliminating the clauses that were so dear to him reawakened in his memory the painful battles he had fought against the intellectuals years ago to preserve those very same clauses. As he wrote, he relived so many sad memories...

The Lord abandoned his *chosen one* at the bottom of the ravine so that he might struggle alone with his own shadow in total darkness. As with the Anointed Jesus, Francis needed to drink it all, up to the very last dregs in this cup of bitterness. When the last sip reached his lips, the *chosen one* would find himself nowhere but in the land of the resurrection.

The Misplaced Rule

The task was completed within a few months. Brother Francis returned to the Porziuncola with his companions and gave the manuscript to the ministers for their evaluation.

It was a matter of delicacy and chivalry that prompted him to retire to his retreat in the *cells*. He felt that his presence might place undo pressure on the ministers with regard to their review of the new Rule.

After several days, Francis descended Mt. Subasio and entered the Porziuncola. The ministers avoided him and no one mentioned the document. This strange silence prompted Brother Francis to take the initiative and he inquired allusively about the new Rule. Some of the ministers evaded his glance; someone gave an evasive response and everyone attended to other matters that had nothing to do with the Rule.

Brother Elias motioned to Francis to leave the assembly. He took him deep into the forest, and said:

"Brother Francis, I regret having to tell you that the document has been misplaced and we do not know who is at fault."

Brother Francis did not say a word. He asked Elias to leave him alone, and he returned to the assembly. The stratagem was terribly humiliating to Brother Francis. That was the kind of thing one does with a seven-year-old. Actually, Francis was a child, but in the best sense of the word. Regarding perception and sagacity, the intellectuals were no match for Francis.

What had they done with the manuscript? Apparently, the intellectuals were dissatisfied and one of them, Brother Elias no doubt, threw it into the flames. What were they proposing with such a "solution"? To exhaust Brother Francis' patience? To stall until Francis' dying day so that nothing of his intents would be written?

Brother Francis stayed in the forest for several hours. He was distressed and very sad. He was not a politician, but he was extremely perceptive and he realized instantly what had occurred and its significance. His soul was in darkness. He fell prostrate to the ground and extended his arms in the shape of the cross.

He said:

"Dear God, I can't go on. Take your hand away; it's too heavy. Birds of prey are circling above me. I'm on the edge of the earth and I don't see anyone. I'm blind and I need your hand to guide me. Take me if there is no ray of light for me. All I have left is one star: your mercy."

* * *

His soul, which used to shine so brightly, had entered a
state of confusion and, at times, of contradiction. An obedience that used to be clothed in joy and chivalry was now
dressed in funereal tones. He approached a loyal group of
disciples and said:

"Take a corpse, leave it wherever you wish, and it will
not protest. It will not make a sound, regardless of where
you lay it. It will not object if you move it. Put it on a chair.
It will not complain. Throw a purple cloak on it, and it will
look paler still."

But sooner or later, he began to contradict himself. A
disciple travelled from Germany to meet Francis and to
consult with him. Finally, the German said to him:

"Brother Francis, I'd like to ask a favor of you: if
someday our brothers stray from the Rule, I ask your permission to separate myself from them so that I may follow
it to the letter."

These words filled Francis with joy. He responded:

"Be advised, it is Christ who will grant you authorization, and, therefore, so will I, and with great pleasure. And
laying his hands on him, he added, "You will be a priest until
your dying day, according to the Order of Melchizedek."

In view of this standard of judgment, he contradicted
himself once again when he gave the following command:
"Although the superior may make contradictory demands
for the good of the spirit, our brothers should never separate
themselves from him, and the more inconsistent the demands, the more they should love him."

Brother Francis had grown tired of listening to details
concerning new and audacious ideas presented by the ministers. One day, he raised his arms, his voice and his eyes to
the heavens, and said:

"For you, Most Holy Lord Jesus Christ, for the celestial court, and for me, a small and insignificant man, may all those who direct by bad example, who shame and destroy what you have built and continue to build with the holy brothers of the Order, may they be accursed."

Actually, the dissident brothers were very few in number, but they were very influential. If an election had taken place, almost all would have voted unanimously in favor of Francis. But a legal governing body had placed itself between Francis and his brothers, and issues of extreme importance were in the hands of the dissident ministers who were politically-oriented intellectuals, some possessing a worldly spirit.

Clare Lends a Hand

Nothing in the world escapes the perceptive qualities of a woman. Clare knew that Brother Francis had a troubled heart, and with her feminine courage she decided to save Francis from himself.

Francis had not visited the Poor Clares in several months, years perhaps.

"I have nothing to give them," Francis said to himself. "Those daughters of God, those women, can see far beyond the scope of human vision. What will they see in me? Only sadness and desolation. I can mask my sadness in front of Brother Leo, even in front of Brother Elias, but never before Sister Clare. I have nothing to give them."

One day, Clare called to Brother Leo and said to him:

"My dear Leo, please express the following to Francis on my behalf: Brother Francis, you ignited our flames. And now you let them die out? You opened our mouths. And now you leave us without bread? You planted these little plants. And now you don't water them? Are you by chance going against your word as a gentlemen? Have you forgotten that we are your Poor Clares? We need you. Who knows, you may even need us. A love feast awaits you. Come."

* * *

Brother Leo transmitted Clare's message to Francis. Brother Francis opened his eyes wide, smiled broadly, and instantly the immortal melodies of the knight-errant filled his soul. He was a different man.

"Oh, yes," exclaimed Brother Francis. "Clare is right. I ignited a flame. Clare was a spark from my flame. Her flame produced many flames, and we have all entered the garden of Love. Yes. I sparked the Great Adventure. I'm responsible. Clare is right. It's wrong to plant roses and not cultivate them. I can't allow those torches to die out. Brother Leo, I'm going to St. Damian. Tell Clare to string together a garland of violets."

"Brother Francis, flowers are not in bloom this time of year."

"Who knows?" Francis replied. "There's every possibility that spring may be waiting for us at St. Damian."

Upon arriving at St. Damian, Clare welcomed Brother Francis with these words:

"We have waited a lifetime, Father Francis."

"Sister Clare, St. Damian is an amphora filled with perfume," Francis rejoined. "Everyday, I raise this amphora before the face of the Lord. You are my children, and live within me. Forget you? It's not possible. Did I not give birth to you and place you in the arms of the Immortal God?"

"Many days and nights have passed since we saw you last," Clare exclaimed.

"Is it so important to be physically present?" said Brother Francis. "Sister Clare, the spirit is what matters. Moreover, you are guided when you take your first steps. Afterwards, you walk without anyone's help. As for the rest, the eyes are perilous windows. Through them, one's interior is scrutinized, and sometimes only shadows reign within."

* * *

"Finally, he's where I want him to be," Clare said to herself.

Here, Clare took the initiative. She was extremely intuitive. The disciples were able to provide only scarce information, but from those fragments Clare pieced together Francis' interior with no difficulty whatsoever. Clare looked at him lovingly, and with a delicate modulation of her voice, as if she were speaking to herself, the words fell from her lips like a shower falling on scorched earth.

"Father Francis," she began, "I'm your little plant. You gave me everything I have, everything I know. You're in the middle of the forest, Father Francis. How can you have any perspective? I'm looking at things from a distance, and for this reason I see things clearly and have more of a perspective. I fear that your problem is one of appreciation.

"A few days ago I read that an old convent was divided over a kitten. One sister grew very attached to that kitten. Those sisters who treated the kitten with disdain were treated disdainfully by the 'owner,' until one day the convent was divided between those who appreciated the kitten and those who didn't. The kitten became the convent's only 'god.' Whether this is a true story or an allegory is not important.

"Father Francis, it's a tiny matter of appreciation! We grow very attached to the *thing* we love. At times I'm not sure whether we grow attached to it or it to us. I doubt there is any difference between the two.

333

"When the *thing* we love is threatened, that is, when there exists the possibility that we will lose it, we grow all the more attached to it. The greater the threat, the greater our attachment. The greater our attachment, the greater the *thing* becomes. Until finally, there is not a *thing* of value in the convent save the kitten."

For Francis, Clare's words were like a refreshing shower on a summer day.

"Father Francis, the ideal, the Order, Poverty are very important *things*. But raise your eyes a little; look around you and you'll find a reality that is beyond measure: God. If you look to God, all your worries will appear insignificant. It's a tiny matter of appreciation! How important are our ideals in comparison to the eternity and immensity of God? When we look at the height of the Almighty, our fears become ridiculous shadows. At that height, things acquire a real perspective, and peace fills the soul."

Clare approached him and said very softly:

"Dear Francis, God! God!"

Clare expressed herself so passionately and honestly that Francis suddenly found himself free of the chains that bound him. Words could not express the joy he felt. Upon realizing this, Clare continued while Francis revelled in this infinite reality, God, a happiness he had never felt before.

* * *

"Father Francis, you were an uncompromising workman. You burned, raked, demolished houses, money, parents, social position. You advanced further still: you conquered the ridiculous, the fear of disapproval. You scaled the mountain, reaching the highest peak of Perfect Happiness. You renounced everything so that God could become your Everything. But at this moment, if a dark shadow still reigns within you, it is a sign that God is not yet your Everything; herein lies your sadness. In short, you have attributed to God what is actually *your* work.

"Only one thing stands in the way of Perfect Happiness: detach yourself from the work of God and attach yourself to *God alone*, completely free.

"You're not totally poor yet, Brother Francis, and for this reason you are not yet totally free, nor happy.

"Let yourself go and take that mortal leap: *God is and that's enough.* Let go of your ideal and enjoy with total abandon this Reality which surpasses all reality: *God is and that's enough.* Then you will know Perfect Happiness, Perfect Freedom, and Perfect Joy."

* * *

Clare said no more. Tears streamed down Brother Francis' face. An intoxicating feeling, very much like witnessing the dawn of a new world, took possession of Francis. He was indescribably happy.

"*God is and that's enough,*" Brother Francis said repeatedly.

He got up very slowly and, as he stared at the ground, he said joyously for the last time:

"*God is and that's enough. This is Perfect Happiness.*"

He turned as he said these words and, without looking at Clare, he left in tears. Clare was also sobbing.

Chapter Six

THE LAST SONG

Mission Accomplished

The manuscript for the Rule of 1223 had disappeared. It had to be rewritten. Therefore, Francis, Brother Leo, and Brother Bonitus scaled the high forests of Fonte Colombo once again. Amidst the savage and sublime beauty surrounding them, between fasting and prayers, Francis finished the definitive Rule. He made certain to include those items specified by the Cardinal protector.

The new Rule was drafted following guidelines proposed by Cardinal Ugolino. It was a precise and concise legislation stipulating explicit precepts and prohibitions. It was four times shorter than the Rule of 1221, with only six biblical references instead of the one hundred or so cited in the earlier version. The manuscript was edited by various persons, assuring a more polished and canonical result. The lyrical and dramatic style apparent in the Rule of 1221 was absent in the new manuscript.

It represented substantially the spirit and manner of life for which Francis had always stood. Absolute poverty was still a must. The disciples should be docile and humble, and should abstain from passing judgment. Labor would be the principal means of sustenance, begging for alms only when necessary. They would not own homes or anything for that matter. They would be brothers in their poverty, expressing their needs to one another, and caring for one another as a mother cares for her child.

* * *

In May of 1223, Francis attended the general assembly at the Porziuncola. Sources do not say to whether there were agreements or disagreements with regard to the Rule. Apparently, the intellectuals avoided public disputes and carried out any negotiations behind closed doors.

Within a few months time, Brother Francis travelled to Rome and placed the document in the hands of the Holy See. Shortly thereafter, the Rule received solemn approbation by Honorius III on November 29, 1223. Ever since that time, the Rule has constituted the official legislation of the Friars Minor.

* * *

The *chosen one* had come to the end of his painful and transfiguring pilgrimage. According to ancient chroniclers, Brother Francis listened to and accepted the *I am.* In fact, according to biographers, peace flooded Francis' entire being when he heard the Almighty express the following words:

"Little one, why do you worry? *I am* the one who made you a shepherd... *I am* your brace and main beam... *I am* the one who entrusted you with this flock... *I am* the one who chose you... *I am* the one who will defend you and keep you..."

In other words, Brother Francis let himself go, taking the mortal leap and accepting profoundly and happily the

God is and that's enough that was communicated to him in the preceding chapter. He was forever free of any worry or sorrow.

His desolation vanished. At that moment Francis of Assisi was almost a citizen of paradise.

* * *

He negotiated his first few climbs alone. Then the Lord gave him disciples and he guided their steps. He gave them an ideal to live by and infused them with a soul. He then established a governing body for them. Now he had finally given them a rule for life. His work with the disciples came to an end, save praying for them and teaching by example.

"I have only a few years left," Brother Francis said to himself. "I have followed in Jesus' footsteps, and have travelled the world with nothing on my back, caring for the outcasts of society, announcing Poverty, Peace and Love. Now I need to go deep, deep within, and contemplate in that space the eyes of my Lord, lose myself in them and make every outline and feature of his blessed countenance mine.

"Brother Leo, now I'm seeing the peaks of the Eternal Mountains. What joy! Very soon my Lord will be a river of honey that will feed my hungry soul. I need peace, Brother Leo; I need to prepare myself for the *great step*. Let's go to the mountains."

A Return to Solitude

In the first days of December, Francis, Leo and Angelo left Rome and embarked on their journey to the Rieti Valley. The first snows had fallen. Francis advanced at a rapid pace. He was very cheerful despite the condition of his dying body. His stomach, arm, and intestines were ailing him, and the strange illness affecting his eyes, an illness he had contracted in the East, caused him terrific pain and, at times, blinded him completely.

"Oh, the human soul!" Francis exclaimed. "It's almost omnipotent. Brother Leo, when you're so consumed with God to the point of tears, there's no fatigue, no snow, no illness. The soul is a flash of lightning emanating from God. For this reason, in some sense of the word, it, too, is omnipotent."

In fact, while in the grip of a snowstorm, neither sleet nor the north winds could mar that ravaged body. He walked gallantly ahead of them. His brothers could barely keep up and they worried about his health. When Francis suspected their concern, he would exclaim:

"God is and that's enough."

These words filled him with abundant energy, and he would pick up the pace. His soul was full of swallows and he felt the confidence and indescribable joy of his earlier days.

* * *

They rested for a day in a nearby hamlet. Brother Francis went up to the bell tower and spent the day curled up against the wall, his soul totally submerged in God's ocean. His brothers went begging for alms. They tried their best to persuade Francis to eat, but he did not taste so much as a morsel all day. The disciples climbed the bell tower several times. Frozen north winds circled them violently, and they were most severe where Francis laid tucked into a corner. He did not tremble and was flushed with color.

"We wouldn't believe it if we hadn't seen it with our own eyes," commented Brother Leo as they made their way down the spiral staircase.

The disciples looked for some straw on which they could lay down for the night. Before falling asleep, Brother Leo said:

"Brother Francis, have mercy on yourself. Doesn't the Rule say that we must care for each other like a mother cares for her child? Why don't you let us take care of you?"

"Oh, Brother Leo!" Francis replied. A radiant light shone in his eyes as he spoke. "I included those statements in the Rule for the benefit of our frail humanity. If we were to jump without inhibitions into God's ocean, we wouldn't need a mother to care for us. God is the mother, God is the warmth, God is the wife, the child, the nourishment. Dear Leo, how many times must I tell you that when the soul thinks of God, cold, hunger, and fear disappear? Oh, it's hard to believe: this day, God has given me more warmth than a fire ever could, and more tenderness than a mother could ever give."

Leo and Angelo were profoundly moved. The three prayed for a long while. Finally, Leo and Angelo knelt before Brother Francis. He imparted a blessing on each of them. It is difficult to imagine a happier group of men in this world.

* * *

When they reached the Rieti Valley, the spectacle before them filled Francis with emotion. It looked like a giant amphitheater completely surrounded by snow-capped mountains. They were able to detect gorges and narrow passes that resembled old wounds left behind by electric storms. They also saw tiny villages on the steep mountain slopes that looked like eagle's nests. What a spectacle!

When they saw, far on the horizon, Poggio Bustone on one side and Greccio on the other, the disciples knelt on the snow and began to pray "We Adore You." The snow gave them warmth.

They walked along the edge of a city without entering it. They went in the direction of Mt. Rainerio and began their climb up the rocky and ancient slopes. Francis rested after ascending a few meters. As he rested, his eyes focused suddenly on the panorama before him: the valley, the city, the towns, and mountain after mountain.

"What peace, Brother Leo!" Francis said. "What joy!"

For a while they did not speak. All of Francis' disciples came to mind and rekindled memories.

"Now I can nourish them with peace," he said to himself.

He felt affection for each and every one of them. As he rested on the mountain of agony, unpleasant recollections of certain ministers knocked on the doors of his memories. As soon as Brother Francis felt his inner wounds opening, he erased the memories and said to himself:

"If there is also a little affection for them, they too will enter the garden of Poverty."

They got up and continued the climb. They reached Fonte Colombo about midday. Lady Columba was very happy to see them. Their "mother" was well aware of Brother Francis' wishes and, following his instructions, had built a hut made of clay and twigs for the disciples. Upon seeing their new dwelling, Francis exclaimed:

"This is truly the Palace of Poverty; blessed be our 'mother' Columba."

In God's Bosom

Francis spent two weeks in total solitude. He would get up early, descend the steep and icy slopes to the cavern where he had written the Rule, and there he would remain all day. He made it clear that he did not want to receive visitors, not even to give them nourishment. The disciples respected his wishes.

Those were days in paradise. He looked out onto an enormous yet bare chestnut tree, completely covered with snow.

"My soul looks just like that," Brother Francis said to himself. "It's naked, free, unfettered. *God is and that's enough*," he would say in a loud voice.

Storms raged frequently, covering the mountain with snow. Suddenly, the winds would push away the clouds, leaving in its wake the splendid contrast between the whiteness of the snow and the blueness of the sky.

The white snow, the blue sky, the power of the mountains, and the brutal force of the tempests evoked God. But Francis' daily chore was to transcend the evocation and reach the Evocative Presence himself, establishing the quiet, ineffable, and marked relationship of I-You.

* * *

He pressed himself against the cavern walls, curling up with his forehead touching his knees. He remained in this position for several hours. At first, he communicated with God out loud. Then the words progressively became only a whisper until there was nothing left but silence. Nevertheless, he continued to communicate mentally with God until his mind also quieted.

Brother Francis entered the very last chamber of his spirit and there in that enclosure he opened his soul to God, and God, in turn, to Francis. Francis welcomed God and God welcomed Francis who gave of himself. Francis established a means of communication with the Lord that was both

343

courteous and intimate, alive and true, a complete mental connection in faith and in love.

All of Francis' mental energies were released and projected onto God and remained with him. And Francis was merged, focused, still, paralyzed with him and in him, in a dynamic and energetic quietude.

For several hours he remained submerged in those divine waters. Francis would feel mysterious energies of "adhesion" surface in the very recesses of his being, along with peculiar powers of "awareness."

In one simple and complete motion, all of Francis was one with God, and God was one with Francis. It was an immediate experience, a deep, penetrating, and possessive experience, without images, nor concrete thoughts, nor representations of God: there was no need to make present that which was already present.

* * *

Francis awakened in order to repose. He was beside himself with joy. The indescribable panorama greeted him when he left the cave, but everything disappeared before his eyes. The peaks, the ravines, the snows, the bare trees, the roaring waters, everything disappeared. Neither above him nor below him was there any universal and unique Reality other than God Himself. Francis was drunk with happiness. Who are you? Who am I?

At that moment, Francis felt that he had lost his identity and had become the Order and all of Humanity. But in the end, Francis also disappeared. The Order and Humanity also disappeared. God was all that was left. God was Everything.

He entered the cavern once again. He began to remember all of his brothers, placing each one in the hands of the Father. In recalling his brothers, he took great pains to feel a special affection for his adversaries, the intellectuals who had caused him much distress. If by chance he felt any aversion toward a dissident brother, he would reconcile himself instantly by kissing mother earth three times.

He felt no shame nor did he reprimand himself as he reflected upon the last four years of his life where malediction and anger had dictated his actions. Instead, he simply fell prostrate, extending his arms and repeating several times with humility:

"Lord have mercy!"

Upon rising and leaving the cavern he would say to himself:

"I'm made of dust, but there is no reason to fear. God's compassion is greater than my own imperfections."

He never belittled himself. Sometimes, when he recalled the sins of his youth, he would say in a loud voice:

"But the Lord is holy, and that's enough."

* * *

Francis left the cavern at dusk and slowly made his way up the slopes. The melted snows on the wet ground made the climb slippery and dangerous. He soon reached the hut. What a reunion! It was as if the disciples had not seen each other for an eternity. They embraced each other as if they had just returned from far away lands. Francis' joy flowed from his eyes, his lips, his skin, his hands. What happiness these among brothers!

"Mother" Columba had prepared a meal.

"Eat something, Brother Francis," said Brother Leo.

"I have other food," Francis replied quite naturally.

The skies were darkening. Suddenly, thunderous clouds released golden rays of light, filling the western sky. The bolts of lightning traversed the wide expanse, colliding with the snow-capped mountains. Francis could not control himself:

"How wonderful! Dear God, how wonderful!"

His eyes moistened with tears.

* * *

It was nightfall. They prayed the psalms and in silent adoration. Afterwards, they had an unforgettable banquet. Their good "mother" served them, and Brother Francis ate heartily. Francis extended a warm and loving blessing in gratitude.

The three brothers embraced their fraternity deep into the night.

"Talk to us about God, Brother Francis," implored his two companions.

Francis was inspired to the core and spoke of God as if he were his most intimate friend. Leo and Angelo drank each and every word; their souls were wide open and brimming.

They were drunk with happiness.

"It's paradise, it's paradise," exclaimed Brother Angelo.

"And paradise is where we find God," Francis explained.

They were not sleepy.

They went on to other subjects and began to recall their bitter fight for the ideal. However, this recollection did not dampen their feeling of peace and happiness, nor did it compel them to feel animosity toward the opposition, not even toward Brother Elias.

346

"A year ago in this same place you dictated the holy Rule to me," said Brother Leo. "I remember the opposition threatening you with defiance. But you didn't act like a frightened little lamb, Brother Francis. You were more like a ferocious wolf. Remember?"

The three laughed uproariously.

"Yes, Brother Leo," Francis replied, "you'll always find a wolf lurking behind the door. But it doesn't matter. God is mightier than the wolf."

They were joyful as they fell asleep. Even Francis had sweet dreams.

A Peaceful Advent

"Brother Leo," said Francis, "if God had a soul, it would be called Peace. They say that you appreciate something most when it is lost. I lost peace. Once I found it, I realized how precious it really is. It would be selfish of us to keep it all to ourselves. Brothers, let's go out into the world and sow peace."

They left their retreat and proceeded down the left side of the mountain along an ancient walkway, until they reached a hamlet called Greccio. The town rested on a rocky elevation, a bare mountain cut in a series of steps.

The townspeople were overjoyed at the sight of the heralds. Francis asked for a cowbell, and he rang it as he made his way to the main plaza. By mid-afternoon all the townspeople had gathered in the plaza. Brother Francis spoke to them of peace and the birth of Christ.

"My children," Francis began, "a child is defenseless. Hence, the child is innocent. He lives in the deep oceans of freedom. He receives everything, whether or not it is earned or merited. He receives everything freely. He is loved freely. This is how we are in the hands of God. What joy ! God is our 'Mother,' my children. He carries us in his bosom, he carries us in his arms."

At that moment, Brother Francis could not contain his tears. The townspeople also cried. When Francis regained his composure, he began to speak to them of the Child of Bethlehem. He spoke with so much emotion that he was unable to continue and wept uncontrollably. The villagers sobbed as they dispersed and walked silently to their homes. They could not recall a more stirring event.

A gentleman who was genuinely moved by Francis' words approached him, took him by the hand and quietly directed his steps toward his home. The gentleman's residence was a stately manor and he was of noble lineage. His name was John Vellita, an owner of exceptional landed property on the opposite side of town, adjacent to a deep ravine which rose to a point. On its rocky surface there were a series of natural caverns which could be seen from his home in Greccio.

John Vellita said to Francis:

"Brother Francis, I'm well aware of your affinities. I know that you enjoy secluded areas where you can communicate privately with God. I would be more than happy to give you and your brothers that place you see out there," he said, as he pointed to the stretch of land in the distance.

Brother Francis was impressed with the imposing view of that rocky expanse.

"There, without a doubt, God is as solid as rock. I accept your offer and may God be your reward.

"Brother John, I would like you to build a hermitage of clay and twigs near the great cavern."

"It will be completed by Christmas," responded John Vellita.

"Christmas! Christmas!"

Upon pronouncing the word, Francis' soul stirred with emotion. "This is the feast of feasts, a day of rejoicing because for our sake a holy and beloved Child was born and placed in a manger, for there was no room for him at the inn."

"Brother John Vellita, if I were to find myself before the emperor, I would kneel at his feet and humbly request that he make a proclamation obliging all of his subjects to sow wheat along the pathways of the empire on Christmas Day so that the birds, especially the larks, could enjoy a great banquet. There's more Brother John: Even the very walls of the empire should eat meat on that day. However, since that is not possible, at least smear them with fat and eat them any way you wish. Furthermore, on that blessed day, donkeys and oxen should eat twice as much barley in memory of the donkey and ox that kept Jesus warm with their breath on that sacred night.

"Brother John, blessed be God! This year, the year peace has returned to my soul, I would like to celebrate the Birth of Christ in a very special way. I would like to evoke in a vivid and genuine manner the suffering the Lord endured for our love.

"Therefore, in the great cavern on that rocky place in the distance," Francis said as he pointed in that direction, "make me a manger in the true proportions of a stall where cows and horses eat. Take an ox and a donkey as well so that we may have a more accurate picture of what occurred in that cavern in Bethlehem. Announce these events to the citizens of Greccio and summon them solemnly on that joyous night."

* * *

Francis returned to Fonte Colombo and began extensive preparations for Christmas. He had always experienced the mysteries of the Lord in meditation. But this time, the mystery of Bethlehem transported him to another world, a world of wonder. The word alone, Bethlehem, was like music that filled his soul with ineffable melodies.

He was at peace. But what he felt during those days was something other than peace and happiness: it was as if rivers of affection ran through his veins.

"On that day," he enjoyed repeating, "the mountains will overflow with sweetness, milk, and honey."

It was the week before Christmas. Brother Francis sent Angelo to the hermitages at Foresta and Poggio Bustone.

"Brother Angelo, you will tell your brothers at the hermitages the following: Brother Francis wishes to celebrate a most blessed Christmas with you. Come, brothers, let's climb God's mountain and contemplate the Great Light. Hills will flatten, curves will straighten, and rough surfaces will be smoothed. Come, brothers, and see Love."

* * *

Brother Leo accompanied Brother Francis to the grotto. Francis spent the entire day in the cavern reflecting on the poverty in Bethlehem, the mystery of Christmas, the universal reconciliation between the body and the spirit, the marriage of heaven and earth. He longed to see the Infant, who is the link between heaven and earth, with his own eyes.

At nightfall, Brother Francis went up to the cabin. After eating, Francis was carried away but did not speak.

"Brother Francis, say something," insisted Brother Leo.

"Words?" inquired Francis. "Here the appropriate words are tears. Oh, Brother Leo, the Lord has been too good to us! When I think of Bethlehem, tears are the only thing I can express. I don't know how to speak, Brother Leo. All I can produce are broken phrases, but a tearful silence is better."

"Share with me those broken phrases that evoke the mystery of Christmas," Brother Leo insisted.

Francis closed his eyes and was silent for a long while. Finally, he opened his mouth as if to say something, but said nothing. He fell silent once again. Brother Francis looked as if he were controlling his emotions, reducing them to words. Finally, in a soft and sweet voice he began to pronounce a string of words: Bethlehem. Humility. Peace. Silence. Intimacy. Pleasure. Sweetness. Hope. Kindness. Softness. Aurora. Goodness. Love. Light. Tenderness. Dawn...

The last words were almost inaudible. Afterwards, Brother Francis did not say another word. Brother Leo fell asleep within a short period of time. When he awoke the next morning, Brother Francis was already up and about. Brother Leo never knew whether Francis had slept that night or not.

God Will Come Tonight

The great day had arrived. On the 24th of December, all the brothers from the neighboring hermitages gathered at the cavern in Greccio. An inexplicable joy united them. Francis was like a being from another world.

It was mid-afternoon. Everyone had gathered in the cavern. Francis spoke to prepare them for the mystery of Christmas Eve. They all sat on the ground. Brother Francis knelt before them sitting back on his heels and began to speak with an air of mystery:

"Brothers, God arrives tonight. God will arrive at midnight, a culmination of all our expectations. God will come on a little donkey, inside the womb of the Virgin Mother.

God will come this night bearing gifts. He will bring a golden box brimming with Humility and Compassion. Tenderness will hang from his arms. God will come tonight."

Francis' eyes were closed as he spoke to them. His brothers were absolutely still, their eyes wide open. Francis continued:

"God will come tonight and tomorrow the Great Day will dawn. God will come tonight and the house will be full of the fragrance of violets and poppies. God will come tonight and a bolt of lightning will strike the darkness and shine on his face for all to see. God will depart from the East, travel over liberating waters, will greet us this same night and break the chains that bind us. God will come tonight and pull out our selfishness by its roots and bury it deep within the ocean. God will come tonight and show us the way, and we will follow in his footsteps. It is not long before the Lord will arrive in splendor and might. He will come bearing the colors of Peace and infuse us with Eternal Life. He's coming!"

* * *

It was nightfall and within a few short hours, the disciples in the grotto witnessed a spectacular event. The mountain was shimmering in white light. In neighboring villages surrounding Greccio, men, women, and children abandoned their homes, raised torches large and small, and descended the mountain amidst songs of joy.

The mass of flickering lights made its way to the ravine and began to climb the ridge leading to the cavern. The light from the torches produced a glimmering phenomenon on the rocky surface, that is impossible to describe.

They had prepared an enormous Nativity scene with hay and straw at the entrance to the cavern. A gentle yet hungry little donkey stood on one side of the manger, chewing constantly. An ox that was no less gentle stood on the other side. The Poor Man of Assisi, calm yet overjoyed, stood beside the crib ready to begin the liturgy.

Francis wore a dalmatic and officiated as deacon. The Mass began. He announced the "good news" of the Birth of Christ in a sonorous voice. He closed the missal and left the altar. He approached the congregation, placing himself between the manger and the faithful.

He began to speak. He looked as if he were about to break down and cry. He echoed several times: "Love! Love! Love!" Later on, he began to say these words repeatedly: "Infancy, Poverty, Peace, Salvation," and at the end of this string of words he would utter the refrain: "Love! Love! Love!" Time and again he would find himself very close to tears.

But something totally unexpected occurred. The threat of tears slowly dissipated, allowing an absolutely serene Brother Francis to emerge. Apparently, Francis lost sense of his own identity and was no longer attuned to any notion of time and space. He was completely without feeling, completely "absent." A marvelous heady feeling had taken possession of him.

He was oblivious to the congregation and began to direct his words to "someone" who supposedly was in the manger, as if no one else existed on earth. He behaved as a mother behaves with her baby: he smiled at the child, made distinct gestures, and expressed all manner of thought and feeling in a language understood only by a mother and her child.

He pronounced "Jesus," "Child of Bethlehem" with ineffable eloquence. It was as if honey flowed from his lips. He pronounced these words with zeal, slowly savoring every drop. He repeated "Beth-le-hem" several times like a baaing sheep in a stable in the Holy Land.

He leaned over the crib as if he were about to kiss a child, or take a baby in his arms, the many gestures mothers show their little ones.

John Vellita could have sworn he saw the sleeping Baby Jesus with his own eyes. Upon feeling the loving strokes of Francis' hand, the Child awoke and smiled at Brother Francis. John Vellita swore it happened.

It was one unforgettable night. To all of the inhabitants of Greccio the grotto was the new Bethlehem. They all talked about miracles.

From Mountain to Mountain

Brother Francis spent the winter and spring moving from one mountain to the next. He remained a while at Poggio Bustone, a place that held fond memories for him. From there he travelled to the hermitage at Foresta, where, according to questionable testimony, he wrote the *Canticle to Brother Sun*. He was mindful to visit the hermitage of pain and suffering, Fonte Colombo, just as he did in Greccio.

He travelled to Narni in springtime. He climbed the nearby mountains along a jagged path and reached the hamlet called St. Urbano. The hermitage was about two miles from the town, accessible by way of an almost vertical cliff. If the landscape surrounding the hermitages made his heart race, it was nothing compared to the vista seen from the hermitage of St. Urbano. It was breathtaking. He also remained a while at prayer in the mountains that surround the city of Spoleto.

The descent from the hermitages was painstakingly difficult, but in time he made his way to the plazas of nearby hamlets. The aura that enveloped him was so irresistible that, in an instant, the entire populace would find itself in the plaza. He spoke to them in the soft and warm voice of Poverty, Peace and Love. Finally, he explained the Passion of Christ with such fervor and emotion that the townspeople would return to their homes silently—as was always the case—and in tears. He inquired about the lepers and would care for them with the same affection he had shown in earlier years.

In June of 1224, Francis attended the Chapter at the Porziuncola. Sources regarding any mediation of his are scant, to say the least. Brother Francis did not intervene, for he had completed his mission and was no longer legislator or director. He was simply a model of simplicity and a venerated father.

I Know the Poor and Crucified Christ

One day he found his afflictions intensifying. Francis was like a lump of clay. He could barely move. His brothers carried him to the hut at the Porziuncola. He spent an entire day curled up in a corner, surrounded by Leo, Maseo, Angelo and Rufinus.

They were like soldiers caring for a wounded comrade. The love they felt for him was astounding. Francis let them love him. It was a warm and beautiful scene. They did not leave his side. At times the pain was unbearable and he let a moan escape his lips every now and then.

There were moments when the pain was absolutely excruciating, forcing Francis to curl up, pressing his forehead to his knees. Brother Leo could not hold back his tears. Brother Maseo cried out in desperation:

"Brother Francis, what medicines could possibly alleviate this kind of pain? We know how consoling the evangelical word is to you. Would you like us to summon Brother Caesar Spira, the man who is well versed in Holy Scriptures? His reading and comments might help to alleviate the pain."

Maseo quieted. Brother Francis remained silent and still. The four disciples stared at him, anxiously awaiting his response. After a time, which, to the disciples, seemed an eternity, Brother Francis raised his head and responded in a modest, unassuming tone: "No. It's not necessary. I know the Poor and Crucified Christ, and that's all I need."

Immediately upon pronouncing these words, he felt his muscles relax and an indescribable serenity permeated his entire being. These words were the synthesis of his ideal and a declaration of his principles.

Brother Leo, wanting to give him further comfort, added:

"Brother Francis, reflect also on the Resurrected Christ; this too, without a doubt, will give you comfort."

Brother Francis responded:

"Those who do not know the Crucified Christ cannot know the Resurrected Christ. Those who do not speak of the Crucified Christ cannot speak of the Risen Christ. Those who do not experience Good Friday cannot celebrate his Resurrection on Easter Sunday."

As soon as he uttered these words, Francis stood up with almost no effort whatsoever, like a rejuvenated man. His disciples stared in fright. Brother Francis raised his arms and spoke exuberantly:

"Write these words, Brother Leo: there is no higher summit than that of Calvary. Not even the Resurrection surpasses it. Better yet, the two are one and the same.

"Brother Leo, I have already celebrated the night at Gethsemane. I have also endured scenes with Annas, Caiaphas and Herod. I walked through the Via Dolorosa. All I need is to scale the slope at Calvary. After Calvary there is nothing. The Resurrection takes place right there. Let's go then to that solitary, desolate, and sacrosanct mountain that Count Orlando has given me. Something tells me that things of some significance might occur there."

In the heat of the summer, about mid-July, Brother Francis, Leo, Angelo, Rufinus and Maseo left the Porziuncola and headed toward Mt. Alvernia.

"Brother Maseo," said Francis, "you'll be our guardian and we'll do as you say, as if you were Christ himself leading the way. We will sleep wherever you wish. You'll provide for us so that our only concern will be devotion to the Lord."

With his handsome face and elegant manner, Brother Maseo had no trouble getting food and lodging during the course of their journey.

After walking for two days, Brother Francis could no longer continue the pace. He was fatigued but his soul was alive and energetic. In view of Francis' decision to arrive at Alvernia at all costs, Brother Maseo entered a hamlet with the object of securing a donkey and muleteer for him.

He knocked on the door of one residence and a man came to the door. He was an older gentleman, getting on in years.

"My lord," said Brother Maseo, "we are five disciples on God's journey. Four of us can walk countless miles. But there is one among us who simply cannot take another step. More importantly, he is the most significant one among us."

"Who is he? What is his name?" asked the muleteer.

"Francis of Assisi."

"You mean the one they call the Saint?"

"The same," Maseo replied.

"It will be an honor to carry such a sacred load," added the muleteer. "Let's go."

* * *

They continued on their way. Francis sat comfortably on the small, docile donkey. The four disciples walked silently and were lost in prayer. Brother Francis kept his eyes closed and, frequently, in moments of intense consolation, covered his head with his cloak. The muleteer kept pace with the disciples and was extremely edified by their modesty.

After several miles, the peasant could not wait any longer and expressed what he had been wanting to say at the outset:

"Father Francis, according to public opinion, you're held in very high esteem. They say that whoever sees you, sees Christ; to look at you is to feel the peace of Christ; and he who touches you is cured immediately of sins and afflictions. Venerated Father, allow me to express a wish: I only hope that you're as holy as the people believe you to be, and I hope you never exploit that good opinion the people of God have of you, for through you these devotees were called to God."

Upon hearing these words, Francis turned his head, his eyes and mouth opening wide in disbelief. When he regained his composure, he said to the muleteer:

"Beloved brother, detain brother donkey."

They all stopped. The disciples helped Francis down. Brother Francis approached the muleteer without saying a word. With great difficulty, he knelt at his feet, kissed them reverently and said:

"May heaven and earth help me give you thanks, brother muleteer. Never has anyone expressed such wise words. Blessed be your mouth."

He kissed the peasant's feet once more. The muleteer did not know where to look, all at once edified and confused.

They rested for a few hours at the side of the road under the shade of a lush fig tree. Francis felt a craving for figs. Brother Maseo reached up and pulled a few from the branches.

Alvernia in the Distance

As they travelled through the Tuscan Apennines, the disciples suddenly stopped: they recognized the proud and solitary summit out in the distance as the indomitable Mt. Alvernia, its peaks piercing the blue sky. To a foe it seemed to take on a menacing appearance, but to a friend its grandeur was inviting.

Francis shuddered upon seeing the majestic alp. It was not the first time he had seen the blessed mountain, rather it was the fifth. He was not sure why his heart began to race. More than likely, he was feeling joy, terror, desire, and fear, all at the same time.

He asked to be let down from the donkey. He knelt on the ground. His disciples and the muleteer also fell to their knees. Francis bowed his head for several minutes, closed his eyes, and clasped his hands together, his fingers intertwined.

Suddenly, he opened his eyes, raised his head, extended his arms, and in a nervous tone, exclaimed:

"Oh Alvernia, Alvernia, Calvary, Alvernia. Blessed be the eyes that gaze upon you, and the feet that traverse your peaks. I greet your fiery rocks and your earthly spruce trees. I also greet my brothers, the falcons, the blackbirds, and the nightingales, and also my sisters, the partridges; and a special greeting to the blessed angels who dwell in your solitude. Cover me with your shadow, sacred mountain, for tempests are fast approaching."

They continued on their way, leaving the wheat fields and vineyards behind, and greeting the abundance of evergreen oaks and chestnut trees. As they walked, these became rarer as the pines and larches appeared, until finally there was nothing before them but the solemn rocky terrain.

"Brother Leo," asked Francis, "what is the emblem that crowns the peaks of our mountains?"

"The Cross, Brother Francis."

"That's right. We need a Cross for the summit of our beloved Alvernia."

"We'll place one there," said Brother Leo.

"Maybe we won't need to trouble ourselves. Who knows, perhaps the Lord himself has taken care of it!"

* * *

They finally reached the foot of the mountain. Before beginning their climb, they rested for a few hours under a lush evergreen oak. What took place at that moment defies explanation. Within minutes, hundreds of blackbirds, larks, robins, nightingales, sparrows, thrushes, finches, and even partridges appeared. Brother Francis, profoundly moved and grateful, repeated:

"Thank you, Lord, thank you!"

Never had they seen anything so festive. The birds whistled, chirped, sang, and fluttered about Francis in joyous pandemonium. Some performed lovely pirouettes and dizzying acrobatics, while others perched on his head, his shoulders, his arms, and on his knees. It was a festival of song and dance.

"Brother Leo, what marvel, what wonder! God is great!" exclaimed Francis, completely overwhelmed by the spectacle, adding: "All we need are the swallows and Alvernia will be covered in the colors of spring."

* * *

They climbed the rocky slopes. Francis' eyes were opened wide with amazement. It was as if he were viewing the slope for the first time. He felt as if he were witnessing the beginning of creation: everything was new. Immense spruce trees, firmly planted in the rocky earth, seemed to touch the sky, and they were so wide that not even four men could circle its diameter.

Francis asked the muleteer to detain the donkey. Poised at the foot of one of the spruce trees, he threw his head back and shaded his eyes with his hands as he contemplated the spruce from top to bottom. After admiring it for a long while, he exclaimed:

"Lord, Lord, how great you are!"

As they climbed, the panorama began to widen before them. Immense beech trees, mighty evergreen oaks, and tall pines of a rare variety created fresh and enormous shadows. Francis felt as if he were in paradise.

"Brother Leo," he exclaimed, "what peace! What freedom! What joy! We are the happiest men on earth."

Upon nearing level ground, Francis felt the need for solitude and manifested his wishes to his brothers. He entered a wooded area and walked in all directions. Afterwards, he descended about five hundred feet. He stood before the rocky terrain, his back to the setting sun. What a sight! It is difficult to find words evocative of God's power and timelessness.

Savage rocks encrusted the mountain, their peaks pressed against the blue firmament. Bathed in golden sunlight, they resembled the blazing fires that erupted in an era long ago. Everything was ablaze on that mountain.

"Bolts of lightning must have created these deep fissures," Francis thought to himself. "What earthquake could form such colossal structures? This must have occurred when the earth protested the death of Jesus."

Francis was overwhelmed as he repeated aloud:

"Lord, Lord!"

The infinite weight of God's sweetness fell upon Francis' soul. This solace freed Francis from himself and fueled his energies, and with renewed vigor he knelt before the gigantic rocks, extended his arms, and exclaimed in a loud voice:

"Almighty God, although I am unworthy to say your name, I dedicate this song to you.

"Lord, Lord, eternal master of the endless horizons!

"You're as beautiful as the landscape, as invincible as these rocks, as eternal as this mountain, as deep as the blue above.

"You have created these rocks, these powerful sentinels, to guard the passing of time.

"My soul feels you and loves you amidst the fires of these peaks.

"Everything is full of your presence. You will shine forever on the rocks of my soul.

"May you be blessed for the power of this eternal mass of rock.

"May you be blessed for its brazen fissures.

"May you be blessed for the eternal snows.

"May you be blessed for the august silence of starry nights."

* * *

He took the long way around as he climbed to the place where Count Orlando had built a few small huts in a circular pattern. At Francis' request, Orlando also erected one solitary hut under a lush beech tree, some distance from the other cabins. Brother Francis gathered his disciples. He sat on the trunk of an old evergreen oak. His disciples sat around him.

"Beloved brothers," he said to them, "the hour of the Great Parting is approaching. I'm a few steps from the House of the Lord. I need to be alone with my Lord. I need to get ready before I present myself all neat and tidy before the Light. I want to be alone. If laymen wish to visit me, attend to them. The only link between you and me will be Brother Leo."

And after My Death?

There is an old saying: the hotter the fire the purer the gold. For Francis, Alvernia was a mysterious alternation between fire and water. He had moments of solace alternating with the suffering and ecstasy of Gethsemane.

It was a year and a half since he had suffered desolation. Now it returned, but it was different: this time it had the quality of deep sorrow and serenity rather than sadness.

The years he had fought for the ideal surfaced in his soul once again. The painful memories of those years hovered overhead like relentless birds of prey and he was unable to shake those thoughts from his mind. Clear images were forming of the stormy Chapters, the *University* in Bologna, the astute and obstinate intellectuals, Brother Elias, Brother John Staccia, the extremely painful period during which time the Rules were drafted...

On impulse, feelings of aversion toward the opposition began to sprout like bitter herbs in a garden. Brother Francis suffered terribly because of these emotions. The past became the present, the present embroiled itself with the future, the Poor Man of God losing himself in the blackest thoughts.

"If, while I was among them," he said to himself, "they dared to conjure up such schemes, what will they do now that they're alone? And, more importantly, when I'm no longer on this earth?"

There were moments when he saw his ideal flap in the wind like a tattered flag, and a future irretrievably lost:

"What will happen to these disciples when I die?"

In one of the worst moments of his life, he ran from the hut as if he were running from danger. He escaped into the woods, stopped in front of a boulder that looked out onto a gorgeous landscape. But the scene did not move him. His heart was troubled and felt as if it were on fire. He ran into the woods once more, kneeling at the foot of an enormous evergreen oak. He extended his arms and yelled as loud as he could:

"Eternal God, extinguish these flames, cool my fever!"

He repeated these words several times with the object of regaining his composure.

"No more," he said to himself. "Ire and apprehension are explosives that destroy the Brotherhood. I shouldn't feel any hostility toward the dissenters. It would be like throwing daggers into God's heart. After the flames are extinguished, I need to feel affection for each of them. Who knows, perhaps in this way they'll immerse themselves in the ideal.

"That's the danger: make an adversary an enemy. Fight for an ideal, which is a noble gesture but, if during the furor, the ideal moves from a mental to an emotional battleground, and if the ideological adversary becomes a cordial enemy, God cannot exist in the middle of all that commotion. When a dissenter becomes an enemy, all channels of communication are destroyed. I cannot resist the one who shows resistance. I cannot allow bitter herbs of rancor to grow in my garden."

And, having said this, he fell prostrate to the ground under the evergreen oak, resting his forehead on his hands. The touch of the earth calmed him, stripping him of negative energy.

For each dissenter that crossed his mind, he kissed the ground three times. He allowed only positive thoughts to permeate his mind until the flames of aggression were completely extinguished and replaced with warm feelings of affection. Then he said in a loud voice:

"Mother Earth, convey this tenderness to Brother Elias, wherever he roams."

And likewise with each brother who formed the opposition.

Afterwards, he asked for God's forgiveness for having offended him by feeling hostility toward his sons and, remembering each by name, he said:

"Father, I place him in your hands; keep him as you would the apple of your eye. Dear God, penetrate the very depths of my being, take possession of my soul, and calm this tempest that rages within. Dear God, I want to feel what you feel for that brother, what you felt when you died for him."

Then, while still on the ground, he imagined his entire being opening wide and receiving the dissident brothers.

"Come, brother," he said as he thought about each one, "I take you affectionately in my arms."

And he would conclude by saying:

"Sister Mother Earth, convey to my brothers the beating of my heart through the deep layers of your earth. Oh Mother Earth, be the great link between my brothers."

He rose, his heart bathed in peace. When he saw a swallow in flight he would say aloud:

"Sister, announce to my brothers the coming of love."

Remembering the hatred he felt toward his brothers, he ran through the woods imparting blessings:

"Blessed be those who work landed property. Blessed be those who guide the disciples."

And he said to himself:

"I'd like to be at the very top of this spruce and smile at my brothers."

* * *

Brother Francis stood up slowly, walked around, admiring the trees and conversing with the creatures of the forest. Then he returned to the cabin.

"Life is a struggle, and in that struggle there is conflict. This is inevitable, yet there's nothing to fear. Reconciliation is a must. This daily task is of primary importance. There can be neither harmony with God nor with the earth if there is disharmony among my brothers. It would be sad if man were a discordant sound in the middle of universal harmony."

It was twilight. The mountain, choked by the flames of day, now breathed with ease. The calm was as penetrating and refreshing as dew drops. Thousand of voices filled the night air, insects flitted from mosses to lichens. The sun still bathed the distant summits in gold. It looked like the dawn of time.

Brother Francis walked slowly to the hut, repeating in a loud voice:

"What peace, what peace!"

* * *

Brother Francis was at peace, spending several days in the depths of God's ocean. Francis' mental energies were focused on the Presence. Once in God, his entire being resonated with emotion. Francis was now in a trance, like a substratum of spiritual energies, totally "outside of himself."

Brother Leo swore he saw Francis' body levitate about three or four meters above the ground, equal to the height of a beech tree. Insatiably curious, Brother Leo spied on Brother Francis with only the most spiritual intentions in mind. He would hide behind trees so as not to be discovered. He would approach him with the excuse of needing to convey a message in order to catch him in a trance or listen to exclamations of ecstasy.

One day, he found him levitated several meters above the ground. He approached him silently, kissed his feet, and he left, saying:

"Lord, have mercy on this poor sinner, and may I find myself in your good graces for Francis' sake."

* * *

Francis said nothing with regard to the blessed curiosity of his friend and confidante. But the matter did not sit well with him. When Francis made the decision to do rigorous fasting for a month in absolute solitude, he asked Leo to stand at the door of the oratory of the disciples. Francis walked away and from a distance he called to Brother Leo. Brother Leo responded immediately. Francis walked a few more meters and yelled as loud as he could:

"Brother Leo!"

This time Brother Leo did not respond.

"This is the right spot," said Francis.

Here, on the day after the Assumption, he initiated his month of fasting and solitude in honor of St. Michael, far away from the curious eyes of his blessed brothers.

The chosen area was a small patch of level ground above a large rock, somewhat like a terrace with a drop of about forty meters, which faced another rock towering above him. This rocky plain was severed from firm ground by this precipice, forming something like an island.

The disciples placed a wooden plank over the precipice that would act as a bridge, and they made a cell of intertwined reeds.

Francis gave them explicit instructions: no one was to come near the area. Once a day, Brother Leo would bring him bread and water, and at midnight he would come for Matins. But Brother Leo could only cross the bridge after stating the password. He would cry out: *Domine labia mea aperies* (Lord, open my lips), and Francis would respond: *Et os meum annuntiabit laudem tuam* (And my mouth will speak your praise). If Brother Francis failed to respond, Brother Leo would have to depart immediately.

Francis' Great Passover

Here, the most sublime period of Francis' life begins. The writer is tempted to offer a colorful anecdote, alluding to the constant dangers that beset Brother Francis in his mountain retreat. In order to unravel the mystery of a man, the writer needs to immerse himself in those waters in some way. Nonetheless, we know very well that all experience is subjective. For this reason, the writer's only access to this experience is by way of deduction and the use of figurative language.

* * *

The following is a narrative attributed to Brother Leo:

"One night, Brother Leo went to meet Francis at the usual hour for Matins. At the foot of the bridge he called out: *Domine labia mea aperies*, as they had agreed, but Francis did not respond. Brother Leo did not turn back, as Francis had previously ordered him to do. Instead, he crossed the bridge and quietly entered the cell. He could not locate Francis and thought perhaps he might have gone into the woods to pray.

"He left the cell and went into the moonlit woods in search of Francis. Finally, he heard Francis' voice. He approached him quietly and saw that he was kneeling, his face and hands looking up to the sky. He heard him say with an ardent spirit: 'Who are you and who am I?' He repeated these words several times.

"Brother Leo looked up and was amazed and overwhelmed by the sight. A beautiful and glorious flame descended the skies and stopped above Francis' head. A voice emanated from the flame and spoke to Francis, but the words were incomprehensible to Brother Leo. Feeling that he was unworthy to stand so close to holy ground, and fearing that he might offend or disturb Francis if he were found out, he walked back slowly to observe the outcome from a distance.

"He saw Francis stretch out his hands three times toward the flame and, finally, the flame rose to the skies.

"While Francis walked back to the cell overjoyed and assured by the vision, he heard footsteps and the rustle of leaves and demanded that the intruder stand still. Brother Leo obeyed, and was so consumed with fright at the thought of confronting Francis, according to what he told his companions, that he wished the earth had swallowed him whole. He knew he was at fault and was careful not to offend his father, fearing that Francis might deny his company. Francis approached him and asked:

"Who are you?"

"I'm Brother Leo, my Father," he said, his voice trembling.

"Why did you come, *little lamb of God*? Did I not tell you to obey my orders? In the name of holy obedience, tell me if you saw or heard anything."

"Brother Leo responded:

"Father, I heard you say several times: 'Who are you, and who am I?'

"Then, on bended knee, Brother Leo confessed his disobedience and, with tears in his eyes, he asked for forgiveness."

* * *

Day and night, Francis immersed himself in God's ocean. Moonlit nights stirred him, but starry nights moved him beyond measure. With the help of Brother Leo's narrative and the "Praises", we can deduce that Brother Francis lived this period of his life in a spiritual *vertigo*, as a result of having measured the distance between God and himself. The Poor Man of God felt that this distance was interminable because it embraced both distance and proximity, transcendence and immanence.

Francis would leave the hut at the darkest hour of the night, sit upon a rock under the stars, and lose himself in the immensity of God, experiencing a mixture of fascination and fright, astonishment and wonder, gratitude and elation.

Looking at the starry spectacle, he repeated numerous times:

"Your name is admired throughout the world!"

He expressed these words in a loud voice and with great emotion. Then he would lower his voice (that voice emanating from areas unknown) and express with the same intensity:

"Who is man that you should remember him?"

One night, he spent countless hours repeating this phrase. After expressing these words, the Poor Man remained in prolonged silence, the phrase vibrating in his bosom all the while.

* * *

On those warm and mysterious nights, Francis, standing on a rock that could touch the stars, contemplated two realities that could never adjoin: on the one hand, God, an admirable reality, overwhelming and burning; on the other hand, Francis, the Poor Little Man, "almost" nothing. And, in between, an immeasurable distance which neither Grace nor Love could ever bridge. However, inexplicably, that distance was more like a bridge paved in gold, constructed by Love. The closer they came to one another (God and Francis), the more discernible the distance between them, for the greatness of the Almighty and the smallness of the Poor Little Man were never clearly perceived.

The intimacy to which we are called does not bridge that gap. Grace proclaims that we are children, but that, too, does little to bridge the gap. During those nights, Francis saw before his eyes, silhouetted against the stars, that extremely tall and lofty rock. Much taller and firmer than the *sasso grande* was this absolute truth: *God is*.

"Who are you, and who am I?" he repeated all night long.

A question? It was something more than a question. An affirmation? It was much more than an affirmation. It was admiration, wonder, jubilation, astonishment. It was the sacred vertigo, an experience that is beyond description.

Francis peered over the precipice that dropped forty meters in front of him under the moonlight. He felt a peculiar and contradictory sensation: the abyss called to him as though it were screaming: Jump! But at the same time, another force was pulling him back. It was vertigo.

Whenever Francis joyfully accepted that *God is*, which occurred every night, he would succumb to a deep intoxication and his life would become one of omnipotence and plenitude, participating in God's eternal and infinite vitality. This transformed Brother Francis into a *troubadour* of a complete and absolute novelty: *God is*. Who are you and who am I?

Upon joyfully accepting that *God is* and *I am not*, the distance was bridged. And at that moment, the distance and the presence merged.

Francis was a man who was seduced by God's abyss. He was also a man who was broken and defeated by the weight of Glory. He was always in a state of wonder. God was always a novelty to Francis. He was always captivated: coming outside of himself and entering Another. He was essentially a *paschal* man.

This is the beginning of Francis' great paschal festival: Brother Francis in a state of tension and openness, coming out of himself and moving toward the Admirable. When his soul "went" toward God, he had at his disposal only a monotonous stream of reiterated words, completely incapable of conceptualizing what was lived:

"Almighty, most holy, omnipotent, alive, all, great, true, glorious, eternal, just, good, direct, divine, honorable, admirable, blessed, immutable, invisible, inexpressible, ineffable, unintelligible, exalted, sublime, noble."

* * *

It was a night of rare beauty and brilliance. The summer air in Alvernia was fresh and warm at the same time. The world slept in eternal peace. Everything was quiet and serene.

Brother Francis, standing on the rocks, raised his arms and dove into the chasms of faith in the immensity of God. That night, new and mysterious energies of "adhesion" appeared in his soul, new forces of profound "knowledge" and love.

Francis said nothing. He ran out of words. The words were communicated as if by sonar between two beings submerged in deep waters.

Francis' mind was paralyzed. Nothing in his mind was distinguishable or capable of being analyzed. It was an act of totality and simplicity: Francis was "in" God. It was a deep and penetrating experience, vivid and immediate, without images, nor predetermined thoughts. There was no need to formulate a representative image of God, for God was "there," "with" Francis, and Francis "with" God.

God was (what was he?) an infinite panorama, without walls, or doors, nourished with tenderness; a forest with a multitude of warm, loving arms ready to embrace; an air dense with golden honey; an incurable dizzy spell, as if millions of arms surrounded and embraced the beloved

Francis; a river overflowing its banks and flooding the countryside.

Everything vanished. The stars disappeared, the night consumed itself. Francis also disappeared. All that was left was a *You* which reached far and wide, within and without.

"You are Holy, you are one Lord God, who works wonders.

You are strong, you are great, you are the Almighty.

You are Good, all Good, Supremely Good.

Lord God, alive and true.

You are charity and love, you are wisdom.

You are humility, you are patience, you are confidence.

You are quietude, you are solace, you are happiness.

You are beauty, you are gentleness.

You are our protector, guardian and defender.

You are our strength and hope.

You are our sweetness.

You are our eternal life, great and admirable Lord."

Francis' "I" was irresistibly drawn to and taken by the One, making it "one" with the Center. This was the great *passover.* However, there was no fusion. On the contrary, Francis not only maintained his own personal identity, which was more concrete than ever, but the closer he got to God, the more diverse they became to the point where the diversity became one of disturbing profiles : "Who are you and who am I?"

* * *

Francis was immersed in the immutable and absolute essence of God. It was not a matter of God having been with Francis, rather God *was* with Francis. God filled him entirely. And, "in" God, there was no far, near, there, here with Francis. Brother Francis transcended time and space : distances disappeared, and Francis began to feel like the *child of immensity*.

On that night, everything was within reach: the evergreen oaks, the rocks, the red stars, the blue stars, the nebulas, the most distant galaxies in the universe. Since God was everywhere, space was nonexistent. Vastness was all that existed. Better yet, all that existed was absorbed and became one with Immensity. Thus: if God "is" with Francis and Francis "is" with God (and God is immensity), then Francis is also "immense," or, as previously stated, the child of immensity: "My God and my All."

Those intoxicating evenings! Nights of awesome experiences "in" God! Brother Francis expanded, proceeded through and possessed the world from one edge to the other. No human sensation can compare to this sense of plenitude and jubilation.

"God, God!" Francis exclaimed aloud. "God empowers man's weaknesses with omnipotence. God bursts open man's horizons, opening even the unfamiliar boundaries."

How can I describe this? Upon seeing himself in God's bosom, Francis' wings expanded, a wingspan that covered the world in its entirety. "My God and my All."

* * *

Once immersed with the One who is immensity, all things became relative to Brother Francis.

That is, all living things lost their individual characteristics, not in and of themselves but as Francis perceived them. On that warm summer night, the night when Brother Francis ("in" God) plunged into creation, the differences between the two beings disappeared. That is the law of differences disappeared and the law of unity materialized.

375

In other words, Francis experienced the internal unity of all living things intuitively in God, because God is the fundamental Creator of all reality, the sole reason for the existence and subsistence of all things. Upon entering the profundity of God, living things lost the distinguishing characteristics that divide them, and, "in" God, Brother Francis began to "feel" all things as part of his being.

Francis reached the one and only "Root" that sustains all things, and "there", all creatures began to be *involved* and *committed* with Francis ("in" God), becoming his *sisters*. Stars, fire, wind, things near and faraway, spruces, rocks, wolves, falcons...all things (and everything) were *brothers* and *sisters*. It was a vivid and cosmic experience "in God," more fulfilling than any other human experience. "My God and my All." God was wife, mother, gift, brother, sister, child, legacy.

All night long, Brother Francis repeated "My God and my All." As he repeated this phrase he felt that he was receiving from the Almighty all the tenderness and enjoyment that creatures could possibly give him. A fuller life does not exist. It was a prelude to Eternity, which is none other than the *total and simultaneous possession of Eternal Life*. My God and my All!

Brother Falcon

That afternoon, Francis witnessed a spectacular storm. From inside the hut, he contemplated the torrential downpour with great emotion. Brother Francis was full of admiration for the giant fir trees which bowed like submissive children, permitting the waters to bathe them, and the rocks which did not resist, and the proud mountain which yielded itself with all humility to the punishing winds and the crashing hail.

"I should be like that," Brother Francis said in a loud voice.

Then he fell prostrate to the ground and extended his arms. He immersed his soul in the earth and, in the hands of the Almighty, he surrendered humbly to the divine currents.

* * *

During that time, Brother Francis established a mysterious friendship with a falcon that inhabited the *sasso grande*. Francis was feeling a closeness and tenderness, a connectedness to all living creatures. One day, a frightful falcon returned from its hunt, its wings flapping loudly in the wind. Francis admired its sense of direction, its swiftness, and its ability to land on a tiny projection with tremendous ease.

Brother Francis felt admiration and affection for the creature. A link was established between Francis and the bird of prey, the latter detecting Brother Francis' affection. Francis mustered all the fire of his sensitivity and addressed these words to the bird:

"Dear bird, brother falcon, God's son, hear me. I'm your brother; don't be afraid of me. Spread your wings and come."

What took place goes beyond human understanding. The falcon extended its wings, and, almost without flapping them, descended as if it had jumped, stopping a few meters from Brother Francis. At that moment, the fondness and respect he felt for the bird reached its peak. It can be said that the powerful bird perceived Brother Francis' warmth and was delighted. Francis did not move. He simply looked at the bird lovingly and with gratitude. The falcon stood absolutely still as well; it looked in all directions quite naturally.

It occurred to Francis to give the bird something to eat. He noticed that all he had in the hut was the bread and water that Brother Leo brought him daily. Remembering that birds of prey eat only meat, he refrained from feeding the bird, and instead expressed these words of affection:

"Where is your nest, bird of God? How wonderful the world must look from such heights! You don't plan out your flights. How do you get to your destination? Where is your compass? Who taught you to fly? What do you do in stormy weather? Are you afraid of lightning? What do you do when meters of snow fall on the mountain? God placed these majestic rocks here to serve as your dwelling. Take care not to show God ingratitude."

The falcon flew by Brother Francis' hut everyday. The two got to know each other well. The falcon was accustomed to staying near the hut and leaving Francis only when it went to hunt for food.

Francis was sad at the thought of the falcon having to eat other little birds, but he avoided thinking about such things. Their friendship deepened to such a degree that at the hour of Matins, at midnight, the falcon would come, flapping its wings vigorously against the wall of the hut to awaken Francis for prayers. There were times when Brother Francis took ill and the falcon did not awaken him or did so much later.

Upon leaving Alvernia, Francis said a special prayer for his brother, the falcon.

The Night of the Stigmata

"Brother Leo, open the missal at random and read the first words you see."

These were the words: "Here in Jerusalem the Son of Man will be taken prisoner, tortured and crucified; but on the third day he will rise."

Francis asked Brother Leo to open the missal at random two more times, and each time words recalling the Passion of Christ were read.

* * *

Francis extended his wings, embraced the passion he felt for the Crucified Christ, recalled his experiences of the last twenty years and, for several weeks, day and night, remained immersed in chasms of pain and love for the Crucified Christ.

His sensitivity, quite sharp by nature, had now intensified beyond human bounds. During these weeks, he gave free rein to this vehement thought: the desire to feel the same pain and love that Jesus had felt on the Cross.

It was as if Brother Francis were seeing the infinite universe through a powerful telescope or diving into the very depths of the ocean with all his faculties intact. In quietude and faith, he reverently probed the intimacy of the Crucified Christ and he "remained" there for several days and nights.

He "perceived" things that are inaccessible through simple human curiosity. Brother Francis, still and immobile, let Jesus' "sentiments" impregnate his being, allowing him to participate in the profound experience of the Crucified Christ. He ventured even deeper, into the primitive origins of the Crucified Christ where impulses, love and pain are born, decisions about life are made, erasing their respective boundaries. In short, Francis lived Jesus' interior life.

Love and pain are one and the same thing.

"My Jesus," said Francis, "you suffered for me because you loved me, and you loved me because you suffered for me. You have loved me freely. Your love served no function and had no end. You suffered not to save me but rather to love me and for that love. You had no other reasons except those of love; the reason for the lack of reasons to love is called loving willingly. You called out my name in the eternal wind that felt like a golden dream. But, when your Hour had come, all the dreams vanished and you loved me with the truth of black spikes and drops of red blood. Where there is love, there is no pain. You conceived me in the love of eternity and you gave birth to me one dark afternoon. Since that time, you have loved me willingly and forever."

Francis left the hut and began to cry out in desperation:

"Love is not loved; Love is not loved."

He screamed at the stars, at the winds, at solitude, at immensity, at the rocks, at the evergreen oaks, at the falcons, and at the men who slept over there in the mountains.

* * *

That night, Francis was drunk with happiness, delirious, aglow, agonizing over Love; and the fact that Love was not loved tortured him no end.

It was a solemn night. The secrets of the earth manifested themselves. Creation was silent, a shroud covering its light. The warm air, an omen of earthly tremors, caressed the forest. Anything could have happened that night; this world could have receded and new worlds could have surfaced.

All the smells, from the most acrid to the sweetest, danced in the winds, creating a strange mixture of fragrances. Francis was acutely attuned to his surroundings. The deluge in Francis had reached the stars. He could either die or resurrect. Why sing? The World was singing a nocturnal calm; but it could well have been a prelude to *Cantata appassionata*. The warriors of old were sleeping an eternal sleep. All their tears had dried.

The moon had not shown its light for days and was roaming about in southern hemispheres. The stars were the only ladies that night. The Lord God raised Francis to heights that challenge the imagination, igniting in his veins a garden of flames. The earth vibrated as if it had a premonition of an impending event of cataclysmic proportions.

* * *

"My Lord, tonight I wish to express the most profound words man has ever expressed. My Crucified Christ, my earth is prepared to weather any tempest. You can throw bolts of lightning, any rays and sparks you see fit to release. I hope they score my flesh with blood and pain. I'm at your disposal.

"I want to 'be' you for just a moment. Release a torrent of love through my torrents of blood. Make my flesh a pyre of pain and my spirit a garden of love.

"My Crucified Christ, I would like, for just a moment, to climb that Cross, remove those nails and lie there in your place.

"I would like to embrace the world from on high, love all men, to love and suffer for them. Tonight, I would like to cover the world with the cloak of peace, gather all the tatters and tumors of the children of these men and erect an altar with that matter in the center of the world and reduce it to a final holocaust so that only the ashes of peace lie on the ground of happiness.

"Tonight, I would like all the ships at sea to navigate on the winds of Love. I want to burn in the pyre of pain so that only Love remains. And afterwards, everything could come to an end, because we would have arrived at the summit of the resurrection.

"Crucified Christ, tonight I renounce everything and for this last coin that I forswear, may a blessed shadow shade humanity and may a smile illuminate the eyes of children. Tonight, may the bees hover over blossoms, may the armies return to be sentinels of peace, may the ailing leave their beds, and may pain retreat forever to its darkest lairs. Jesus, envelop me with the world's pain so that I may transform it into total love, and may no one ever suffer pain again. May the world feel the embrace of sweetness.

"Tonight, I want to light the way for all wanderers, captives, and outcasts. I want to plant a rosebush in every garden, wash the dry countryside with rain, release winds of hope, wait at the door for all repatriates, run with a basket in my hand sowing peace, be a staff for the crippled, a blind man's guide, and a mother to all orphans."

* * *

This was how he spent the night. Something resembling a stampede occurred when the first glimmers of light on the horizon announced the coming of day. It was a flash of pain and love entering Francis' arteries like a tempest. The beloved Crucified Christ descended from the skies like a meteor. The atmosphere filled with sweetness. Jesus was a wave of fire, energy, strength, pain, and delight over the Poor Little Man.

At that moment, Francis was looking toward the East. An apparition resembling a seraph with six fiery wings appeared before his eyes. But as it approached, Brother Francis was able to discern the effigy of a crucified man under its wings. The Poor Little Man suffered delirium: it was fright, jubilation, admiration, infinite sorrow, crazed delight, and excruciating pain. All the swords of the world were falling on Brother Francis. Francis felt as if he were dying. He was walking the interface between life and death.

He felt as if he were in the middle of a furious storm, sensations similar to bolts of lightning striking his body. He let out an agonizing scream. The pain was beyond description. Moreover, the Poor Man was not sure whether it was pain or pleasure he was feeling. Within minutes he felt something similar to bolts of lightning striking his body once again, five all together.

Francis thought that this was the end, that very soon he would be reduced to nothing but ashes.

"My Crucified Christ, let all your pain fall mercilessly upon me. Lord, what is more, I wish to end the world's pain and suffering and transform it into Love."

But there was no need for words. The hour had come. Francis was crucified.

The vision disappeared. Dawn was approaching. Francis had the impression that the storm had ceased and everything had returned to normalcy. In the incipient light of day Francis was indeed able to ascertain that his hands, feet, and side were burned, wounded, pierced, and bleeding.

The wounds caused him terrible pain.

Farewell, Mt. Alvernia

After attending Mass on September 30, 1224, the Crucified Brother gathered his disciples and said to them:

"My brothers, every morning, the Lord walks barefoot on this mountain, and angels with golden wings fill the air. Thus, it is a holy mountain. The ministers should appoint to this Brotherhood only those brothers who are as holy as the mountain itself.

"I'm leaving today with Brother Leo and I will not return. I'm just one step away from eternity. Brothers, you will remain here, but you will always be with me. Love one another as a mother loves her little one. Be chivalrous and faithful to Our Lady Poverty, and treat her with respect. Above everything else, including Poverty, render eternal worship to Sacred Love. You are knights of Eternal Love.

"Farewell Brother Maseo. Farewell Brother Angelo. Farewell Brothers Silvester and Illuminato. Peace be with you. Farewell to you all. Farewell Mt. Alvernia. Farewell beloved mountain of the Angels. Farewell brother falcon. May you be blessed for your sweetness. Farewell lofty rocks, I will never see you again. Mother of the Eternal Word, I place in your arms my children who are here with me."

"We cried inconsolably," the chronicles continued. "He, too, departed in tears and carried us in his heart."

* * *

The Crucified Brother and Brother Leo descended the mountain slowly and carefully along a narrow route opposite the rocky slopes that leads to Chiusi. But they did not enter the castle. The brothers continued their descent in silence. Francis had been sobbing, but soon stopped. Brother Leo, sensitive and sensitized, cried and cried, not caring who might see his tears. Brother Francis travelled by donkey, with Brother Leo pulling the reins.

After travelling some distance, the Crucified Brother looked back. Mt. Alvernia was still visible. But as soon as they turned toward La Foresta, the last traces of the holy mountain began to disappear. Francis ordered Brother Leo to stop the donkey. Brother Leo helped him down. Francis knelt on the road, and extended his arms in the shape of a cross as he looked at Alvernia. In the distance, the black silhouette of the mountain gave it a menacing and somber aspect beneath the clouds. Francis blessed it for the last time, saying:

"Farewell, holy mountain. May the blessings of the Almighty fall upon you. Peace be with you always, beloved mountain; I will never see you again."

They got up and continued on their way. Suddenly they lost sight of Alvernia's black silhouette. They penetrated the shadowy gorges of La Foresta in silence. The Crucified Brother broke the silence, saying:

"Brother Leo, everything is coming to an end. I am at the threshold. All I need to do is enter. The swallows are in flight. Sometimes I feel as though I'm going out of my mind with happiness. Brother Leo, *little Lamb of God* and comrade in battle, The One who has no name is signaling me to leave. This might very well be our last journey."

He said no more. Brother Leo did not respond. They continued in silence. After a while, Brother Francis looked at his companion and saw tears in his eyes.

"Brother, you cry just like those who have no faith," said Francis.

"What will become of me? You're my father and my mother."

"How many times must I repeat this: neither the moth nor the sword will ever reach the wide expanse of the soul. Oh Brother Leo, after the Father takes me in his bosom, I will be at your side more alive than ever. Is the body of any value? Well, look at mine: it's a sad sack of bones. The soul, Brother Leo, the soul possesses eternal youth. Dry your tears, *little Lamb of God*, and let a smile shine in your eyes."

These words consoled Brother Leo, and he dried his tears with the sleeve of his habit.

They continued in silence.

"Brother Leo, write: The flesh crumbles like a wall in ruins. When the last block falls, a brilliant light will appear. I'm so happy, Brother Leo. We are victorious! It is the victory of God's infinite mercy. Hallelujah!"

That night they slept in a cavern along their route. For the first time, Brother Leo cleaned the wounds of his Crucified Brother with warm water and aromatic herbs. The Poor Man of God acquiesced like a submissive child.

"I have a fever, a very high fever, Brother Leo. At times I feel so dreadfully ill..." said the Poor Man.

"The wounds and the loss of blood are causing your fever, Brother Francis," explained Brother Leo.

"If that is so, imagine the fever my blessed Crucified Christ suffered that afternoon on Calvary! May he be blessed for his pain and his love."

Francis was shivering. Brother Leo left the grotto in search of wood to light a fire. He moved Francis an adequate distance away from the flames. They produced an excessive heat, nonetheless. So Leo moved Brother Francis further away from the blaze, placing a cloth over his eyelids in order to protect his ailing eyes from the light of the flames. The flames began to die out, leaving only embers. Leo moved Brother Francis once again, bringing him closer to the flickering light. He removed the cloth from his eyes, since what remained of the fire was only a faint light glowing in the embers. Brother Francis had always enjoyed sitting before a fire in contemplation. Brother Leo was like a mother to Francis, and like a child, the Poor Man acquiesced. What a spectacle!

Francis did not sleep that night. He was a mosaic of pain, love, fever, and nostalgia for the Eternal Hills. Every day was like an eve, and he kept vigil before the great adventure of death.

Brother Leo went to rest in a corner of the cavern, but not before covering Francis. He awoke at intervals to make sure the Poor Man was comfortable. When he saw that Brother Francis was uncovered, he would go to his side and cover him again. The Crucified Brother, his eyes closed, his soul curled up in the arms of the Father, did not sleep at all that night. At around midnight, Brother Leo noticed that the night air was getting colder in the grotto. There was no wood. He went outside. He felt his way through the darkness and managed to cut a few branches to light a bonfire once again. And after covering Brother Francis, he laid down to rest.

A horrible dream woke him up at dawn. The Poor Man had already left the grotto. Brother Leo went in search of him and found him on a small hillock, his arms stretched out before him as he looked toward the East. A brilliant dawn was announcing the rise of the sun. The Crucified Brother was as resplendent as the morning sun. He saw Brother Leo approach and went to greet him with this look of expectation, as if he were anxious to communicate something.

"A multitude of angels visited me last night. They were all master musicians. They were tuning their zithers, lutes, harps, oboes, violins and flutes. The Father commanded them to perform a great concert for me. What joy, Brother Leo! Eternity is within sight! The fight is over. No more sadness or sins. I also saw a mountain made of gold. But do not fear, *little Lamb of God*, it was wheat, not gold. Have you not heard Christ say that we must store the harvest in the granaries of eternity? I've done that and nothing else all my life. I've seen other things as well: there are no signs of moths eating away at the rafters in the house the Father has prepared for me. Thus, my treasures are in a secure place. I'm so happy, Brother Leo!"

"Well, I'm not so happy, Brother Francis," said Brother Leo, and he started to cry. Brother Leo was a sensitive and emotional man.

"What's wrong, my beloved *little Lamb of God*?"

"I too had dreams last night," Leo responded, "and they weren't as delightful as yours."

"My son, open your heart and tell me everything."

"I dreamt that after your death, the ministers will persecute me, throw me in prison and beat me. And I'll be a fugitive on the run, hiding in the mountains, escaping the ire of the intellectuals."

Fortunately, upon saying these words, Brother Leo lost himself in a flood of tears and covered his eyes with his hands. I say *fortunately* because Brother Leo was therefore unaware of Francis' reaction. A dark shadow of sadness immediately covered Brother Francis' entire face, a face that, up until that moment, was radiant. Instantly, all of his old wounds resurfaced.

"I know them well, and they're quite capable of doing all that," Francis said to himself while Brother Leo cried in silence.

Suddenly, the future clouded his mind, a panorama full of shadows.

In fact, Brother Leo outlived Francis by some forty years and was a victim of all kinds of persecution on the part of the ministers and intellectuals, including flogging, imprisonment, etc.

Francis was in utter despair, not so much because of the omen but rather the trepidation that had consumed him. He was a man of peace, and when that peace dissipated, he felt nothing but death.

But if he himself were a victim of desolation, how could he possibly console the inconsolable Brother Leo? He reacted instantly. He repressed the sadness, approached Brother Leo, gave him a warm embrace, and, as he tapped him lightly on the face, he said:

"Champion, remember: I will wait for you under aurora's arch and watch you enter eternity triumphantly. You will come from the battlefield covered with scars; each scar will shine like an emerald forever and ever. The more wounds you endure, the more you'll shine in paradise."

These words consoled Brother Leo, and they began their slow descent down the hillock. Brother Leo walked in front of Francis, guiding his every step. They walked in silence. For a moment, Brother Francis gave into feelings of aversion toward the traitors who renounced his ideal. He was deeply saddened for having these sentiments, even though these hostile thoughts invaded his mind for only a moment. When they reached level ground, the Crucified Brother knelt before Brother Leo and said:

"Bless me, father, for I have sinned. Brother Leo, hear my confession."

Francis confessed his sins. Brother Leo was the secretary, nurse, and confessor of Brother Francis of Assisi. Brother Leo gave him absolution.

* * *

Francis got up and said to him:

"Let's sit down."

They sat on some rocks and the Poor Man began to speak:

"Tell me, Brother Leo: What is God's finest attribute?"

"Love," responded Brother Leo.

"No it's not," said Francis.

389

"Wisdom," Leo replied.

"No it's not. Write the following, Brother Leo: The rarest and most precious pearl on God's crown is patience. Oh, when I think about God's patience, I have this irresistible urge to burst into tears, cry my eyes out before the whole world, because tears are the most eloquent way of celebrating this invaluable attribute. And, instead, a bitter sadness takes hold of me when I realize I have not exercised that patience with my adversaries. How I would love to have them here before me so that I could go down on bended knee and kiss their feet.

"Continue writing, Brother Leo: Malevolence is the excrement of Satan himself, a nasty subterranean sewer that poisons the fountains of life. How I long to have a pure and patient heart! And when the shadow of malevolence appears in my heart, even for an instant, all I want to do is fill my mouth with dirt.

"Benevolence, in contrast, is a mysterious current (subterranean as well), something like an invisible sacrament that purifies the springs and sows harmony in those fraternal spaces. Brother Leo, write: If ever I give birth to a good sentiment, all of humanity will rise four hands above the ground.

"Oh, the patience of God! Brother Leo, always write this blessed, blessed word with very large letters. I don't know how to say it. When I think of God's patience, I just go crazy, out of my mind with joy. I just want to die of pure happiness."

He repeated several times, as if in ecstasy:

"God is patient! God is patient!"

Francis' joy was contagious. Brother Leo began to shout this phrase over and over again.

Finally, Brother Francis said:

"Sister Mother Earth, bear witness to this oath," and, as he placed his hand on the ground, he added: "In imitation of God's patience, we will never give into feelings of hostility toward anyone. May Sister Earth denounce us if we violate these words in any way."

The Power of Love

They embarked on their journey once again, reaching Borgo San Sepolcro on that same day. Without entering the city, they began to scale the mountains. They climbed along a smooth cliff and reached a rocky *projection*, that looked like a roof covering the entire world, and was called *sasso spicco*. From there, scaling a lofty cliff some several meters high, they made their way to the hermitage of Monte Casale.

Upon reaching the hut, a disciple ran out, apparently beside himself with emotion, and exclaimed:

"Father Francis! Father Francis!"

He knelt at Brother Francis' feet and embraced his ankles, kissing his feet over and over again as he bathed them with his tears. The Poor Man was stunned, and inquired:

"My brother, who are you?"

"Don't you remember, Father Francis? I'm one of those three bandits who, by your mercy, abandoned that life and entered the Brotherhood."

In fact, for several years now the ex-outlaw had been leading a most exemplary life. At midnight, he would rise for Matins. At times, he would stay up and spend the rest of the night in adoration. He worked silently in a little garden his brothers had planted for him on a mountain side. He was very hospitable toward his guests.

After hearing the news, the Crucified Brother took Brother Leo by the arm and walked hastily into the woods, and in the depths of the forest he began to scream in exaltation:

"Wonders of Love, wonders of Love! Write this down, Brother Leo: There are no prisons where there is love. There are no mental barriers, no egotistical bonds, no combative energies at death's beck and call that can resist Love. Brother Leo, what is the difference between God and Love? They're two sides of the same essence. Keep writing, Brother Leo: Love transforms cemeteries into gardens. Love's vestment is silence. There is no sweeter melody. Harps made of gold, the vibrant energies of spring, and the splendor of the dawn are no match for the melodies in Love's bosom. All miracles are possible with Love. Have you not witnessed the latest miracle, Brother Leo? Have you not seen an outlaw become a saint through the magic of Love? How can I say it, Brother Leo? I'll say it with this one phrase: God is Love."

Francis' ailing eyes were shining like two brilliant stars. This, indeed, was Love's latest miracle. How had Love revived those two dim and lifeless orbs?

* * *

Francis and Leo spent several days in the hermitage. One fine morning, they descended the mountain retreat and, as they passed through Borgo San Sepolcro, the tiny village trembled with delirium. What was it about this man? It was as if his reception had been prepared weeks ago. Not even the procession of a victorious captain could match this euphoria. Perhaps it evoked the Master's triumphant entrance. Everyone wanted to touch him. The workers left the field; the women, their homes; their children, the schools. They cut olive branches and branches from other trees and waved them in the wind, exclaiming:

"Ecco il Santo!"

The multitude crowded together, pressing against the Poor Man. Many times, he came close to falling to the ground. Women, with sickly children in their arms, risked their very lives in order to touch him. The crowd screamed, cheered, cried.

Francis, constantly pushed to and fro, for the most part was oblivious to it all, as if his spirit were somewhere else. At times, he looked annoyed, and at other times, resigned himself exclaiming:

"Lord, Lord."

Suddenly, he felt the impulse to speak. He got off the donkey and went to stand on a rock in the plaza. And with unusual vigor, he began to say:

"I'm an insignificant worm, a useless man, a sinner..."

He could not continue. The multitude rushed forward, screaming:

"Santo di Dio, Santo di Dio."

Francis' manner was one of hopelessness and resignation.

When the crowd quieted, Francis shook his arms and shouted:

"Love, Love, Love. May your self-centered and antagonistic feelings burn in the fires of Love. Oh Sacred Love, the wings of protection, the nest of life, the die of happiness, the dwelling of infants, the endless chain, the guardian of peace, refreshing shade, the eternal mother, the sleeping child, the endless ocean, the music without words, the everlasting melody..."

Francis was drunk with ecstacy. He continued:

"Love one another. Love your enemies. Love the rocks, the trees, the birds, the fish, the frogs... Love the flies, the toads, the spiders, the bats, the owls... Love the serpents, and they will not bite you. Love the wolves, and they will not devour you. Love your enemies, and they will become loving children. Raise the flag of Love, and rivalry will disappear, wars will end, envy and offenses will vanish."

It seemed that Brother Francis had lost his mind and that an immortal youth had risen from the ashes. He began to move and pronounce these words with the rhythm of a dance:

"God is Love. Love is mightier than death. Place Love where there is hate. Where there is offense, place forgiveness. Where there is discord, place union. The lamb will lie with the wolves. The sparrowhawk and the nightingale will sing the same tune. Swords will become orchards; soldiers will become sowers; battering rams will turn into windmills; battlefields will become wheat fields; neither frontiers nor homelands will set brother against brother; peace will cover the earth's orb, and God will be all in all."

From a distance, one could detect the flames of delirium in the eyes of the masses. Francis was on the brink of collapse. At that moment, he took deep breaths and did his utmost to regain his composure. He raised his arms once more and said aloud:

"God, give me strength, God give me strength...!

He could not go on. From one minute to the next, he lost all self-control and cried inconsolably. The crowd went wild. The people cried, screamed, roared:

"Santo di Dio! Santo di Dio!"

The multitude came dangerously near, almost suffocating the Crucified Brother. Brother Leo cried uncontrollably. Instinctively, a group of robust men formed a chain around the Poor Man of God, and it was a miracle that Francis came out unharmed from among the throng that day.

The scene repeated itself, to varying degrees, in other cities.

At the Gates of Creation

They continued on their journey in this manner: Brother Leo in front, guiding the donkey; the Crucified Brother sitting quietly on the animal and with his eyes closed.

"A minute longer and the crazed crowd would have devoured you whole, Brother Francis," said Brother Leo.

"God! God! Brother Leo, it's God that they want to devour. The people are hungry for God. When they smell God, they lose their heads and lunge at him like wild, hungry animals. God, Brother Leo, God!"

They quieted and continued in silence. It was late autumn. The high peaks of the Apennines were covered with snow.

They travelled the whole day tolerating bad weather and poor roads. Almost without realizing it, night had fallen and there was no shelter in sight. They sought refuge in a crag and were glad to spend the night in that hollow break in the cliff. A man who had accompanied them that day was freezing from the cold and mumbling to himself, almost cursing Brother Francis. The latter approached him and placed his wounded hand on his shoulder. Francis barely touched him and the chills disappeared. The heat penetrating his body was so great, he could have been standing next to a lit stove.

* * *

The following day, Brother Francis said to Leo:

"Brother Leo, let's dedicate the day to our blessed Love, Lord God, our Father."

They began to climb a small rocky mountain, its summit peering out in all its splendor. They climbed very slowly, for there were no clear paths to follow. Brother Leo guided the donkey and its sacred load, making wide turns in order to facilitate their climb. Evergreen oaks, black cypresses, chestnut trees, thickets, boxes, and boulders were everywhere.

They sat down and rested for a while. Francis was happy. His sense of smell became much more acute as his sight deteriorated.

"Brother Leo, could I be smelling thyme?"

Brother Leo got up and soon returned with a handful of sprigs. Francis took a whiff of the perfume, breathing in deeply, and said:

"Blessed be God for this splendid thyme. Brother Leo, I have always heard it said that the most pleasurable sensation God can bestow is the ability to inhale the perfumes of thyme and rosemary. Isn't that right?"

Instantly, Brother Leo got up and within a few minutes returned with a bouquet of fragrant rosemary.

Francis took both handfuls and inhaled. The perfume was absolutely intoxicating:

"Oh... Lord, Lord..., oh... gifts from God! I'm the happiest man on earth. Life is so beautiful, Brother Leo. The day I enter the gates of eternity, I will plant thyme and rosemary in the mountains of paradise. Write the following, Brother Leo: only the poor will experience the intoxicating and surprising sensations the earth has to offer. Only the poor will enjoy the delicate wonders of the Father. How wonderful it is to be poor for the sake of love!"

* * *

They got up and continued on their way. This time, Brother Francis preferred to walk. He was in front; Brother Leo, to his side and trailing a bit behind, watchful of Brother Francis' every step. Francis climbed very slowly, hunched over, carefully eyeing the ground as though he were looking for a lost object.

"Brother Francis, what's wrong?" inquired Brother Leo.

"The rocks, Brother Leo, the rocks! Have you ever heard psalmists compare Christ to a rock? Whenever I see a rock on the ground, I can't help but think of Christ. And I would feel so much grief if I were to step on one. It would be like treading on the consecrated host."

He fell to his knees and kissed a plain old rock with so much veneration and warmth one would think he were kissing Christ.

"Brother Leo, write: Every creature on earth bears the image of Christ. How many times must I tell you, Brother Leo, that that which is essential is invisible! Close your eyes, look with faith, and under the very first rock you'll see the handsome image of the Lord. The world is full of wonder to the eyes of faith."

"Brother Leo, I'd like to share a secret. You don't know how many times I was tempted to include the following article in the Rule: to urge my brothers, in the name of the Lord Jesus Christ, to pick up any piece of paper they spot on the ground and display it, for there they might find written the name of God; or, at the very least, compile the letters that will spell out God's name. Blessed are those who endeavor to do it."

* * *

They continued their climb up the rocky mountain. When they reached the summit, Francis rested while Brother Leo searched for an adequate place to stop for the day. Having found it, he brought the Crucified Brother there and prepared a rock for him to sit on.

"Brother Leo, we will stop here for the night as well. The night air will probably be very cold. So, gather some wood. You'll gather all kinds of branches, even thick ones, but listen to me, Brother Leo: no tree trunks, don't even touch them, because...our blessed Christ's cross was cut from that wood."

His eyes were moist with tears.

"Listen to me, Brother Leo: Be careful not to cut the roots of the thickets, so that they may grow again."

While Francis remained in contemplation, Brother Leo went out in search of wood. Suddenly, a swarm of larks flew by the cavern, singing joyfully. Brother Francis trembled with emotion. He walked out of the grotto in case others might fly by. They did not come.

"Our sister, the lark," said Francis, "is an example to the friars. She wears a tiny hood very much like ours! Her feathers have the same earth tones as our habit. She looks humbly for nourishment along her route. She soars through the skies singing happily. In short, our hearts should always reach those lofty heights. We should be like larks."

* * *

At nightfall, Brother Leo lit a fire, heated some medicinal herbs, and, with extreme delicacy, treated Brother Francis' wounds, caring for him as a mother would a child. Francis spent many hours before the blaze in a state of ecstasy. It looked more "beautiful, vibrant, and joyful" than ever.

"Brother Leo, brother fire's strength and magnificence makes me tremble with emotion. Look at that constant motion. Look at how the flames rise and fall, how they magically appear and disappear. Look at how the flames rush from one side of the wood to the other. They're yellow, later blue, then red, and then greenish-blue. It's like sorcery performed by Mother Earth. Fire, ocean, God: they have so much in common! Brother Leo, write: In all creation, what most resembles God is fire. They are both full of life and movement. They both illuminate and give warmth. They both move and are resplendent. They both blacken, purify, cauterize, depending on the circumstances. They're both vibrant and magnificent. Praise to you, Lord, for brother fire."

The next morning, Brother Leo took what remained of the burning pieces of wood and carelessly threw them outside. He also threw dirt on the burning embers to ensure that the fire was completely extinguished.

"No, Brother Leo," said Francis, "don't do that. We must not smother anything on this earth. If the intellectuals of the Order did not think it ridiculous, I would have included the following precepts in the Rule: Do not extinguish candles or flames; do not cut tree trunks; do not step on rocks; do not cage birds; do not cut flowers; do not burn anything; do not destroy anything; do not disparage anything; nourish the bees during the winter; have compassion for every living thing; show affection to tiny, insignificant things; ugly, repulsive animals like toads, rats, flies, roaches, lizards, serpents...should be favored among you. Oh, if the intellectuals had permitted it, what a Rule the brothers would have had! Oh, Brother Leo, the entire world is one enormous sacrament of God."

* * *

Francis felt the same tenderness for all of creation.

A large young hare accompanied Brother Francis, like a faithful puppy, on the days he spent in reflection in the mountains of Greccio. In the same region of Rieti, on the days Francis dedicated to prayer sitting near the banks of a lake, a kingfisher and a medium-sized trout came at the same hour every day to ask for blessings.

In Siena, a handsome pheasant kept company with the disciples. It would go on a hunger strike during Francis' absence, and would not eat for several days.

At the Porziuncola, a large cicada would poise itself on the branches of a juniper tree and sing piercing notes. When Francis called it, the cicada would gladly acquiesce, landing on his right hand while singing songs of praise.

A devout little lamb also stayed with the disciples for a while at the Porziuncola. Whenever Brother Francis prayed, the little lamb would go to his side and lie on the floor. During consecration, the lamb would bend its two front legs; and it would greet Our Lady with affectionate "baas."

Francis asked a gardener in a nearby hermitage to allocate space in his vegetable garden for some flowers. In springtime, when the countryside burst into bloom, the following frequently took place: Brother Francis would stop before a flower (he never cut flowers) and speak to it as if it were a person. He would use the amorous words of a lover, inviting it to praise the Almighty. He would touch the flowers delicately and caress their petals. It was as if they were conscious of his affection, almost human in their response.

In short, Brother Francis had penetrated the secrets of creation.

One day, to the great wonder of Brother Leo, Francis went begging for wine. He returned with a jug full of foamy red wine. He boiled it and then let it cool. Afterwards, he mixed it with honey and took the mixture into the forest and placed it near a beehive.

"Brother Leo," said Francis, "we cannot allow these beautiful creatures, the bees, to die of hunger. We're in the middle of winter and there are no flowers."

One spring, he spent time making turtledove nests. For hours he would observe the birds while they carefully constructed their nests. He made his nests with precision, almost duplicating the originals, and placed them in bushes and thickets.

"Brother Leo," he would say, "I like turtledoves very much. Do you know why? Their finest attributes are those of my Lord: compassion and humility."

Brother Pain

They continued on their journey to the Porziuncola. Brother Francis was absorbed in thoughts of eternal life. He spoke of nothing else except the grand festival awaiting the poor, coffers full of treasures, brilliant diadems crowning their heads.

Brother Francis spoke as if the end were imminent. Could we say that Francis was happy? He felt something other than happiness. He was almost anxious to step on the pinnacle of eternity. He was suffering. Abdominal pains, hemorrhages, constant fevers caused by the stigmata, and ailing eyes made the Poor Man of God an open wound. Eternity meant, among other things, rest and the end of his pain and suffering.

They arrived at the Porziuncola. However, they stayed there less than a day. Feeling that death was fast approaching, he was consumed with the desire and the need to proclaim the Word of God. During the winter and spring months, he travelled to most of the Umbrian villages. He was a tireless apostle, travelling to three or four hamlets every day.

The daily excursions were debilitating and weakened him further to the point where, on several occasions, he even feared for his life. His sight was almost completely gone. His eyes were bandaged and he suffered terrible headaches.

He met Pope Honorius III and his retinue in Rieti. Ugolino insisted that Francis see the doctors in the city. Francis had always been allergic to doctors and refused to come before them. They convinced him by way of a verse from *Ecclesiastes*: "The Lord has made medicine available. Man will not look upon it with contempt."

The Crucified Brother agreed to a medical consultation and, eventually, to undergo surgery.

* * *

"I'm a wall in ruins," said the Poor Man of God to himself. "Only a few hours remain until the dawn of Day. The pinnacle of eternity is within sight. I'm going to say my farewells to Sister Clare and the Poor Ladies. It may be our last farewell."

Francis and Brother Leo travelled to St. Damian with the intention of visiting for a few days.

"Father Francis," said Clare, "the larks, the nightingales, the swallows, the carnations in the cloister, the Minoresses and I welcome you. We have but one wish, Father Francis: that your stay at St. Damian be a prelude to paradise."

Knowing the things he enjoyed, Clare prepared a garland of violets for him to wear. He took them in his hands and smelled them. They filled him with inspiration:

"Oh, humility," he began, "mother of saints and cradle of the Brotherhood. Sister Clare, how can I express this? Strong and free men dwell in the bosom of humility. Where there is humility there is no fear. It is the school of wisdom where the aristocrats of the spirit and the most commendable of the human race are forged. Where there is humility there is spiritual beauty, the serenity of twilight, the elegance of a lady, the tenderness of a mother, the strength of a champion, the resiliency of steel, the grace of a dove. How can I say this? Sister Clare, a humble woman is an invincible woman. The violets smell wonderful, Sister Clare! The stars help me to give you thanks for this garland."

The Crucified Brother looked as if he had been reborn that day. But the feeling did not last. During the night, pain and suffering were on the prowl, and they pounced on the Poor Man of God like a pack of hungry wolves.

"Brother Leo, do you know what fire is? Well, that's what pain is: it's a fire that burns to the marrow of the bones, biting, tearing, burning, stripping. It becomes impossible to breathe. The body becomes nothing but flames, better yet, a pyre. The only difference is that it devours, but does not consume. Brother Leo, I can't go on. Please ask the Almighty to remove his hand for a moment."

Brother Leo was never so discouraged in all his life. That night, the Crucified Brother was in contortions, moaning in pain. His eyes were two flames of blood and pus. His liver was about to burst. His wounds were ablaze. Brother Leo did not know what to do. It occurred to him to seek help, and he called at the convent of the Poor Ladies.

"But what can they do?" he thought.

"Brother Leo, I take it back. Do not ask the Almighty to remove his hand. He is my Father. He cannot ask his son to live this violent attack. Tell him to do what he feels is right, and may his will be done. Brother Leo, is pain the worst form of human existence, or the ultimate? Why did the Son of God use this method to redeem the world? What is there after pain? Redemption? Extinction? Peace? What is pain in the hands of God? Affection? Punishment? Predilection?

Purification? Mercy? Admonition? I've heard it said that pain and pleasure are one and the same. Could that be true?"

* * *

It was morning.

"What a relief! Brother Leo, write the following: The dawn is a kiss from God. Praise be to you, Lord, for the morning: it is the end of pain and the beginning of hope. If it weren't for the dawn, we would succumb to hopelessness. Nights are awful."

Nevertheless, Francis' suffering did not subside. At sunrise, Sister Clare arrived with a bowl of chicken soup containing ingredients which, according to her, were very stimulating. Brother Francis had no desire to eat. However, as a courtesy to her, he began to drink it slowly. He could not finish it however. Spasms of pain induced regurgitation. Brother Leo ran to a corner and cried. Clare, with tears in her eyes, did all she could to make Brother Francis comfortable.

"Sister Clare, I'm crucified," said Francis. "The pain is tearing at me like a rabid dog and my bones are pulverized."

"Father Francis, what can I say that can possibly help you? You know everything. You've spoken so many times to us about the Crucified Christ."

Upon hearing these words, Brother Francis opened his eyes as if he were recovering from lethargy.

"You're right, Sister Clare. I shouldn't complain. How could I have forgotten about my Poor Crucified Lord? Brother Leo, if during the night I murmured any kind of lamentation, erase it from your writing tablet immediately. I've not been a true gentleman to my Lord. Praise to You, God, for brother pain, the inseparable companion of my Crucified Lord. Blessed be God for that infant who has given us life. Brother pain purifies us, undoing the worldly chains of bondage and placing us in the arms of God. Write the following, Brother Leo: Happy the man who, ambushed by pain, wears the armor of faith and love. He will be as pure as gold, a fountain of virtue and life. Unhappy is the man who, in the grip of agony, finds himself unprepared and without faith. Without a doubt, he will suffer annihilation. Oh my glorious Lord Jesus Christ, valiant companion of pain, do with me what you will!"

He relaxed and slept a while. Clare and Leo left his side for a moment.

"What do you think, Brother Leo?" asked Clare. "How much longer do you think we'll have Father Francis with us?"

"Sister Clare, I thought that pain and suffering ended with the crucifixion. Mysteriously enough, the Almighty continues oppressing Brother Francis. What can we do? What would one gain by resisting or asking useless questions? Brother Francis has taught me that it is best to close one's mouth, open one's heart, and bow one's head before the mysteries of God. As for the rest, there's nothing we can do."

"Brother Leo," said Clare, "now that we're alone, tell me about Francis' crucifixion. Did Christ appear in the form of a bolt of lightning? A spark of light? Did his flesh burn? Any gashes? Tell me."

"Sister Clare, if, as they say, heaven is full of mysteries, all the more reason do I have in stating that the night of the stigmata will be left to the imagination. Gashes? Yes, Sister Clare, in his side. I can tell you that his hands and feet have deep wounds, much like the color and shape of the nails that pierced Jesus' hands and feet."

"Do you think that Father Francis will permit me to wash and treat his wounds? It would be a tremendous privilege for me to do so."

"Erase that thought from your mind, Sister Clare. Francis guards his divine secrets with a passion. He will not share them even with his most beloved friends. He has told me several times: Beware the man who does not have secrets with his Lord!"

* * *

They entered the room once again. Francis' eyes were wide open.

"Sister Clare, is it day or night?" he asked.

"It's midday, Father Francis," Clare responded.

"I can't see, I can't see. Not even a shadow. I'm blind. It looks like midnight."

He sat up and opened his red eyes as wide as he could.

"I don't see anything," he said once again.

He lay down on the bed and said:

"Lord, Lord, I am your servant; I have no right to complain; do what you will. Everything is fine."

There was a long silence. Clare and Leo looked at one another sympathetically. Brother Leo went and stood by the door. Clare's eyes filled with tears, but she did not cry. She remained at the foot of the bed.

"Where are you, Sister Clare?" Francis asked.

"Right here, Father Francis."

"Sister Clare, the flight of the swallows! The flight of the swallows!" gasped the Crucified Brother.

"What is it that you wish to say, Father Francis?" asked Clare.

"When I was young, I devoted my energies to repairing these walls. I would stop working, sit in the cloister of St. Damian and spend hours admiring the swallows in flight.

Their delightful pirouettes, their daring acrobatics, their incredible speed were emotionally stirring. At times, I was so overcome with emotion that I cried. Oh, there's no greater spectacle than the flight of the swallows. I've dreamt of seeing them once again. I came to say my farewells, but also (I've told no one) to catch the swallows fluttering about in St. Damian. Now, the Lord has taken away that privilege. I will never see the flight of the swallows again. Sister Clare, this is what I regret the most. Regardless, do what you will."

Clare was silent. She felt sorry for Brother Francis. He would no longer witness the swallows heralding the spring.

The Violin

During the course of the day, the Crucified Brother managed to steer his spirit through the oceans of tranquility. He was a docile child in the face of divine battles. He did not resist. He did not ask questions. He accepted the new situation peacefully and quietly. He walked the fine line of total abandonment and fell into the arms of serenity.

His spiritual attitude helped to alleviate the pain. Brother Leo did not leave his bedside. Sister Clare would come in and out frequently, bringing aromatic waters, then a change of clothes, later homemade remedies she prepared herself. Brother Francis went from sight to sound. Losing his sight amplified his vision of faith.

"Brother Leo, what's happening? Are we in paradise? I don't see light, but my ears are ringing with harmonies. From Spoleto all the way to Perugia, I hear voices in the valley, birds, crickets, toads. The sounds fill my soul with an eternal symphony. And that goldfinch that is singing in the cypresses against the window... I could die of happiness. I've never felt such sweetness."

He lowered his voice and said:

"God! God! How great you are!"

Leo and Clare were relieved and overjoyed. Now and then they would look at one another, acknowledging and in accord with the words Francis had expressed.

"Brother Leo, write the following: Only the blind will see God. Just close your eyes and the universe is one with God. Oh, what's truly important lies beyond the retina. Brother Leo, forget your eyes, your ears, your sense of smell, your sense of touch and we will find ourselves in paradise. Behind death stands the wall of immortality. The divine One will appear when the walls of the body fall in ruins. Oh, Brother Leo, when will I finally rest in the arms of my Father?"

His expression was an exquisite study in serenity. Sister Clare signaled Brother Leo to the door, and said to him:

"Brother Leo, I've seen many ailing faces and I know how God works in these matters. The relief Father Francis is feeling at the moment is nothing more than a respite. The pain will come back and perhaps more intense than ever. I'm anxious about tonight. Anything can happen. Allow me to suggest several courses of action."

At nightfall Sister Clare gathered all kinds of cloth, special medicinal herbs, prepared various remedies she had previously used with those in her care, and brought in various liquids. She also lit a small stove just outside the room for boiling water.

She took her leave and asked for Brother Francis' blessing. The Poor Man of God placed his wounded hand on her head. After a few minutes of silence he raised his voice and, with words of profound inspiration, asked the Almighty to keep her and guide her footsteps.

When Clare left, Francis said:

"Don't be shocked by what I'm about to say, Brother Leo, just write: Oh, women... the most exalted mystery on earth. They smell death, Brother Leo. Women were placed on the face of the earth in order to give life. And where there is death, be it body or soul, from deep within the mysteries of life, they extract the energies needed to mount a defense. Without women there would be no *Life*. Women, Brother Leo, are always in touch with the earth and life. And don't let what I'm about to say frighten you: God, the source of life, is closer to women, and they are closer to God. They wear the truer Face of God, without even knowing it. I'm remembering the great lady, Lady Pica... And now, don't let what I'm about to say shock you, and continue writing: Ever since I experienced the spirituality of my mother, Lady Pica, I've been tempted to invoke the name of God with the word *Mother*."

* * *

Sister Clare was not mistaken. As soon as Francis said these words he was overcome by a wave of pain. Within minutes, the Crucified Brother was a pyre of pain. The flames were higher than ever. Brother Leo was frightened and gathered all the medicines Clare had prepared. He read the list to Brother Francis in the hopes of calming his spirit, but Francis failed to react.

The pain was reaching a crescendo. Brother Francis was contorted in agony. And when the pains surpassed what was humanly tolerable, no one could even hazard a guess as to what truly happened to the Crucified Brother.

Pain and pleasure were face to face. Calvary and Tabor embraced and blended together. No one can explain whether Francis was having an out-of-body experience or suffering a momentary lapse, having fainted as a result. The fact remains, Brother Francis had begun to hear the strings of a violin as played by an angel. The music made the boundaries between pain and pleasure disappear. Pleasure had either seized or conquered pain, forcing it to submit and be sublimated.

Brother Leo saw that Francis' convulsions had stopped and a smile was forming on his lips. At first, Brother Leo thought that Francis had indeed passed to the next life. But he took his pulse and realized that his heart was beating normally, that is, on the outside.

On the inside, Francis had reached the zenith of human resistance. God had become music, having the fingers of an angel perform a *partita* that blended all the melodies of paradise.

God himself, in his omnipotence, hurled all of his infinite sweetness on Francis' mortality, shaping, focusing, and concentrating all of Brother Francis' energies on his musical sensitivity. God had become an ineffable *Stradivarius*. With this powerful *visitation*, all energies (energies that are one and the same for pain and pleasure) were being pulled by a "torrent of delight," resisting the sphere of pain and immersing themselves in the sphere of pleasure.

* * *

The Poor Man of God felt as if he had been dreaming:

"Brother Leo, if the angel had played one more note, surely I would have died right there. Mercy (you should also right this word in capital letters, Brother Leo) lifted me to the first, the third or the fifth heaven, and I heard melodies a man can only hear when dying. I no longer need Sister Clare's remedies. Blessed be brother pain who purifies us and prepares us for the music of eternity. Brother Leo, write: There's not a dictionary in the world that adequately defines what awaits those who love God."

The pains returned. Even if they had been fires from hell, Francis would have confronted them undaunted. The smile never left his face for the remainder of the night and the next morning, no matter how much he suffered.

"Father Francis," said Clare, "in view of the fact that the pains have worsened, it has now become impossible to move you to the Porziuncola. Would you like me to prepare a little cabin for you, similar to the one at St. Mary of the Angels?"

"I'm most grateful for your concern, and I accept your humble offer," Francis replied.

A hut made of intertwined twigs and branches was constructed near the rectory and the cloister, according to Francis' specifications. Clare personally supervised the construction, making sure the norms of poverty were considered. She did everything possible to alleviate Brother Francis' pain and suffering.

The Crucified Brother stayed in the hut for about a month and a half. Not once did he leave the narrow confines. The pain was relentless.

Nocturnal Transfiguration

One night, however, the unexpected happened. The intensity of consolation equals that of desolation. That night, desolation had reached its maximum intensity. The Almighty Father had abandoned his son, allowing him to wander aimlessly through the cracks and crevices of despair. After the night of the stigmata, this was Brother Francis' *grand night*, even more memorable than the night in Spoleto.

The Father denied him all manner of consolation. It was as if all of the turbulent fires of hell had attacked the poor soul in one final assault. That night, Brother Francis wanted to die and end his pain and suffering.

The old wounds in his heart began to bleed. The Poor Man of God was saddened by the fact that he was incapable of reacting peacefully. He yearned to turn back the clock and begin again, to live a solitary life in the Apennines. His ideals lay scattered on the ground, like soiled and tattered flags. To make matters worse, he had the distinct impression that all the rats in the region had been summoned for the sole purpose of torturing him. They covered every inch of the hut, screeching relentlessly. They climbed onto his bed and trampled his body, even biting him at times. His pancreas was blazing hot, red flames shone in his eyes, his wounds were on fire, all was fire, delirium, agony.

Francis of Assisi had reached the point of no return, the most precarious moment in his life, the abyss of total despair.

At midnight, the moment of truth had arrived. On impulse, he sat up and let out a desperate scream:

"Lord, my God, how much longer? I can't go on. Take me, please."

The following words resonated throughout his entire being with extreme clarity:

"My dear Francis, if, in compensation for your suffering, someone were to give you a treasure that was larger than anything on earth, you would gladly take the gift, would you not?"

"Of course, my Lord; it would be an invaluable gift."

"Well then, dance with yoy, Poor Little Man of God; sing out in your pain, for you have been promised the eternal reward."

* * *

Suddenly, terrestrial and celestial forces began to stir. From deep within the invisible currents of the earth there arose... what? Winds blow from the four corners of the earth and its wings... what? Like showers of stars falling from the heavens... its name? It was called *jubilation*. It was a dizzying tide. It was an intoxicating tenderness.

"Brother Leo, pass me the violin," said Francis.

Leo thought that Brother Francis was delirious, and he spoke to him as if he were a child:

"You're dreaming, my dear Francis. This thing with the violin happened the other night. There are no violins now, Brother Francis."

"How many times must I tell you, Brother Leo, that only the blind see wonders. Go outside. Cut two thick branches from the cherry tree just outside the door and bring them to me."

Francis took the branches, placed one on his shoulder, as though it were a violin, and took the other one in his right hand, holding it like a bow. And Francis "lost" himself in music all night long, as if he were performing a sonata. He did not stop passing one branch over the other until the break of dawn. He opened his mouth as if he were singing. His blind eyes looked upward, as if they were actually focused on something. This was how he spent the night. His soul was lost in another world.

A radiant morning loomed in that ethereal space. Flowers were blooming and the world wore raiments of hope. First and foremost, Lady Pica appeared standing on a rock. In his infancy and youth, she had embraced him with loving arms and fostered his high ideals. There, the night in Spoleto was visible like a morning star. The Byzantine Christ paved the way.

The Lord, in all his mercy, had taken him by the hand and they walked together among the lepers and along the walls in ruin. He had conquered ridicule, disrobing in front of all of Assisi. His first disciples were there, along with the approbation of their new way of life by the Holy Father, the happy days in Rivo Torto, the poverty at the Porziuncola, his brothers and their increasing numbers, the fights for the ideal, the wonders in Greccio and those of Alvernia... It was all very beautiful!

Like a grand lord, the sun had presided over this glorious procession, illuminating the way. Its warmth, beauty and might accompanied him by day, and especially by night. The delightful cascading waters near the hermitages had quenched his thirst. Oh, the unforgettable starry nights, rich with the Presence, and those nights when the moon was full. The earth had given him her mountains for prayer, her caverns for rest, her winds that rocked him to sleep, and her bosom for olives, wheat, nuts, grapes, and plums. It was all very beautiful!

Higher still, beyond the sun and stars, was the Almighty who, in power and love, had made this singular existence possible. It was all very beautiful!

The Crucified Brother, always "faraway," clearly sensed that his existence had been a privilege, a gift from God, the Father. He was eternally grateful to the Father, fire, the sun, the waters, the earth...and, on the most desperate night of his life, a night filled with rats, fever, and delirium, the Crucified Brother of Assisi gave the world the happiest and most optimistic hymn the heart would ever hear: the *Canticle of Brother Sun*.

At the break of dawn, Sister Clare brought a change of clothes and some chicken soup to her sick brother. Before entering the room, she called to Brother Leo and asked:

"Did Father Francis rest last night?"

"Sister Clare, all I can tell you is that his heart is still beating. But Francis is no longer in this world. Very strange things happened last night, Sister Clare. Brother Francis had reached the limits of desperation. I can't begin to tell you what occurred when he crossed that fine line: I'm not sure whether it was delirium or ecstasy... He asked for two branches and he moved them in such a way one would think he were playing a violin. He passed one stick over the other all night long, opening his mouth as if he were singing arias."

"Brother Leo," Francis called from inside the room.

"Here I am, Brother Francis."

"Has Sister Clare arrived?"

"Yes, Brother Francis, she's here."

Francis looked as if he had awakened from a deep sleep, as if he had visited another world.

"Last night, the Lord, in all his mercy, reassured me that my place is secured in paradise. I have written a song, as a token of my appreciation. And I would like you, Brother Leo, faithful comrade in battle, and you, Sister Clare, my most precious flower, to be the first to hear it."

He sat up comfortably in his bed. He placed one branch on his left shoulder and took the other one in his right hand, and began to rub one with the other with great enthusiasm. He opened his mouth and sang:

Omnipotent, Almighty, good Lord,
praise, glory, and honor are yours;
only you are worthy of blessing,
and no human being is worthy to pronounce your name.

Praise be to you Lord for all creatures,
especially for the honored brother sun
that shines at the dawn of day, radiant in all his splendor,
and heralds the news of his Creator.

And for sister moon for her white light,
and for the stars your power did ignite,

so pure, so lovely, so vivid they are
shining in the heavens: Praise the Lord!

And for sister water, precious and pure,
useful, chaste, humble: Praise the Lord!
For brother fire, the sun's absence lures
its power, its attraction, its joy: Praise the Lord!

For sister earth who brings every blessing.
Sister mother earth, who on every occasion
bears herbs, fruits, flowers, and much more,
sustains us and prevails: Praise the Lord!

Serve with humble and contrite hearts!
Show gratitude and sing the praises of creation!
All creatures, praise the Lord!

Even before Francis reached the fourth verse, Brother
Leo lost control and began to cry. Clare listened peacefully.
As soon as he finished the hymn, Brother Leo, in a flood of
tears, threw himself on Francis, kissing his shoulders, his
hands, and his pierced feet, saying:

"Lord, have mercy on me, for I'm nothing more than an
insignificant worm. Who am I to be so honored, to live side
by side with a saint?"

"Brother Leo, your emotions are getting the better of
you. Write: Only God is a holy saint."

The Crucified Brother put the breviary aside for a while
and spent hours reciting the *Canticle of the Sun*. When the
pains became somewhat acute, he reflected this change in
his intonation and pitch, and invited Brother Leo and Sister
Clare to sing along with him. There was no better medicine
for his pains.

* * *

"Brother Leo, I would like to found another Order or, better yet, I would like the Order of the Friars Minors to be known as the Order of the Friars Minstrels. Brother Leo, go and search for the *King of Verse* and bring him here promptly."

As soon as Brother Pacifico arrived, Francis asked him:

"Brother Pacifico, do you have your lute with you?"

"Brother Francis," Pacifico replied, "what's a soldier without his sword? A herald without his trumpet? A singer without his lute? What good is he? My dear Francis: it's right here in my hands."

"You have responded well, my brother. How I'd love to play that instrument!"

"I can teach you, if you like," replied Brother Pacifico.

"It's late, my brother. Night is approaching. I will soon take my leave."

"I'll teach you the fundamentals. They'll serve as background music for the *Canticle*."

It was quite a sight to see this blind, useless man, this obliging student of music, take the lute in his hand, position his fingers, and cheer like a child when he managed to strum a correct chord.

"Brother Pacifico," said Francis, "choose a group of brothers who are musically inclined. After I teach you the *Canticle*, I want you to teach it to them. You will go to hamlets and cities, and gather the people in the town square. Before and after preaching, you will sing the *Canticle*, accompanied by the lute and the flute, like true minstrels of God, just like Provençal troubadours. As soon as you finish the Canticle, one of you will tell your listeners: 'We are the minstrels of God, and as a reward we ask the following: live by Love.'

417

"Brother Leo, write: I want the Friars Mirors to be troubadours of God walking the earth proclaiming that there is no Almighty other than God. Fill men's lives with joy. Aren't God's servants minstrels destined to lift the hearts of humble men and lead them to happiness?"

Ambassador of Peace

The Crucified Brother was still at St. Damian when he got word that a violent confrontation had taken place between Bishop Guido and the *Magistrate*, Messer Oportolo. The matter under debate had reached scandalous proportions.

This situation was a cause for worry and greatly distressed Brother Francis. It was upsetting to see no one negotiating an agreement.

"It is most shameful to see servants of God—the bishop and *Magistrate*—exercising malice toward one another. No one is taking the initiative to help them make peace with one another."

Therefore, he made the decision to be that instrument of peace from his sickbed. He added a verse to the *Canticle*, which said:

"Praised be the Lord, for those who
forgive in the name of love,
and endure tribulations and infirmity.
Happy are those who suffer peacefully,
for they will be crowned by you, God Almighty.

"Brother Pacifico: Go to the *Magistrate* on my behalf and invite him to join the other dignitaries in the bishop's plaza to hear my *Canticle* with the extra verse."

At the appointed hour, the plaza was crowded with citizens. Brother Pacifico and his chorus walked onto a platform. The *King of Verse* raised his voice and said:

"Citizens of Assisi: you are going to hear the *Canticle of Brother Sun* which Brother Francis has just written on his sickbed for the glory of God and harmony among all brothers. He himself has begged on bended knee that you listen attentively."

Brother Pacifico sang the verses alone, the chorus repeating them in unison. The *Magistrate* "stood up and, with clasped hands and tearful eyes, listened attentively and with devotion." Likewise, his attendants got up "just as one does upon hearing the Gospel at a Mass."

The congregation was profoundly moved by the verses of the venerated Brother. The multitude burst out in tears upon hearing the last verse in the song about forgiveness. The emotion stirring in the crowd was contagious and touched the hearts of the two quarrelers.

The *Magistrate* walked through the throng and approached Bishop Guido. He knelt at his feet, saying:

"Even if my son were to suffer at the hands of an assassin, there is no man on this earth I will not pardon at this very moment for the love of God and Francis, his servant. For this reason, I am at your disposal and will give you satisfaction, my lord bishop, in any manner that you may require."

Bishop Guido took the *Magistrate* in his arms and gave him a warm embrace, saying:

"I, too, ask your forgiveness. For the sake of my office, I should exercise humility. However, I am by nature an irascible and obstinate individual. I beg of you, forgive me, for the love of God and his servant, Francis."

On that day, the whole town exalted the Poor Man of Assisi. His ambassadorship paved the way for renewed peace and harmony.

A Farewell to Clare

The Poor Man of Assisi spent some fifty days on his sickbed in the hut at St. Damian. Clare was his nurse. She showed goodness and bestowed countless acts of kindness with the object of alleviating his pain. Her concoctions were her own tried and true remedies. In short, she was his nurse, his mother, and a feminine presence during his entire illness.

Francis recovered, thanks to her undying care and concern, and was ready to embark on his journey to Rieti.

Intuitively, Clare sensed that Francis had only a few days to live and that, most likely, they would never see each other again.

"Father Francis," said Sister Clare, "the archangel hovers above you. The crown is ready, the symphony has been rehearsed. The light in your throat will soon die out, but before it does, we would like to hear your last song. Come to the convent and give your last message to the Poor Ladies."

Leo, Pacifico, Maseo, Rufinus, and Angelo accompanied him to the parlor. The Poor Ladies, like radiant doves, appeared on the other side of the grill.

Francis sat in a rustic chair, and his brothers stood on either side of him.

"Brother Pacifico," said Francis, "take the lute, tune it, and practice some notes."

The prelude sounded better than ever, like music being performed by angels. Suddenly, Brother Francis opened his mouth and sang the first verse. The silence was like a massive dome absorbing his fragile yet firm voice. His brothers sang the chorus, repeating the verses in unison.

One by one, the Poor Ladies slowly glided down the slopes of emotion, giving way to a flood of tears. Clare was the last one to be overcome by this contagious display of feeling. Even the disciples were overwhelmed. They were all sobbing, except for Francis.

While their tears dried as they regained their composure, Brother Francis observed a moment of silence. Soon afterwards, he expressed his words of parting, saying to them:

"My Ladies:

"The reception is ready. The musicians have the zithers in their hands. The banquet will soon begin. I must take my leave.

"My Ladies: I kneel before you to ask that you remain forever faithful to our Most Holy Lady Poverty.

"I also pray, on bended knee, that your lives be burning candles that will shine forever before the Sacred Love. May you be emeralds pinned to the white tunic of the Beloved.

"My Ladies: I will wait for you beneath the arch of eternity. Farewell."

Amidst a flood of tears and sobs, Clare calmly approached the Crucified Brother, and placed a gift wrapped with laurel and olive branches, violets, lovely roses, and carnations in his hands. She kissed his two wounded palms, and said:

"Father Francis, until the Great Encounter. Farewell."

Only at this very moment did Clare's eyes moisten with tears.

He opened the wrapping and found a pair of felt sandals that Clare had made to measure for Francis' pierced and bandaged feet. Clare and Francis never saw each other again.

Entreating Fire

From this moment until his death, the Poor Man of God was in the company of the four comrades who had accompanied him from the very beginning: Leo, Maseo, Angelo, and Rufinus. This, at the request of Brother Elias who, in acknowledging Francis' wishes, arranged that his four loyal brothers accompany him day and night.

They made him a large hood to cover his head and help alleviate his terrible headaches. They covered his eyes with a thick, smooth cloth. They procured a small donkey, the most docile one they could find. And they embarked on their trip to Rieti. Elias and Ugolino insisted that he seek lodging in the episcopal palace where all amenities would be made available to him.

But the Crucified Brother made plain his wishes to lodge at the hut in Fonte Colombo, about an hour's walk from the city. The pains in his stomach and liver soon worsened.

During this time, the Poor Man of God maintained a presence of mind that was absolutely extraordinary. One can say he was divided into two elements. His body was a pyre of pain, but his soul was so radiant it shrouded his pains with serenity.

The Pope's physicians used all the remedies at their disposal to lessen the pain in his ailing eyes. They labored in vain. They decided on a more aggressive approach: to begin cauterization at the ear and run the incision to the more damaged eye.

The Crucified Brother agreed to undergo the prescribed therapy. But when he felt the cauterizing agents, and heard the clanging metal of the surgical instruments heating in the oven, a paralyzing fear seized his entire body.

Then a scene of indescribable tenderness took place. Brother Francis began to modulate his voice like the sweet sounds of a mother entreating her most beloved child. He could be heard as he spoke these words to the incandescent iron:

"My dear brother fire, I love you with all my heart. I've always been courteous with you for the love of the One who gave you life. Now be courteous with me and do not harm me too much so that I may endure this operation."

And, making the sign of the Cross, he blessed the fire as a sign of friendship. When the surgeon took the cautery in his hands, Leo, Angelo, Maseo and Rufinus, horrified and agitated, ran from the hut into the woods. They did not wish to see the torment that was about to take place.

Francis placed himself in the hands of God and clearly invoked the image of the Crucified Lord. He identified with the Crucified Christ as he did in Alvernia, totally immersing himself in the love and suffering of the Lord. With this, the surgeon took the cautery and made a very deep incision from his ear all the way to his eyebrows. Brother Francis did not so much as flinch.

When the surgeon completed the surgical intervention, Francis said to him:

"If you like, you can burn me some more. I didn't feel a thing."

Friendship and Enmity with God's Creatures

After several hours, the frightened brothers returned. They saw a serene Francis, a man who was not suffering any pain whatsoever. Brother Leo in all simplicity screamed:

"A miracle, a miracle!"

Brother Francis said to them:

"Men of little faith, why did you run? Brother Leo, write the following: There are no miracles, only reconciliation. I loved the wolves, and the wolves showed me affection. I loved the trees, and the trees gave me shade. I loved the stars, and the stars showed me their splendor. I was kind to fire, and fire showed me the same courtesy. There are no miracles. Better yet, everything is a miracle.

"Continue writing, Brother Leo: Paradise is in the heart; hell is in the heart as well. When God is absent from the heart, man experiences creation as a mute, deaf, blind, dead individual; even the Word of God lacks God.

"When man's heart is filled with God, he sees God all around him. He lifts a rock and God appears. He looks up at the stars and he sees God's shining light. The Lord is smiling in the flowers, murmuring in the breeze, asking with the wind, and responding with a storm. He sings in the rivers... All creatures speak of God when one's heart is filled with God."

* * *

The crucified Brother's head was completely bandaged, yet he resonated with peace and tranquility. It appeared as if pain itself had become a *brother*, the last one of all, and this new brother loved and respected Brother Francis. The Poor Man of God had immersed himself in universal harmony. He had entered paradise even before crossing its gates. His four loyal brothers were at his side every minute, day and night, completely overjoyed at seeing a happy Brother Francis. They treasured every word the Poor Man of God uttered as if it were a precious relic.

"Continue writing, Brother Leo: It was also the heart of man that injected enmity into the roots of creation. Man uses his superior intellect to torture defenseless animals. Man wants to domesticate them, that is, dominate them, transform them into beasts of burden. The hunters are not the poor who hunt because they are hungry, but rather the rich who have everything. They kill for pleasure.

"Man is disrespectful because he feels superior to everything. It is the law of the jungle. He fells trees thoughtlessly, cuts flowers needlessly, cages birds, kills fowl, burns waste, and constructs prisons called zoos for the amusement of others.

"Creation feels overwhelmed and enslaved by man's selfish pride and arrogance, and that's why she reacts with hostility. And for this reason, waters inundate and drown, fires burn, wolves tear and devour, lions gnaw, serpents bite and kill, tempests wreak havoc, hailstones destroy the harvest, atmospheric forces conspire and transform themselves into bolts of death, subterranean forces become devastating earthquakes, diseases plague man, and, above all, death rides victoriously on a black charger in an inevitable retaliation against the arrogance of man. This is creation's response."

Brother Francis seemed to stir with emotion, moist tears forming in his eyes. But he soon recovered and continued:

"Brother Leo, continue writing: I have loved. That's all I've done all my life. And the first commandment of love is to let the living live. Oh, Brother Leo, if we would only respect and revere everything that lives, everything that exists, creation would be a happy place. And allow me to be precise, Brother Leo: to respect particularly the weak and the small. Big things take care of themselves. What is the point of honoring a lion or a rhinoceros? Man should use his superior intelligence to protect and help all living things. As for me, I have endeavored to be the smallest among all living things, especially among the meek. Brother Leo, I would love to have included the following clause in the Rule: I,

Brother Francis, useless servant, ask on bended knee that all my brothers not only respect every living thing, but also venerate and revere everything that exists."

Peace and Love

"Brother Francis," said Brother Leo, "how can one possibly honor so many injustices in this world?"

"Answer me this, my beloved *little Lamb of God*: Have you ever seen murky waters cascading from cliffs on a mountain range?

"My dear Leo, write the following in very large letters: If the source is called Good, then everything that springs from that source will be good. If you lift the face off every living thing, you will find the image of Christ underneath it. Brother Leo, have you ever thought about light? Light is that which diffuses. If it didn't diffuse, it wouldn't be light.

"By some 'necessity' which is both entirely free and loving, God exploded in an expansive universe and that is the origin of creation. One by one, he created all living things, shaping them according to one image: the Eternal Word.

"Brother Leo, how thrilling it is to discover that all creation is a replica of the Lord. All things are sacred. All things have been blessed and sanctified. All things are good. That is why I tell you to venerate everything that breathes and everything that exists. And for this reason, one must extend the same courtesy not only to roaches and spiders, but also to rocks and metals. Creation is an enormous sacrament of God.

"Write this carefully, Brother Leo: A friar must be poor and elegant at the same time. Cleanliness, order, and neatness are the attributes of one who venerates the very chair he sits on, the table where his meals are served, and the clothes on his back.

"A truly poor person is an aristocrat. Vulgar persons cannot be poor. Be courteous, Brother Leo, not only to people but to things as well."

With this, Brother Leo looked at his habit and checked to see that it was clean. Brother Angelo got up and started to put things in their place, and Brother Maseo began to carefully sweep the floor of the hut. Brother Francis was tired but happy. His brothers gave him some chicken soup to help restore his energies. After about an hour, the four disciples sat on the floor near Francis. They were anxious to listen to him once again, for they knew he had but a few weeks to live. So Brother Francis continued:

"Yes, Brother Leo, everything is good. The first commandment consists in believing in the good. What is gained by cursing the darkness? Just light a candle and darkness vanishes. If you're bent on obliterating one war with another, you'll soon have universal conflagration. You may find it hard to believe, but peace is mightier than war, just as good is superior to evil. Why? Because God is the Supreme Good.

"Write, Brother Leo: No enemy on this earth can resist kindness and love. There is no hate which does not recoil in the face of Love. Which is stronger, fire or water? The world says: the strong hate. Christ answers: he who forgives is the strongest one of all. Hate is fire; forgiveness, water. Have you ever seen fire overcoming water? When they encounter one another, fire is always the submissive one.

"What is gained by complaining about all the injustices in this world? When people say: 'all is lost, this is the end,' hope raises its flag and says: this is the beginning. If hope is greater than despair, good is superior to evil.

"Write, Brother Leo: The Friars Minors will go around the world with a banner raised on high: the banner of

427

Poverty. The flag will have the following inscription: Peace and Love."

* * *

The four disciples sat very still. They were sons listening ever so carefully to the last words spoken by their venerated father. Francis continued:

"Is there any point in attacking iniquity? Every lie holds a grain of truth and many good intentions. All you need to do is wave the flag of truth and the lie vanishes. And those who were seated in its shadows curl up under the eaves of truth. Truth is mightier than lies.

"Write, Brother Leo: Do not attack anything. Do not destroy anything, because everything is good. Truth defends itself. Brother Leo, do you remember the Lateran Council we attended more than ten years ago? The Holy Father, Innocent III, wanted to prepare us for a crusade to thwart the efforts of the Albigenses. I wanted no part of that crusade. I said to you: We will show the Albigenses kindness and love, and they will, without a doubt, cease their implacable course of action and follow us like docile sheep.

"This has always been our way. Isn't that right, Brother Leo? How many times have we encountered proselytizing groups such as the Albigenses and the Waldenses? They insulted us in the beginning. We answered the insults with Peace and Love! They were amazed by our reaction. They let their guard down and we conversed with them. When they perceived that our love was genuine, they became docile sheep, eager to hear anything we had to say.

"Oh, Brother Leo, when Truth and Love march together, there's not an army in this world, whether from above or below, that can foil their mission."

The two of them, Brothers Francis and Leo, began to recall countless episodes when they had opposed the forces of evil with good: heretics, sinners, fanatical Ghibellines, assaults by highwaymen...

"All by the mercy of God!" Francis exclaimed.

Upon remembering so many wonders, Brother Francis was overcome with an enormous sense of gratitude, and said to them:

"Brothers, let's go to the grotto and sing the *Canticle of Brother Sun.*"

This was the same cavern where, years before, he had suffered much agony and distress while writing the definitive Rule.

Brothers Maseo and Angelo took Brother Francis by the arm and they began their descent down the perilous cliffs. They descended very slowly, practically carrying Brother Francis in their arms. Brother Leo walked a few meters ahead of them, and Brother Rufinus walked behind, just in case one of them might slip. What a spectacle! There is not a mother on this earth who has loved her sons as Brother Francis loved his disciples.

When they reached the grotto, the Poor Man of God said:

"How wonderful it would be if we had our dear Pacifico here with his lute. But, since that is not possible, I'd like Brother Leo to go and bring me two branches from that chestnut tree."

While Brother Leo was cutting the branches, the other three prepared a place for him on a rock.

His illnesses were progressing; but Brother Pain was courteous with the Crucified Brother, and the latter looked tranquil and radiant. He took the two branches and held them as if he were holding a violin. And as he rubbed one over the other, he sang the first verse of the *Canticle*. The cavern of agony became the cavern of the resurrection. The song reverberated throughout the grotto. As usual, Brother Leo was the first to break down and cry. Later, Brothers Angelo and Maseo followed suit. All the while, Rufinus was serene and composed. Brother Francis was in another world.

They repeated the *Canticle* three or four times. After-wards, they began to reminisce, recalling events of earlier years in that same cavern. However, not once did sadness enter the picture. They went up to the hut. The disciples separated: one went in search of medicinal herbs, another for cloths and soft bandages, the third went to beg for food. Brother Leo, the nurse, stayed with Brother Francis.

At nightfall, the four companions made certain that their ailing brother was resting comfortably on the rustic cot. They sang the *Canticle* once again. Brother Francis was not tired. The four disciples sat around his bed and were eager to hear and grasp the Crucified Brother's final words.

* * *

Brother Francis remembered the thousands of followers who were traveling around the world sowing Peace and Love. He recalled many touching moments of his brief yet prolific life. Finally, he began to speak to them about the eternal festival, the eternal music, the sacred hills of para-dise... He soon began to say very little, as if he were slowly falling asleep. He did not sleep, however. It seemed that he had "crossed" to the other side.

His disciples blew out the candle and each went to rest on goat skins in a corner of the hut. They slept very little. Instead, they kept vigil all night, alerting one another to the slightest movement of their ailing brother.

They spent several weeks in the cavern. These days were happy ones for Brother Francis. He devoted his energies to writing letters to kings, princes, and emperors, all of whom he most certainly had never met. He also wrote to all the brothers of the Order. Instead of saying the Divine Office, he sang the *Canticle* repeatedly, and generally only in the cavern.

Brother Francis was eager to go out into the world once again to proclaim Peace and Love. Although he was near the end, he was anxious to leave that same day and visit city after city teaching the Franciscan ideals. In parting, they went into the grotto and sang the *Canticle*. Then they walked out to that rocky projection and sang the *Canticle* one last time before a panorama of snow-capped mountains, cascading waters, and majestic chestnut trees. This is how Brother Francis said his farewells to Fonte Colombo, a truly Franciscan retreat.

The Last Journey

They went from hamlet to hamlet. Francis travelled by donkey, his companions walking beside him. They climbed up to the hermitages and down to the villages. They stopped at the plazas. Brother Francis spoke invariably about Peace and Love. He celebrated Christmas at Poggio Bustone. The townspeople believed him to be a miracle worker. He was already canonized in the eyes of the public. They went from village to village all the way to Siena. There, they met a Dominican monk, doctor of theology, who was bent on ridiculing the rival Order. He asked its Founder a capricious question with the intention of cornering him:

"Reverend Father, can you tell me how one should interpret these words from the prophet Isaiah: 'If you do not denounce the wicked for his impiety, can I continue to seek after his soul?' I know many a man who has committed mortal sins and, despite this fact, I find myself turning a blind eye. Do I assume responsibility, yes or no?"

A wise man such as Francis of Assisi need not concern himself with intellectuals. The latter usually abuse their high office and risk losing themselves in irrelevancies when they transform universities of sacred sciences into schools of rationalization. There, the students learn various intellectual maneuvers that justify their positions about life and other matters of interest. They soon have an answer for everything, lose sight of their spiritual simplicity, acquire a knack for the complicated, and sometimes even distance themselves from life itself.

The Poor (and wise) Man of Assisi said the following to the Dominican monk:

"I belong to the Order of Holy Ignorance. I don't understand these things. I only 'know' about the Poor and Crucified Christ. I don't 'know' any other science. The Lord did not call me to be a doctor of theology, but rather to live as a poor servant."

According to sources, the professor insisted that he answer the question. In spite of this, Francis resisted the pull of intellectual platitudes (there he would be truly lost), and responded as a true witness of God:

"Yes, the true servant of God reclaims the wretched without oppression; but he reclaims him mainly by his conduct, the truth that shines in his words, the example he has shown, all the splendor in his life."

A truly wise response!

* * *

One night, Brother Francis began to vomit blood and to suffer terrible spasms. He hemorrhaged until morning. Everyone thought that the hour had come. His four loyal followers did not know what to do. They sobbed and cried out in grief:

"What will become of us poor, abandoned orphans without our father, our mother, and our shepherd?"

Brother Francis was totally exhausted due to the loss of blood. His pallor, however, shone with the beauty of twilight, a beauty that can only come from the other side.

"Brother Leo, is it time?" asked Francis. And without waiting for a response he added: "Maseo, Angelo, Rufinus, and Leo, sing the *Canticle of Brother Sun*, and do not stop."

After singing it several times, the four disciples asked him to dictate his last will and testament.

"Brother Leo," said Francis, "I found my life in the Porziuncola; I'd like to leave my soul in the Porziuncola. But if God the Almighty wishes something else for me, call Brother Benedict Pirato."

When he arrived, Brother Francis said to him:

"Write: I bless all my brothers, those that are in the Order and those that will enter the Order until the end of time, and since I can no longer speak, I will say but a few words: forever worship the Sacred Love, be forever faithful to Lady Poverty, and live by the Holy Church."

* * *

Alarmed, Brother Elias decided to take him to the Porziuncola. They spent a few days in the lovely hermitage of Le Celle, near Cortona.

They continued their journey, without following the most direct route through Perugia for fear that the townspeople might trample the saint. So they took the long way around, passing through Gubbio and Nocera. They stayed a few days in the hermitage of Bagnara.

One day, the retinue arrived in Assisi. The city exploded with joy. It was absolute delirium. It was no longer about the son of Bernardone, but rather the Saint of Assisi. The multitude, the municipality, Bishop Guido and Brother Elias decided to place Brother Francis in the bishopric. The Porziuncola was a public place and, therefore, dangerous. The Perugians might come and take him away, leaving Assisi without her Saint.

The Last Sister

Brother Elias allowed Francis' old companions to stay with him, caring for him day and night in the bishop's palace. It was a large room with all the amenities and it looked out onto a courtyard.

On the first day, sadness shrouded Brother Francis' face. He would have liked to remain at the Porziuncola.

"There's a contradiction here," he said to himself. "Someone who has lived in a hut to die in a palace."

But that was not as distressing as his other thoughts:

"What's worse, my Lord has died on the Cross and here I am on this splendid bed."

In addition, he found the very reasons for his presence in the palace absolutely repulsive: his holiness made him a target for those who wished to abduct him. This was so disturbing that he preferred not to dwell on the matter.

"Brother Leo, this is usurpation, a vulgar theft. Holiness applies only to the Almighty. Attributing this distinction to a simple man is an act of theft. And all the more in this case: I have said it a thousand times, Brother Leo, I'm the worst sinner in the world, and this is not an exaggeration, nor is it false modesty. Any mortal receiving what I have received would have responded much more magnanimously. Bernardone's son, a saint! What an abomination!"

He lowered his voice as he uttered those last words.

However, there was something else troubling him that first day. He learned that the bishop's palace was surrounded by guards assigned to protect and defend the bishopric against a possible assault by the Perugians. This hurt Brother Francis to the core. He wanted to die.

"Brother Leo, all my life I've denounced worldly possessions. For this reason, I have been a man of peace. Soldiers and swords defend property or conquer it, and where there are possessions there is violence, more so now when I and my holiness are that property in question. Oh, Brother Leo, I feel as if I'm going to die of grief."

However, he did not protest. He remembered God's patience and a halo of serenity veiled his face. He did not sleep that night. The stigmata raised his temperature and the severe hemorrhaging he suffered caused acute dehydration. Brother pain, notwithstanding, was forever courteous to Brother Francis.

His four loyal companions did not rest that night. His nurse, Brother Leo, did not leave his bedside. He treated his wounds through the night. The three other disciples spent the night washing bandages, preparing homemade medicines, boiling water.

The Crucified Brother was faraway. He seemed not to hear anything. Despite his fever and dehydration, not once did he cry out in pain. He acquiesced like a puppet on the strings of those caring for him, and he did not say a word. A blessedness covered his entire crucified body.

* * *

It was a summer morning. It looked like the dawn of a new world. The aurora, like an incandescent meteor, shone a glorious light. A shimmering cloak covered the valley from

435

Mt. Subasio all the way to the Sabine Hills. Millions of swifts and swallows took flight into the valley that pressed against the blue sky and the scene exploded in jubilation, chirping, song, acrobatics, vertical dives... It was life. An intoxicating mixture of perfumes impregnated the air: basil, geraniums, carnations, roses, orange blossoms, jasmine... Blackbirds, nightingales, thrushes, goldfinches, and canaries burst into song, creating a symphonic explosion in the morning air. It was ecstatic.

Brother Francis sat up in his bed. His eyes were wide open, and he said:

"My God, what is this? It's paradise, Brother Leo. Open the windows and let creation in. It's horrible being in this palace, Brother Leo! Happy are the poor who open their eyes and find themselves under a sky filled with stars; they extend their arms to embrace a tree, they wet their hands in a stream, and warm them by a fire. Brother Leo, I'm suffocating in this mansion. I want to go to the hut, to feel the earth underneath my feet, the water, the snow, the frost. I'm a caged bird. I want to live among my sisters, the creatures and sing. I can't stand it, Brother Leo."

"It is the Almighty, Brother Francis; it is his will that you dwell here for a while."

"God, have patience! God, have patience!" Francis exclaimed in a low voice.

Brother Francis calmed down immediately upon uttering these words, the sweetness of paradise caressing him like the dawn.

"Brother Leo, find Brother Pacifico."

When the *King of Verse* arrived, Francis received him with open arms:

"Welcome, swallow of God! Take the lute. Come brothers, let's form a chorus and sing the *Canticle*."

The robust voices of his disciples singing the *Canticle* resonated through the princely quarters for the very first time. Francis and Pacifico sang the verses one by one and their brothers repeated them in unison.

* * *

A physician from Arezzo arrived the following morning. Buongiovanni, which means "Good John," was a friend of Francis'. Since Jesus says in the Gospel that "only God is good," Francis called him simply *Brother John*, or Benbegnate (Welcome).

"Tell me, Benbegnate, how sick am I?" asked Francis.

"With God's help, everything will turn out fine," the other responded.

"Don't deceive me. Tell me the truth. Don't be afraid. I've already placed myself in God's hands. All I wish to do is follow the Will of God."

"If that's the case, I'll tell you the truth: according to my calculations, you have until the end of September or, at most, the beginning of October."

Upon hearing his prognosis, the poor, blind man trembled with delight, and he sat straight up in his bed with no difficulty whatsoever. He raised his eyes to the heavens, extended his arms and repeated several times, aloud:

"Welcome, my dear Sister Death. Brother Leo, call Rufinus, Maseo, and Angelo so that we may all sing together."

Before they began, he said to them:

"Brothers, I have just received word that my Sister who is going to take me to paradise is on her way here. She is the one who will open the gates of eternity for me. What news! Let's celebrate it in song."

Brother Leo was in a flood of tears even before they hit the first note. His emotional response was contagious. Even so, they all sang more enthusiastically than ever, despite the tears in their eyes. Upon singing the last verse, Francis signaled them to stop and he improvised a new verse in honor of Sister Death:

"Praise the Lord for our sister death
which no man can resist.
Woe is the person who dies in mortal sin!
Happy is he who lives by your holy will,
for a second death will do no ill."

The new verse completed the *Canticle*. Chroniclers say that "they sang the Canticle of the Creatures (to Francis) several times a day in order to raise his spirits, and at night they sang it to the sentry guarding the palace as a show of support and for their entertainment."

Farewell to Assisi

Brother Elias was not too fond of all the singing. He believed that a man who was considered a saint in the eyes of the public should exercise more self-control, some measure of restraint and not sing for countless hours in the shadow of death. Thus, the Minister-General entered the chamber of the ailing individual and said to him:

"Brother Francis, it is comforting to see you so cheerful, but the townspeople do not understand this. I fear that the citizens, who venerate you as a saint, might consider this a bit scandalous. They do not see you preparing for death in a proper manner."

Francis replied:

"Brother, let me sing. There is no better way to express the joy I feel being so near to my Home. I'm suffering, Brother Elias. Singing helps to alleviate the pain and I feel close to my God and my Father when I sing. Brother Elias, you would have nothing to worry about if I were at the Porziuncola. There, in the forest, we can sing and not call attention to ourselves and welcome death with song and festivities."

The Minister-General decided to move Brother Francis to the Porziuncola. The municipality suggested that a small band of bodyguards accompany him to guard against any attempt at abduction. Brother Elias agreed.

The four disciples placed their ailing brother on a stretcher. The procession moved slowly and carefully through the city streets. They soon passed the principal gate called the *Portaccia*. They walked along a stretch of olive groves until they reached the plains. Now and then, the blind man inquired as to their progress.

When they reached the leper colony at San Salvatore delle Pareti, the ailing brother motioned them to stop and place the stretcher on the ground facing the city. His brothers helped Francis sit up. His eyes were closed. He maintained this position for several minutes.

Within minutes, a cavalcade of memories appeared before his mind's eye, emotionally stirring memories of special moments, moments of surprising solace, and so many wonders of love in the last twenty years in this city and its environs. There was his maternal home where he first caught a glimpse of Grace. There were the city streets where, on one of his nights of merrymaking, God appeared with all the weight of his sweetness upon Francis. There were St. Damian, Rivo Torto and the Porziuncola. Mt. Subasio was there, with its hermitages and smooth cliffs.

Now he was travelling to the Porziuncola to greet death. He wanted to stay there at the side of the road and express his gratitude to his city and say his last farewell.

He raised his right arm with great difficulty, made the sign of the Cross in the air, and said:

"Assisi, my beloved city, may the blessing of the Almighty fall upon you like the fresh breezes of dawn. Assisi, my beloved city, yesterday you were a hideout for outlaws, today a mansion for saints. Yesterday, there was the rumble of war, today the silence of peace. May you always provide wheat and oil for the sons of your sons. Lord Jesus Christ, extend the shadow of your wings over her walls, her bell towers, and her plains. Generation after generation will herald her name through the centuries. Assisi, my beloved city, I'm leaving you; I place you in God's hands. May you be happy. Farewell."

The procession moved on and they soon arrived at St. Mary of the Angels.

The Fire Goes Out

The four disciples placed Brother Francis in the dark hut at the Porziuncola. They were in the middle of the forest, some four meters from the chapel of St. Mary, the chapel that Francis had repaired with his own two hands.

"It's spring, Brother Leo."

"No, no, Brother Francis. We're in the first days of autumn.

"I smell the perfume of every flower, the rustle of leaves in all the forests, the freshness of every garden. It smells like spring. What joy! Who knows, maybe spring has exploded in my veins. I'm so happy, Brother Leo! Tell Brother Pacifico to gather the friars minstrels, so that they may accompany him in song like lively troubadours. Tell them to come to the forest and have them sing the *Canticle* day and night, without stopping. Have them stand there, a few meters from this hut. Sing until I'm with my Lord."

Francis' return to the Porziuncola, theater of many divine scenes of comfort and solace, seemed to have restored his strength. He was only glowing on the outside, however. His extremities and abdomen were bloated, giving him a deformed appearance. He only had a few days to live. Brother Pain treated him with more sensitivity with every passing day. The beauty of dusk and the peace of twilight weaved an exquisite pattern on his countenance until his last breath. His soul was navigating the waters of eternity.

"Brother Leo, I hear the silent music of violins and harps of gold," he said. "The melodies are coming from afar."

Brother Francis looked as if he had just returned from a long journey.

"When will I rest in my Father's arms! I have the errant spirit of travelers... When will I see the hills of my Homeland!"

"Brother Leo, write: I'm a river. When will I reach the Sea?

"Every afternoon, great birds fly from my nests to the Eternal Mountains. When will they get there? Where is the One who is looking for my soul? You are the Immortal Waters. Please quench my thirst.

"The strings of my harp are taut. Play, my Lord, don't be afraid; it doesn't matter if the strings break, so long as you play an everlasting melody.

"Turn out the light, my Lord. I want to sleep."

* * *

His four loyal companions did not leave his side. The *Canticle* could be heard incessantly throughout the forest. Francis' entire body was deteriorating. Why was the amphora still intact? His stamina was absolutely amazing. Brother Pain was ever delicate and courteous with Francis.

"It was wonderful," Brother Francis said to himself as he looked back on his life. "On that morning, God's mercy gave me the most important victory of my life."

He was referring to that episode in his life when he disrobed before all of Assisi and handed his clothes to Peter Bernardone.

"Leo, Maseo, Angelo, Rufinus, come here and remove my clothing."

His disciples were startled.

"Could he be suffering from delirium?" they said to themselves.

Sensing their hesitation, Francis said to them:

"My old comrades who have weathered countless battles, don't be so indecisive. I came into this world naked, and naked I wish to return to the arms of my Father. I want to die totally disrobed, as Jesus Christ did. I want to die in the arms of Lady Poverty and in the bosom of Mother Earth, my sister. Go on, then, and remove my garments."

They removed his vestments, one by one, until he was completely naked. The four disciples lost their composure and they began to sob. They cried like children. Even Rufinus, the most serene one of all, could not control his emotions. Francis covered the wound in his side with his right hand. It was a bloated, pale body, tortured by sorrows and infirmity. What a spectacle!

"Now take me and place my body on the naked earth," he said to them.

They picked him up very carefully and placed him on the soft earth. Brother Francis closed his eyes.

Twenty prolific years flashed before his eyes and he felt gratitude and immense satisfaction on completing his mission. He opened his eyes and looked at his brothers, and said in a spirited voice: "My work is done, thanks be to God. May Christ help you accomplish your mission.

"Sister Mother Earth, I want to rest deep within you. But before I sleep, hear the beatings of my grateful heart. Thank you for your streams: they are born high in the mountains; their waters are refreshing because they run down shaded ravines and quench the thirst of many a weary traveller.

"Thank you, sister earth, for your caves and caverns. The face of the Lord shines within their walls where pilgrims spend the night, where beggars keep warm in the dead of winter. In short, they are dwellings for the poor.

"Thank you, sister earth, for your flint that gives us fire which illuminates the night, keeps us warm, gives us joy, cauterizes our wounds and purifies the earth.

"Thank you, sister earth, for your winds and breezes. They refresh us in the summer, disperse the seeds of life, and move the sails of the windmills.

"Thank you, sister earth, for your vegetable gardens, your wheat fields, your fruit trees, your springs that give us fresh water, your trees where your birds nest.

"Thank you, sister earth, for your bed that you lend us for the eternal sleep."

Brother Francis closed his eyes while expressing these sentiments, as he lay on his back. He tried to turn his body so he could kiss the earth, but he was unable to do so. He decided then to place the palms of his hands on the ground, and he said:

"Thank you."

"Brother Leo, tell Brother Pacifico to sing the *Canticle of Brother Sun.*"

It was a spectacle beyond belief. The disciples were just a few feet from the hut; they sang the *Canticle* as loud as they could. His four companions, including Brother Bernard, sang in a flood of tears. Brother Leo, with one knee to the ground, pressed his head against the wall of the hut, and cried inconsolably. Brother Francis, naked, eyes closed, and calm, repeated the verses while his brothers sang outside the hut...

They completed the "liturgy" of courtesy to Lady Poverty and in gratitude to Mother Earth. Brother Francis wished to remain on the ground for a while. He waited until someone passed him a garment to wear which he would receive as alms, since he was truly poor. He made his wishes known and a protector of the Porziuncola brought him some garments, and he handed them to him, saying between sobs:

"I am lending you these undergarments, this tunic, this hood, and let it be clearly understood that you do not own anything. Therefore, I forbid you, in the name of blessed obedience, to give these articles of clothing to anyone."

It was the absolute and highest order of poverty.

Upon hearing these words, the ailing brother seemed to revive. His body shuddered; his soul trembled with indescribable happiness. He raised his arms and said:

"May you be forever blessed, Holy Lady Poverty. You break the chains of bondage and place us naked and free in the arms of God."

He then asked them to take him to his bed once again. They did so lovingly.

* * *

The Crucified Brother was dying like the flame of a candle. His voice grew softer with every passing day. His face shone with the sweetness of paradise. Day and night, the *Canticle* could be heard echoing through the forest. Different groups of disciples took turns singing. During one of those moments, Brother Francis said:

"It's the prelude, it's the prelude to the eternal symphony."

He began to say his farewells to everyone.

"Brother Leo," Francis said to him, "faithful comrade in battle, secretary and nurse, my mother on so many occasions, I say farewell. Forgive me for having taken you across rocky terrain on our chivalric journeys for Christ. Words cannot express my gratitude. I bless you beyond what I am able. And I'll be waiting for you under the great arch of eternity. Farewell."

Brother Leo did not hear a word. He was beside himself with grief and in a flood of tears.

He directed his attention to his first companion, Brother Bernard, placed his hands on him, and said:

"I absolve and bless you. A thousand blessings for my brothers who are not here today. Make sure they hear these words, and bless them in my name."

Believing that Bernard would be the object of persecution (and he was not mistaken), he added:

"It is my wish that the Order be particularly affectionate towards you, my beloved Brother Bernard, who was the first to renounce all his worldly possessions and join me on the path of the Word of the Lord."

* * *

At this time, a friar from St. Damian arrived with news from Clare and her sisters. They had been crying inconsolably. He sent this message to them:

"I, little Brother Francis, wish to imitate the poverty of the Lord and of his Holy Mother, and I ask on bended knee that you, my ladies, never deviate from this path, no matter what others may advise you to do."

He turned to the messenger, and added:

"Tell Sister Clare that I forbid her to lose herself in sadness, and that she continue being the great lady she has always been."

Remembering his Roman friend, Jacoba de Setesolios, he said:

"She'd never forgive me if I left this world without telling her my time has come."

And he began to dictate a letter to her which said:

"To Lady Jacoba, servant of God: Brother Francis, the Poor Little Man of God, greets you in the name of the Father and the Holy Spirit. My dear friend, I wish to inform you that the end of my life is near. In the meantime, embark on your journey if you wish to see me before that hour arrives. Bring a shroud with you for my body and however much is necessary for the tomb. I ask you also to bring me some of those almond pastries that you used to prepare for me during my convalescence in Rome..."

He had to stop the dictation. At that precise moment a disciple entered the hut, saying:

"Brother Francis, Lady Jacoba has just arrived with her two children."

"Praise be to God!" Brother Francis exclaimed. "Let her in. The law that prohibits women from entering doesn't apply to 'Brother' Jacoba."

It was quite a spectacle: the elegant lady of Roman nobility, with her children, her entourage, her perfumes and lavish gown, in the house of mourning of the Poor Man of God, going well beyond the mores of monastic life: complete freedom to the children of God...

After greeting one another, Francis asked if she had brought almond pastries. At her affirmative response, the Poor Man invited all to gather round, and he said to them:

"Come brothers, and let us eat these delicious pastries prepared by 'Brother' Jacoba."

It had been written that his life would be full of surprises. On the eve of his death, when all should be agony and suffering in the house of mourning, all were happily eating sweet morsels! It is a unique episode in the history of the spirit. What freedom! What maturity!

* * *

Brother Francis seemed to revive with the arrival of 'Brother' Jacoba; but he soon fell into the grip of agony. Actually, he had only a few hours to live.

He directed his attention to the disciples who were present and said to them in a loud voice:

"When you see that I am taking my last breath, place me on the ground as you did yesterday and leave me there for the time it takes to walk a mile."

An impassioned *Canticle of Brother Sun* could be heard deep within the forest. The voices in the hut mixed with the voices in the forest, and the tenuous voice of the dying man joined the voices in the hut, and the whole world seemed to sing the last verse of the *Canticle* to sister death.

* * *

There was no death rattle. The Poor Man of God expired like a dying candle, like the light in a lamp that has no more oil to burn. His four comrades and his loyal brothers remained absolutely still, not moving even an inch from his deathbed. At this stage, administering medication was pointless. He was beyond help. They simply waited for the light to go out. They cried quietly and almost without a sigh.

Only Brother Leo was convulsed with emotion, sobbing uncontrollably. For this reason, he got up, stepped aside to a corner of the cabin, went down on one knee, rested his elbow on the other, and pressed his head against the wall of the hut. He maintained this position for hours and cried inconsolably. He was oblivious to those around him, and his tears seemed endless.

* * *

Francis' voice was ever so soft. When his lips began to move, his disciples huddled around him to hear his last words.

"Brother Leo," he said, "I hear the bells of eternity. They are calling me to the feast. What joy!"

There was a long silence.

Suddenly, unexpectedly, as if he had returned from regions unknown, the Poor Man of God raised his voice and said:

"Brother Leo, write my final words: My Lord, I will crawl on my knees to your feet, I will sit in your shadow and cover my nakedness with my hands. Your hands will take my hands, you will help me to my feet, you will embrace me and say: 'You are the son of my Love and shadow of my Essence.' You will kiss my forehead and place a garland around my neck. You will place a gold ring on my finger and cover my nakedness with the vestments of a prince.

"And you will say: My son, look at me. Look at me and there, deep within your heart, I will find my name. And I will say to you: Let me into that ocean. And you will say to me: Come. And I will dive into its depths, and lose myself in it, lose my head, and dream.

"I will ask: Aren't you ashamed to have me for a son? And You will respond: Haven't you seen your name written in the most bountiful corners of nature? You will place your cheek next to mine and say: in the wide expanse, there is no other, You are the one and only.

"My Father, is it true that you dreamt of me even before the blush of dawn appeared? Is it true that your feet walked across the centuries and the worlds behind my fleeing shadow? Tell me, is it true that when you pointed to the heavens, it melted in song? Is it true that when my eyes surrender and I place myself in the arms of sleep, you will stay at my bedside?

"I will ask: What do I give you? Your response will be: Giving belongs to Me, and only receiving belongs to you. I will ask: Why don't you speak? You will respond: Silence is the language of love.

"Tonight, I will arrive at your house. You will place me on a bed of flowers. You will draw the curtains so that the moon does not shine in my eyes. I will say to you: I've travelled from afar; I'm a tired and wounded child, and I'm sleepy. With the hands of a mother you will touch my eyes and say: Sleep. And I will lose myself in your ocean..."

There was a long silence. No one said a word. Everyone stared at the dying man.

A disciple read the Passion of Christ, according to St. John.

It was the afternoon of October 3, 1226. The last rays of golden light covered the high peaks of the Apennines with nostalgia and the aura of eternity. The earth had produced a golden harvest and wore a look of satisfaction, like one who has completed her mission.

Unexpectedly, the dying man opened his eyes, hunched forward and said:

"It's coming! It's coming!"

The tone of his voice and the expression on his face betrayed a look of anxiety, much happiness, and a certain sense of relief like a man being released from prison. His disciples wore a look of expectation. The dying man lay down on his deathbed once again. He was silent and breathed with difficulty.

After a few minutes he opened his eyes once more, and this time, he said without any anxiety or emotion:

"It's time!"

In a weak voice, he added:

"Brothers, help me sit up."

His four companions assisted him, showing extreme veneration, and helped him to sit up on his deathbed.

He extended his arms and, while looking at the door of the hut, said in a soft voice:

"Welcome, Sister Death. I don't know why the world fears you so much, my dear kind sister. You are full of mercy and release us from life's burdens. What would those in despair, those imprisoned in the cells of sadness do without you? You free us from this *body of sin*, from perdition. You close the doors of life and open the doors of Life."

Then he said to those present:

"Knights of my Lord, if, in the course of our brief life, we have been chivalrous and courteous to Our Lady Poverty, isn't it fitting that we do the same with Lady Sister Death who has just arrived to release me from the prison of my body and take me to the eternal paradise?"

* * *

He improvised a chivalric "liturgy." He told the doctor to stand at the door and, like an ambassador, announce solemnly and joyfully the arrival of the illustrious visitor.

He asked his disciples to place him on the ground. With extreme reverence his four loyal companions placed him on the earth one last time. His body lay on lambskins. Brother Francis told them to sprinkle dust and ashes on his body, in honor of Sister Death. They did as he commanded.

After a few minutes, the dying man began to pray the psalm: "With my voice I cry out the name of the Lord." His disciples joined him in prayer.

Brother Francis was forty-five years old. In twenty brief years he had lived an extraordinary history of the spirit.

In the woods and in the hut, the disciples continued to sing the *Canticle of Brother Sun* with impassioned voices.

Brother Francis lay on the floor. His body was absolutely still.

Francis had passed on.

* * *

At that moment, a spontaneous and triumphant procession accompanied the Poor Man of God to the gates of paradise.

Angels, archangels, cherubim, and seraphim paraded in the heavens. They covered the wide expanse from one end to the other and sang *Hosannas* to the Almighty and to his servant Francis.

There were wild boars, wolves, foxes, jackals, dogs, pumas, oxen, sheep, horses, leopards, bisons, bears, donkeys, lions, pachyderms, antelopes, rhinoceroses. They were all marching together, like old friends.

Behind them, bats, butterflies, bees, condors, hummingbirds, larks, hornets, swallows, cranes, thrushes, finches, partridges, sparrows, nightingales, blackbirds, roosters, chickens, ducks. There was such a feeling of familiarity among them that one would think they had shared the same farmyard all their lives.

Later on, the procession continued with alligators, dolphins, hippopotamuses, swordfish, whales, monkfish, goldfish, flying fish, trout. It was amazing: the larger fish did not prey on the smaller ones. They acted like members of the same species, like siblings of the same family. Finally, the procession ended with cobras, anacondas, vipers, boas, large lizards, small lizards, dinosaurs, and rattlesnakes.

Meanwhile, in the woods of the Porziuncola, the *Canticle of Brother Sun* resonated endlessly. These *brothers* were singing, screaming, crying out, squawking, braying, whistling, hollering, howling, barking, bellowing, baaing, wailing.

The world had never heard a symphony of voices that compared to this. All of God's creatures were singing *hallelujahs* to Francis, their friend and brother. Together, Francis and his friends were praising the Almighty Creator.

Behind this triumphant band of brothers, Brother Francis of Assisi, seated on a little donkey, rose from the ground and soared into the heavens. The great gates of paradise were opened. Those gates had not parted since Ascension Day.

All of creation followed the Poor Man of God into paradise.

The earth was reconciled with the heavens, matter was reconciled with the spirit. The flame no longer burned on the log. God's mercy had crossed the threshold. It was home once again.

Slowly, very slowly, Brother Francis disappeared into the celestial spheres like a blue meteor penetrating the depths of eternity.